Wine Sense

Wine Sense

The Art of Appreciating Wine

Steve Shipley

InkIT Publishing
Pokolbin, NSW, Australia

Wine Sense © 2014 by Steve Shipley.
All rights reserved. No part of this book may be used, reproduced, or transmitted in any manner without written permission of the author and InkIT Publishing.

Cover Art Design: Sheamus Burns
Layout and Preproduction: Sheamus Burns
Editor: Deanna Lang, InkIT Publishing

Published by InkIT Publishing, Pokolbin, NSW, Australia
ISBN: 978-1-925200-01-0
Printed by CreateSpace, An Amazon.com Company
First edition. First printing.

Acknowledgments

Wine Sense would not be possible without the financial support and contributions of many. I thank the Publishizer (http://www.publishizer.com) team, especially founder, Guy Vincent, who encouraged me to use crowd funding and a preorder campaign. Doing so made me commit to publish within a specific deadline and propelled this book to market months earlier than originally intended. More importantly, I wish to thank those who provided the funding and financial support to make this happen based on your faith and trust that you are buying a quality product before it was completed. *Wine Sense* would not have been possible without your financial support, and for that, I am eternally grateful.

Platinum corporate sponsors:

- Cognizant Australia (http://www.cognizant.com/)
- Rumble Asia (http://rumbleasia.com/)
- Up 2 Speed (http://www.up2speed.biz/)

Patron sponsors:

- David Andrews and Sarah-Jane Tarr
- Michael & Kris Axarlis
- Andrew and Rachel Baartz
- Scott Bales: Author, Speaker & Advisor
- Amit Banerji, PMWorks
- John Barry, wine enthusiast

- Tim Blake
- Jamieson Bryan, Partner, Deloitte & Touche
- Phil Cave
- Antony Challinor
- Beny Chun: an overworked individual who just wants to fish, golf and drink wine
- Greg Clarke
- Marianne and Jim Covington
- Nessa Doyle
- Mark S Drummond
- Stephen Kowal
- Angelo Lim
- Denis and Glenda McGee
- Taraneh & Morteza Ansari
- Shane and Kylie O'Connor
- Gwen and Roger Pratesi
- Jeannie Radcliffe
- Steve Ramsden
- Riccardo Raso, Principal - McBurney & Partners Pty Ltd
- Ramona Roach and Toni Gluseski
- Dr. Ramtin and Anahita Shams
- Paul and Colleen Sommerin
- Tack Kuang and Sook Ching Soon
- Graeme Stephens
- Richard Switzky
- George Sykiotis
- David Tonuri
- Virginia Trombley
- Guy Vincent

I also want to thank the many authors and stalwarts of wine appreciation who took their time to share their in-depth knowledge. The books from which I have learned and used as part of the research for *Wine Sense* are included in the Bibliography. In particular, I want to thank Emile Peynaud and Steve Charters, MW, for their dedication to the field and clear articulation of insights. I also reviewed ideas and gained insights through the time provided by Mark Baulderstone of Riedel Australia, Greg Clarke on philosophy and aesthetics, and Jessica McLeish, owner of McLeish Estates winery.

Finally, I would like to thank my wife, Deanna Lang for teaching me how to live and how to cook. Both have been instrumental to integrating wine into our lifestyle and becoming passionate about it. Deanna also provided ongoing technical and editorial support bringing *Wine Sense* to fruition. Most importantly, she willingly accepted and encouraged my writing and learning the publishing trade even though it took several years away from pursuing other interests.

Preface

This book is intended for a global wine drinking audience. As such, it has been difficult to cater to each locale's standards and customs with regard to language, currencies, and references to vendors and research. I have tried to make the book both appealing and useful to as large an audience as possible. When reading and contextualizing the information within, please be aware of the following:

- Language conventions are English United States (US).
- Currencies are specified in US$ and are approximate in range. Currencies in US$, your local currency and other currencies may change, based on foreign currency exchange rates determined by global market conditions.
- I have done my best to define and adhere to 'common conventions' for subjective wine terms and phraseology (such as 'fine wine'), but these terms mean different things to different people and are interpreted differently by each of us. Therefore, there may be some evaluative assessments made with which you may disagree or describe differently.
- Any assessment of wine quality or value is mine and mine alone, and may be assessed differently by the reader.
- Measurements of temperature, if not specified, are in Fahrenheit. I have endeavored to present temperatures in both Fahrenheit and Celsius.

- Volumes are presented in metric (liters and milliliters [ml]) as this is a common form of volume measurement for liquids universally.
- All other measurements are Imperial.

In an attempt to further your knowledge and experience drinking and appreciating wine, I mention a number of products such as glassware, wine cellaring and storage systems, and books by brand and title. I do not have any commercial relationship with these vendors. I do not work in the wine industry nor am I associated with any winery, manufacturer of wine equipment, or wine industry associations. I present brand names and book titles so you can quickly learn and explore the wine subject matter more thoroughly. References to these products are based on my personal experience and are not a recommendation to buy a particular brand. However, where I have mentioned a particular brand or book, it is because I have had a positive experience with it myself and believe many others may also. Hopefully, you will find these references useful to help navigate more effectively your wine drinking and appreciation journey.

The book is intended to be read from cover to cover, but can be read in any order if you have specific areas of interest. *Chapters 3 & 4* may be skipped all together if you are not interested in the background of the philosophy of the senses or wine as an aesthetic pursuit. *Chapter 5* (and all of *Part Two* can be passed over if you do not care about the language, science and physiology of how the senses work when drinking wine. However I recommend reading *Part Two* as it provides an understanding and foundation to help you improve your wine drinking experiences. Regardless of any other choices you make about parts of the book to read or ignore, it is highly recommended you read *Part Three* as it provides useful tips on how to enhance wine drinking enjoyment. And if you are content after finishing *Part Three* that no further information or education of wine drinking is necessary, you can skip *Part Four*. If you want to continue the journey (and why wouldn't you?) to further your wine drinking education and improve your wine drinking experiences further, then *Part Four* is highly recommended. Therefore, the book can be used as an ongoing reference and refresher course as required.

With that in mind: happy reading and happy drinking! Let's get started.

Table of Contents

Acknowledgments — iii
Preface — vi
Introduction — 10

Part One
Wine and the Senses

Chapter 1: Wine Enjoyment — 15
Chapter 2: Enjoying Wine through Our Senses — 22
Chapter 3: Philosophy of Wine & Primary and Secondary Senses — 26
Chapter 4: Wine as an Aesthetic Experience — 38
Chapter 5: The Role of Language in Wine Appreciation — 49

Part Two
How Wine Interacts with the Senses

Chapter 6: Overview of Wine & Sense Interaction — 59
Chapter 7: Wine and Sight — 66
Chapter 8: Wine and Smell — 78
Chapter 9: Wine and Taste — 90
Chapter 10: Wine and Feel — 111
Chapter 11: Wine and Sound — 117

Part Three
Enhancing the Wine Drinking Experience

Chapter 12:	Improving Smell and Taste Sensations	120
Chapter 13:	Improving Sight Sensations	159
Chapter 14:	Improving Feel Sensations	166
Chapter 15:	Improving Sound Sensations	171
Chapter 16:	Other Ideas for Improving Wine Drinking	176
Chapter 17:	Buying and Storing Wine	179
Chapter 18:	Wine Drinking Practice & Experience	230

Part Four
Where to Next?

Chapter 19:	Tools & Systems for Managing Wine Inventory	264
Chapter 20:	Further Wine Education	268
Chapter 21:	Other References	298
Chapter 22:	Final Thoughts	302

Appendices

Appendix A:	Castro's Categories of Wine Odors	305
Appendix B:	Wine Database Format and Field Listing	307
Bibliography		314

Introduction

I have enjoyed wine for most of my adult life. My wine drinking pleasure has improved markedly over the last fifteen years as I became more knowledgeable of wine, the grapes, and winemaking processes. The appreciation of sensual pleasures possible when drinking wine has resulted from a deeper understanding of how wine interacts with the senses, and understanding and becoming comfortable with the underlying reasons as to why, when and how I drink.

There are a number of excellent books on wine and philosophy, books and courses on how to taste and appreciate wine, and how to match wines to foods to enhance your dining and social experiences. Some are overly academic and detailed, making it difficult for people without prior experience (or a background in science or philosophy) to engage. Other wine compendiums present themselves as 'the single volume on the subject you will ever require,' but are often overly simplistic and miss important points on how to enhance your wine drinking experience. It is my hope this book offers a path in the middle of those two extremes and provides an easy and quick, yet pragmatic, approach to help you more fully enjoy wine drinking as part of your life style.

Wine Sense has two objectives:

1. Enhance your wine drinking enjoyment and experiences through understanding why and how the experience works, especially in regard to how your senses respond when drinking wine

2. Provide you with enough knowledge, understanding and confidence to buy good wines at good prices (without having to trust in others to explain what that means)

Introduction

This book has been written for you as a wine enthusiast and consumer. The wine industry has implied authority and 'experts' who often dictate what wines should be drunk and how much we should pay for them. Listening to 'experts' and accepting their guidance can be useful. I pay for their services on a regular (small annual fees) basis as I value their input. I use the expert critics to help describe how wine tastes, but not if I will enjoy it; only I (or you) can determine that. With regard to personal taste, wine is highly private and subjective. Augustine refers to the sense of sight and hearing to be public senses, used for exploring and sharing a common experience (such as in the appreciation of art), whereas he noted that "taste and smell take unique portions of their objects into their bodies, making the sensory event more private."[1] Our response to how a wine tastes is a private experience unique to us individually. You can value wine industry authority and expertise to assist in making choices: however the decision on what wine you like is ultimately yours and yours alone.

I have confidence now to trust my tastes and judgment and my appreciation of what constitutes fine wine. The intent of this book is to provide you with the background and knowledge to be able to achieve similarly. I selected wines previously based expert critic opinion or the recommendation from wine sales people and I ended up overpaying for those wines. Throughout my wine drinking history, I have overpaid approximately 25% - 35% for wine. By reading this book, you should be in a better position to trust what you like, why you like it, and what you are willing to pay for it.

There is much debate on if wine tasting is only possible for those who have been born with the capabilities to be able to appreciate wine or if our capabilities can be developed over time. Sense experts who have studied this question and the science that underpin how the senses affect our overall enjoyment when drinking wine are quite certain that with a little knowledge, practice and experience, that almost everyone's wine drinking can be significantly improved. Michael Schuster says, "If you want to be a good taster, and work at it, the likelihood is that you can be."[2] Terry Robards, wine writer for The New York Times, in the introduction of his *Book of Wine* breaks apart the myth that only special people are empowered to know and understand wine by claiming, "Anyone can become just as knowledgeable simply by applying himself - by taking the time and trouble to taste wine and learn about what he is tasting."[3]

The book is written in four parts:

Part One: Wine and the Senses
Part Two: How Wine Interacts with the Senses
Part Three: Enhancing the Wine Drinking Experience
Part Four: Where to Next?

Part One: Wine and the Senses provides an overview for understanding how wine interacts with the senses and why this is pleasurable. It provides useful background information on the philosophy of wine, philosophy of the senses, pursuing wine as an aesthetic experience and how the language of wine shapes those experiences. *Part Two: How Wine Interacts with the Senses* provides a thorough explanation of how wine interacts with each sense to heighten your wine drinking experience. *Part Three: Enhancing the Wine Drinking Experience* offers simple, pragmatic tips to make wine drinking as enjoyable as possible. *Part Four: Where to Next?* provides direction to other resources and ideas to continue to mature your wine drinking pleasure.

This book is about 'tasting' wine for pleasure and becoming 'intoxicated' through the experience; it is not about drinking wine to become drunk. Wine contains alcohol and should be consumed with care. I have my RSA (Responsible Service of Alcohol) certificate. It is inexpensive and easy to obtain in Australia. I enjoy wine for its flavor, the sensual pleasure it provides, and the intoxicating effects provided - on its own or with a meal: I do not drink to get drunk.

The knowledge encapsulated in this book has come from a number of years of personal wine drinking experience supplemented by further research. Enjoy a good glass as you read this book. I continue to write the wine blog *SAZ in the Cellar* (http://sazinthecellar.com/) and can be reached through my blog or via email or Twitter for feedback or questions.

Steve Shipley
Email: shipleyaust@yahoo.com.au
Twitter: @shipleyaust
SAZ in the Cellar (http://sazinthecellar.com/)

Notes

1. Korsmeyer, *Making Sense of Taste*, 35.
2. Schuster, *Essential Winetasting*, 17.
3. Robards, *Book of Wine*, xi.

Part One
Wine and the Senses

Chapter 1
Wine Enjoyment

My first introduction to wine (or 'wine-like' alcoholic drink) occurred 45 years ago. My father made 'wine' in his basement using strawberries, dandelions, sweet potatoes, or any other ingredient that could add flavor to the crude fermentation process used. Since it was free, it was my wine of choice while studying at university. When we ran out of my father's homemade wine, we would buy a bottle of Boones Farm Apple or Strawberry wine which cost approximately $0.93 per bottle in the early 1970s.

Why do we start drinking wine in the first place? Notable British philosopher, Barry Smith, says: "It doesn't attract us immediately; we have to acquire the taste. The reason we start isn't hard to seek. As Jamie Goode puts it: 'it's alcohol and it gets you drunk; what greater lure is there for teenagers than that?"[4] That is why I and most others started to drink. I was not looking for the pleasure that wine could bring; I was looking for an alcoholic escape from reality! Ken Bach says, "But so-called adult food and beverages, including wine, generally are acquired tastes." He goes on to ask the question "Does this mean that you have to learn about them in order to enjoy them? Developing a taste about them isn't a matter of learning about them but of getting accustomed to them, as your palate matures."[5] So why do we like wine if it took an effort to become accustomed to it in the first place? Why, unlike most other adult beverages, do we continue to drink wine and value the experience more over time?

During my university days, I did not realize that what I was drinking at the time was not really wine. It was just a flavored alcoholic beverage. I cannot remember when I had real wine (made from grapes) the first time, but it would have been sometime late in my university life or graduate school. It probably was introduced to me through a meal with friends, attending a BBQ or some similar function. I must have enjoyed it more than my father's homemade wine and Boones Farm, as my first 'on my own' wine buying memories are from going to Surdyk's (a liquor store with ample wine choices) in Minnesota to buy wine while I was attending graduate school. There was an early attraction to wine that made me desire it as part of daily life and as a compliment to studying, dining and socializing.

Fortunately, good, extremely inexpensive ($3 - $5 per bottle) Chilean wines could be purchased back then and comprised the majority of my first 'cellar.' By cellar, I mean a box at the bottom of the linen closet which usually held somewhere between a half-dozen and dozen bottles. When inventory fell below a half-dozen bottles, I was off to Surdyk's to buy more.

I could tell that the cheap Chilean wines and my other wine purchases were far better and more enjoyable to drink than my father's or the Boones Farm wine, but I did not know why. You may ask the question "Why do you care? If you like it, just drink it and be happy!" (We will explore this question later.) I knew I was drinking wine which I enjoyed more and that was good enough. However, I was choosing bottles by being attracted to the label as a representation of perceived quality. I was not able to select my own wine, and had to rely on the help of others to understand what a good choice might be whenever I tried a new bottle.

At that point in my life, I consumed as much beer and hard liquor as wine. All sources provided inspiration through alcohol and provided a means for socialization. However, over the following decade, I found hard liquor was too hard on my body, and taste-wise, was not to my liking. I admire and envy people who can truly enjoy their scotch, whiskey and cognacs, but I do not enjoy beverages with that much alcohol in them. I still enjoy the occasional beer, but it is wine that became my drink of choice by the time I turned thirty.

I cannot remember clearly why this was, but with some confidence believe it to be for the reasons that follow:

- I liked choice across a variety of grapes and the many different flavors of wine.

- I liked the many different styles made, and how each winemaker can impose their thumbprint on a unique wine style.
- The alcohol content was to my liking, being between 10% and 15% instead of higher.
- Beer caused bloating and I could only drink several beers without feeling uncomfortable – wine was easier to drink slowly over a period of time.
- Philosophically, I viewed wine as being part of the annual renewal of life. It followed the seasons and connected us to the soil and annual rebirth.
- Wine presented a mysterious quality in that I could buy one bottle for several dollars and a similar one for much more and my curiosity demanded I understand why there existed such a vast difference in price when I could not detect difference in quality.

Wine continued to surprise and mystify. It seemed to compliment my lifestyle without intruding upon it as hard alcohol did. Barry Smith eloquently puts it: "The body has no struggle in accepting this harmonious liquid - it feels good for us, like a blood transfusion with several vital elements to it. You delight in the experience and in that of those with whom you share the bottle. The moment is fleeting, ephemeral and transitory, yet utterly memorable. And you know, at that moment, that you want more opportunities like this, not to drink this very wine again, because this is an unrepeatable experience. You want more opportunities to drink other wines as great as this because now you know great wines exist and that you are capable of responding to them. At that moment you learn something about wine and something about you. You are astonished that wine can reach such heights, provide such a complex and yet harmonious experience; and in understanding that wine can do this, you want to know more."[6]

The question of wine appreciation and enjoyment is "do I need to learn about wine to enjoy it, or do I need to enjoy it to want to learn about it?" This question is easy to answer. You must enjoy wine drinking in the first place. There are other food products - take butter for instance - that can be studied in terms of the molecular structure, flavors added, how hard or creamy the texture is and what is likely to be most salable to a mass market. But butter and most other food and drink products do not captivate the way wine does. These products do not drive us to need to understand more in order to appreciate them. Wine is almost unique in that regard.

When I started drinking wine, I knew almost nothing about it. I knew there were wines made from red grapes and white grapes, and that white wines should be chilled before drinking them. That was about the extent of my knowledge and experience. I could tell that certain wines made of certain grapes tasted better than other wines, but did not know why or how to determine this. With more experience, my ability to appreciate wine grew. I was fortunate to be able to participate in meals that included fine wines with people who knew more than me. I had greater enjoyment in drinking wine (and eating food) when dining with them. I did not understand why that was, nor could I recreate those experiences on my own. But by asking some questions and getting some pointers from others more knowledgeable than myself, over the next 25 years, I picked up some basics. I still lacked the confidence to be able to review and choose wines on my own and made mistakes by buying wines I did not enjoy, and I overpaid for a bottle when a comparable bottle next to it was available at a fraction of the cost! And when bringing wine to a meal or BBQ, if I knew my more knowledgeable business friends were attending, I was fraught with apprehension as I was guessing more than knowing what constituted an acceptable wine.

However through continued experience, I came to realize that I (and anyone else) could improve their wine drinking experience by gaining a little knowledge. I wanted to make each experience with regards to wine a better experience by taking the risk out of it. There was still the risk (which actually leads to more excitement and anticipation) that a bottle may be corked, or someone else changed the food and the wine is no longer a perfect match for the food. However, I was certain a little knowledge could help me enjoy my wine drinking experiences far more than I had been. Therefore, I set out to learn more about different grapes, styles, and regions for wines; what wines to match with food (and more and more, now I reverse the process and determine what food I want to eat based on the wine I want to drink!); and how I could enjoy each sip more.

This does not require drinking more expensive wine. In fact, by gaining some basic knowledge, my average bottle cost is now significantly lower than previously. With some knowledge and continuing to partake in more drinking experiences, I have gained the confidence and ability to choose far less expensive wines, knowing they are of high quality. And by storing, opening and serving wine properly, I get more flavor and taste out of every bottle, even when drinking less expensive wines. Without basic knowledge and experience, you are at risk of significantly overpaying for your wine drinking experiences. Research has shown that consumers often make simple mistakes about the wine they are consuming and are relatively poor at discriminating and re-identifying wines, as they are affected by prior biases and prejudices.[7] Wine buying and consumption is more of a gamble if we do not have some basic knowledge and experience of what we are doing. My personal experiences have been evidence of this as I have purchased too many bottles of the wrong wine at too high a price.

Over time, and as one learns and experiences more wine drinking, it is a natural progression to insist on drinking better wine most of the time. But even with a mature palate, you may often want to drink a simple wine instead of a fine wine. Cain Todd states, "I may prefer a simple, rough table wine to a complex fine wine, even while acknowledging that the latter is *objectively* better and more interesting, just as I may at times prefer to listen to Mozart rather than Schoenberg, or read Asterix comics instead of Proust, without this entailing anything about the respective objective value I attribute to each."[8] Knowing more and having more experience does not limit our choice or preference at any given point in time. It makes us realize there exists fine wines which are complex and worthy of consideration, and by approaching them with consideration in an attempt to understand, we will be rewarded.

Additionally by experiencing and learning more, we come to know what wines to drink to improve our health, what wines to avoid (such as wines high in sulfite), and how to drink to achieve enjoyment without bodily wear and tear (described further in *Chapter 14: Improving Feel Sensations*).

As with many things, some knowledge and understanding can go a long way to increasing enjoyment. I have found this to be true with wine. Over the last fifteen years, I have increased my study of wine, shaped my experiences with wine to make sure I was continually learning, and have taken a more systematic approach to understanding what makes wine so pleasurable. Wine is almost unique in its ability to be enjoyed as nourishment, be appreciated as an art form, provide sensual pleasures, and enhance our thinking and ability to experience. I find wine also continues to surprise. Just when I think I understand how wine is made, why it will taste the way it does and how much I will appreciate it, wine continues to reveal new truths and humble me. I have often established an initial viewpoint that has changed over time as my tastes and preferences have changed. Wine continues to be an acquired taste, and one that evolves and changes. I used to enjoy the bigger red wines with high alcohol content. 14.5% - 15% alcohol Shiraz from the Barossa Valley was my wine of choice. Yet, over time, I came to really appreciate the subtleties of an old-world style red blend which has an alcoholic content in the range of 12% - 13.5%. Our tastes and viewpoints on wine continue to evolve and sometimes provide a new mystery or beauty that was not expected. This is one reason wine is so alluring.

Our first reaction to wine is sensual. We experience wine through our senses, primarily smell and taste, but also to a high degree through sight and feel. The next chapter and *Part Two: How Wine Interacts with the Senses* focuses on how our senses are used to respond to wine in more detail. The sensory input must be enjoyable for us to like wine. Our first reaction to wine is through the senses, and our judgment limited to if we do or do not like it. Therefore, much of this book focuses on how our senses work when interacting with wine and how to enhance that to make wine drinking more enjoyable. Wine, once bottled, is not going to change in terms of potential. But by knowing how to best store wine, how to serve the wine, and how to taste and drink the wine, we can maximize the enjoyment from every bottle.

Wine is more than just a sensory reaction from which we derive pleasure. Wine is also a cognitive and affective experience according to Steve Charters, Master of Wine (MW). Drinking and appreciating wine is both a quantitative and a subjective experience. Charters provides an overall framework for how the sensory, cognitive and affective inputs work holistically to provide wine drinking pleasure.[9] His approach is similar to the approach and framework presented in this book. A detailed focus is provided on understanding how our senses interact and respond to wine. It then focuses on how to gain more knowledge and practical experience to increase the cognitive awareness and ability to enjoy and appreciate wine more fully. And finally, through the use of providing the right experiences in terms of drinking together, sharing experiences, and using wine language to discourse wine, how your affective experience make wine drinking a fuller experience.

Paul Draper, the prominent American winemaker was once asked, "Paul, why did wine appeal to you? Why does wine matter?" Draper responded, "Certainly it appealed for the pleasure it can bring to each day. And it matters because when wine is present as we break bread with family and friends, it brings a sense of ritual and of community, of caring about one another. Enjoyed in this way, in moderation, it opens our heart and civilizes us."[10] I was provided similar advice at university which I never forgot, but failed to understand and incorporate into my life until later. A professor once told us that if you cannot find time each day to break bread and drink (wine) heartily with friends and family, then there is something wrong with life. I find that true and try to take far more meals and drink with those that matter.

I enjoy drinking wine when I am alone, while reading, or writing, or watching television. This enjoyment when drinking alone is derived from my sensory and cognitive responses. But wine almost always seems better when sharing the experience with friends and being able to discourse over the wines being consumed. We tend to learn more from each other and social interaction on its own adds to the experience. There are many aspects that impact our affective experience, but being in community and sharing with others is a large part of creating a positive affective experience. While the early Greeks did not respect the senses of smell and taste as much as they did sight and hearing, they "extolled the virtues of wine in liberating social intercourse, lubricating intellectual thought, and facilitating the unification of the good, the beautiful and the true."[11] Similarly, intellectuals and philosophers throughout the ages have agreed with the value and wonder of wine from the Greek Symposiums to the best European salons of the last several centuries. And wine plays a similar role in society today.

Notes

4. Smith, "The Objectivity of Tastes and Tasting," 52.
5. Bach, "Knowledge, Wine and Taste," 26.
6. Smith, "The Objectivity of Tastes and Tasting," 53.
7. Todd, *Philosophy of Wine*, 29.
8. Ibid., 97.
9. Charters, "On the Evaluation of Wine," 168-172.
10. Jefford and Draper, "The Art and Craft of Wine," 200.
11. Todd, *Philosophy of Wine*, 2.

Chapter 2
Enjoying Wine through Our Senses

The *Merriam-Webster Dictionary* defines 'sensual' as "relating to or consisting in the gratification of the senses or in the indulgence of appetite." By this definition, wine drinking is one of the most sensual activities there is as it interacts with each of the five basic human senses to varying degrees. The two most predominant interactions would be smell and taste, followed by sight and feel, and then sound to a lesser degree.

In *Part Two: How Wine Interacts with the Senses,* we explore this interaction in more detail. In *Part Three: Heightening the Wine Drinking Experience,* ideas are provided to increase the sensual pleasure achieved through wine drinking.

There are five basic human senses:

- sight
- smell
- taste
- feel
- sound

This ordering is my view of the sequence and predominance of the sense in the wine drinking experience. You may argue that you hear wine (decanting process or swirling) before you see and smell it, but since hearing wine is far less important for achieving sensuality when drinking wine, it is last on the list. As explained later, while smell and taste are more predominant for achieving wine drinking pleasure than seeing wine, seeing it is clearly first in order and significantly shapes our expectation of how the wine will smell and taste. Therefore, it is ranked first in order.

SPD (Sensory Processing Disorder) Australia defines two additional human senses being a sense of balance and sense of spatial positioning.[12] While this is an evolving field, these last two senses are unimportant to the wine drinking experience (unless you are drinking too much and having a tough time standing up!), so we will focus on the traditional five human senses mentioned above.

For the most part, we invoke our senses through various body parts:

1. sight, through our eyes
2. smell, through our nose
3. taste, through our mouth
4. feel, through our skin
5. sound, through our ears

However, it is more complex as many of the senses simultaneously interact with each other to alter the sensory experience. The taste sense is highly influenced by smell. It is impossible to separate smell from taste as separate, identifiable responses. Taste is highly influenced by feel, the manner in which wine rests on the palate (mostly due to alcohol content), and the amount of tannin in the wine is felt on our tongue and inside our cheeks. Aristotle questioned if taste was actually two different senses (those experienced through our taste buds and the feeling inside the mouth).

The cross-modal sensory experience between sight, smell, taste, and mouthfeel provides complex, yet pleasurable nuances to tasting wine and other foods and liquids. Dr. Charles Spence studies cross-modal sensory response and provides strong evidence of how senses enhance each other. He emphasizes with learning and experience, we can be trained to significantly improve our ability to detect nuances when drinking wine and increase our appreciation and enjoyment of wine. He has studied how listening to music has increased our desires and response to certain wines over other wines.

Spence conducted studies, proving our sight influences our perception of taste and states this influence is so prominent that he refers to sight as 'visual flavor.'[13]

A clever wine parlor game is to conduct a blind tasting, where red dye is placed into white wine to see if people can determine what grape variety is in the wine. Even if the wine is Sauvignon Blanc or Riesling (the two strongest and most easily identifiable white grapes), if the wine has been dyed red, about two thirds of people will guess the wine has been made from a red grape such as Merlot or Cabernet Sauvignon. There is no scientific reason that sight should influence smell and taste, but our sense of sight is so strong that it causes us to perceive smells and tastes incorrectly. Sight is important as it conditions and prepares us for smell and taste by reviving memories from previous tastings. But, it is so prejudicial; it can mask even obvious smells and tastes.

There are a variety of different wine assessment and scoring systems, but they all are similar and evaluate wine on sight, smell and taste. The scores provide an assessment of the overall quality of the wines being judged by the panel of industry experts (and highly influence consumer purchasing decisions, especially among those who do not yet have confidence in their sensing abilities). One interesting element to note in the differences among scoring systems is how each values the importance of the various senses for evaluating wine. Robert Parker's 100-point system (which works off a base of 50 points, so it is really only 50 points for scoring) allocates 5 points for sight. This represents 5% of the total score (or 10% if you only use it as a percentage against 50 points) for sight. The remaining 95% is allocated to smell, taste and overall characteristics. I interpret this philosophy in scoring to reflect a belief Parker has in the ability to objectively assess smell and taste. Whereas the original and other major scoring system, the UC Davis scorecard gives a full 20% of the wine's overall score to the sense of sight. Clearly, this reflects a strong belief in how important sight is when assessing wine.

While the scoring systems vary in terms of individual sensory response, it is unlikely these differences would have one system assess a wine positively while another system assesses it negatively. There is enough underlying scientific basis and similarity across the various scoring systems to provide for consistent results. Yet, the systems reflect different views of how important each sense is for wine assessment.

Earlier, we discussed the role of cognitive and affective responses as important in the overall enjoyment and appreciation of wine. Yet, it is the manner in which the physical human senses interact with the wine that provides the most concrete and intrinsic enjoyment from wine. How this works is presented in *Part Two: How Wine Interacts with the Senses*. But first it is worthwhile to tap into several millennia of philosophical thought on how accurate and trustworthy our physical senses are in objectively evaluating wine and other gustatory pleasures.

Throughout history, many philosophers have derided the role of smell and taste as being inaccurate, and less important and worthy than how the world is perceived through sight and hearing. While there is merit in this position, more recently, studies and scientific evidence have shown that with learning and practice, we can significantly improve the ability of our bodily senses of smell and taste to the point of trusting them as a good judge in assessing a wine's characteristics and its quality.

Notes

12. "The Seven Senses."
13. Spence, "The colour of wine," 122-9.

Chapter 3
Philosophy of Wine & Primary and Secondary Senses

Throughout human history philosophers, scientists and others have studied the human senses. Common conventions have centered on there being five senses that humans (and animal life forms) possess:

- sight
- smell
- taste
- feel
- sound

This chapter discusses the philosophy and physiology of the senses; the next chapter, the cultural and possibly aesthetic consideration of wine as part of our lifestyle. You may not care about these topics and proceed to *Part Two* and *Part Three* of the book to focus on how to better understand and improve wine appreciation and drinking. But if philosophers and other learned individuals have paid serious consideration to these topics over several millennia, I believe it is worth us taking several minutes to understand why. It also provides a broader and deeper context for what is presented later.

Discussion of how the human senses are used as sensual input has occurred since antiquity, with most conventional worldviews enduring for several millennia. The view of sense was initially shaped by Plato and Aristotle. Reviewing wine appreciation from the broader philosophical perspective is relatively recent, occurring mostly during the last fifty years, with most published material on the topic occurring during the last decade. Many of the key questions relevant to our discussion that have been considered included:

- Does all learning occur through our senses?
- Can we trust what our senses tell us?
- Are all or some of our senses more objective or subjective than others?
- Does response through (some of) our senses improve or compromise our moral character?
- Can wine (and food) be viewed as an art form or an aesthetic pursuit?
- Are wine and food of more value than just providing nutrition?

Plato and Aristotle articulated their beliefs on the hierarchy of sense functions based on broader metaphysical belief systems. Plato took the view that our visual and auditory senses are more noble and higher-ranking than other senses (smell, taste, feel) which were considered senses of the flesh and appetite, and therefore cannot be part of a higher purpose in life. Plato cautioned that information provided through bodily experiences could be unreliable.[14] It was the pursuit of knowledge as best directed through our eyes and ears that made men worthy as members of the human species. Any indulgence of the flesh was a potential compromise of our intellect. Aristotle accepted the role our body and its senses played as an important part of life, but recognized that the senses of smell, taste and feel needed to be controlled. When taken to excess, bodily senses could ruin us via obesity, alcoholism or sexual deprivation. These appetites were necessary for us to nourish ourselves and propagate life, but too much of a good thing could be ruinous. Plato goes on to say that "appetite is a powerful, relentless force that must be kept chained like a wild animal lest it overtake the whole being."[15] With the formation of these views several thousand years ago, the bodily senses of smell, taste and feel were relegated to a lower level of respect and importance.

Ancient philosophers debated heavily the role senses played in our development, especially of our intellect. They downplayed the role bodily senses played, yet they used wine as part of their symposiums to facilitate social interaction, intelligent dialog and debate. "Wine moistens and tempers the spirit, and lulls the cares of the mind to rest. It revives our joys and is oil to the dying flame of life. If we drink temperately, and small draughts at a time, the wine distills upon our lungs like sweetest morning dew," said Socrates several millenniums ago.[17] More recent philosophers such as Hume and Kant enjoyed wine and believed moderate imbibing helped the mind function and the soul become peaceful, even while distrusting taste as a sensory input.

Over time, most philosophers have distinguished and segmented the senses of vision and hearing as being nobler than smell, taste and feel. Various frameworks emerged regarding this segmentation, including:

- cognitive versus bodily;
- distal versus gustatory;
- objective versus subjective;
- moral versus immoral;
- intellect-pursued versus appetite-driven;
- pure versus distractive;
- upper versus lower;
- primary versus secondary;
- distance-perception versus closeness-perception; and
- aesthetic versus utilitarian.

Ophelia Deroy states, "that smells and tastes have been noticeably despised by philosophers and aesthetes."[16] Korsmeyer claims that taste as a sense has been underrated in philosophy annals throughout history and deserve more prominence.[18] Cain Todd states, "Philosophical reflection on the nature of wine, our experience of it and the pleasure in drinking it has been firmly rooted in the ordinary, everyday observation that, in the hierarchy of importance, our senses of taste and smell seem to lie well below vision, hearing and touch."[19] Todd continues: "that we trust of taste and smell perceptions and memories less than our visual, auditory and tactile perceptions and memories, and we are wary of sharing and comparing our gustatory experiences."[20] Clearly, the smell, taste and (sometimes) feel senses have not established a positive reputation at any time in history!

There is validity of these views on the segmentation and ordering of the senses. Aristotle developed the view that the senses (sight and hearing) that could perceive things far away had a cognitive, moral, and aesthetic advantage while sense perceptions up close (smell, taste, feel) were distracting and less controllable. Amerine and Roessler point out when the senses inter-relate with each other that our sense of sight can deceive our smell and taste senses through stimulus errors.[21] Seeing a bottle with a screw cap versus a cork, for example, influences our sense of taste and can make us perceive a wine sealed with screw cap to be of less quality then one sealed with cork.

Recent scientific and philosophical studies of human senses have been reasonably consistent in defining sight and hearing as more accurate senses than smell and taste. For most of us, our eyes and our ears can discern with no or little margin of error the characteristics of objects we see or hear. Most of us can determine an object's shape, measurements and color accurately. We consider these to be attributed to the object as perceived through the sense of sight. This is not true for everyone as some people suffer from color blindness, or have other sight impairments such as cataracts or poor eye alignment which cause issues with depth perception. Amerine and Roessler present studies that 8% of males and 4% of females are color blind,[22] making their sense of sight less objective and reliable.[23] And there are illusions of nature such as a straight pole looking bent as the light is refracted when the pole is placed in water. But largely, most of the human population has a consistent gift of sight interpreted in a systematic and normalized manner. Similarly for sound, almost everyone can determine if one sound has a higher or lower pitch than another. And a number of people are trained to be able to discern a musical note's exact pitch.

When it comes to sight and sound, there are also known, systematic models to consistently and accurately evaluate the objects characteristics with which our sense of sight and sound are interacting. The distal characteristics of these objects, according to many philosophers, mean the objects can be more systematically defined, and objectively measured and categorized. They claim the smell and taste of wine cannot be so easily defined or categorized. Senses such as smell and taste are much harder to categorize and appear to be more inconsistently interpreted among those doing the sensing. However, it is rare to find people who are anosmic (cannot smell due to congenital defect, disease or accident). If one is a poor judge of odor quality, it is unlikely to be due to an inability to smell.[24] More and more, scientists and philosophers are starting to understand and appreciate that a lack of consistency in assessing and judging a wine's characteristics through our senses is more an issue of experience and practice and not limited by human physiology. Does that make wine less desirable as an object? No! In fact I would argue the opposite. From a philosophical perspective, I believe objects which are more difficult to define and categorize are far more mysterious, interesting, and worth examining.

We can put our sense of sight to a bottle or glass of wine to determine its size and shape. However, this is not why we enjoy drinking the wine. It is because of the way wine smells and tastes. Philosophers criticize objects that are ingested through our bodily senses (instead of our cognitive ones) as being less complete, less interesting and less worthy of attention. But think of the things that interest and impassion you the most, be it artwork, music or wine. While we can accurately assess distal characteristics of artwork, such as the size of the piece, the content and the colors used, we do not have a systematic framework to determine if a painting is excellent, good, or bad (its quality or worth). And it is our reaction to it by the interaction of the content or subject matter of the painting, the style of brush strokes used, the adherence to or away from reality (think Van Gogh in terms of someone who paints in a representative, but not realistic style) that really makes a given piece of art be appreciated by one person and not by another. Few of us are attracted or turned off by the actual size of art pieces.

Arguments regarding the ability to appreciate wine often center on if our response to it can be categorized objectively and accurately. There is no question as to there being some subjective aspects of tasting and describing wine. Every individual has a different perspective and cumulatively, these can make wine tasting appear to be a solely subjective, even farcical experience. Subjectivity is introduced at multiple levels:

- our individual capabilities / sensitivities (physiologically inbred) to various wine chemicals and other elements
- ability to analyze / judge (experience based)
- ability to describe (experience based)
- differences in personal preferences (inherent bias)
- context / environmental (the point-in-time lens we use as filter - including things such as mood, psychological well-being, temperature conditions, background music, etc.)

The position that our smell and taste senses are limited by our capabilities (and differs from person-to-person) appears to represent a small part of the argument for subjectivity. Through learning, practice and experience, each of the responses from our bodily senses becomes more objective, less subjective. There are common norms in terms of how people respond through their senses. Systematic approaches to judging wine, describing wine, and continued technological advances recording and replaying smells and tastes have shown, that while more challenging, each of the bodily or gustatory senses can be treated objectively. The empirical evidence exists that wine can be viewed objectively. Scoring systems, such as the UC Davis 20-point wine judging system and the Parker 100-point evaluation system for wine, provide a solid and consistent structure to evaluate wines according to the responses provided through our gustatory senses. Wine judges require training and certification that their sense of smell and taste work well and in a consistent manner. A plethora of wine writing and wine reviews (which a large portion of the population is willing to pay for) implies we believe the manner in which the writer or reviewer has evaluated a wine is objective and meaningful for us, not just a private matter of like or dislike on the part of the reviewer.

People often point to the debate and disagreement that Jancis Robinson and Robert Parker had over their review of a particular wine, the 2003 Château Pavie, during a tasting and review in 2007 as to how subjective the response can be when evaluating wine. In fact, their objective evaluation of the wine's characteristics and qualities were assessed as close to identical. It was their preferences and biases that made Robinson despise the wine and Parker delight in it. Robinson found the wine to violate the traditional old-world style Bordeaux she was expecting, while Parker embraced the overripe, intense fruity flavors as a bold new style even when considering it in the Bordeaux category.[25] This would be similar to two music critics being able to objectively evaluate a musical performance with regard to being in tune, properly paced, melody and harmony, composition, etc., yet one judge disliking it because they had a preference or bias for rap music and the piece was a classical one.

Barry Smith claims: "the stubbornly persistent view that when we speak about a wine's taste we can only be speaking about our response to it is based on the idea that tastes can only be experienced as sensations, and that sensations, being utterly subjective, cannot provide any basis for drawing conclusions about the world, or about other people's experiences."[26] His view is this is overstated, as we can all tell if a wine is severely chilled, or possesses other characteristics such as vanilla flavors or a long finish we can all agree on.[27] Sensitivity levels may differ somewhat by individual, but the influence of training can greatly overcome that for almost all of wine's characteristics. Yet, the prejudice persists that wine is subjective as it is experienced through our 'lower level' sensory responses.

Another factor that makes wine tasting seem to be a subjective experience is the ability to define our smell and taste responses accurately and consistently. (Discussed in more detail in *Chapter 5: The Role of Language in Wine Appreciation*.) Not being able to consistently and accurately describe our responses does not mean it is not an objective experience, only that our ability and training to discuss wine has been limited. (Wine language is a growing field of importance and one of the main requirements to become a Master of Wine, one of the highest accreditations one can achieve in the field of wine.)

The other troubling aspect which has been difficult to address is that every bottle of wine is changing over time. It changes during fermentation and initial storage, when moved from metal container to oak, and changes further while cellared. Once opened, the taste continues to change as the wine interacts with air and warms in temperature. How can something that is constantly changing be evaluated objectively, or at least consistently, when it is relative to different environments and context? However the changes and differences can be explained and described scientifically and accurately so they should not be considered to be subjective in nature.

The glass used is one of the biggest influences (as explained in more detail in *Chapter 8: Wine and Smell* and *Chapter 9: Wine and Taste*) on how a wine smells and tastes. For these reasons, official wine judging always uses the International Standards Organization (ISO) tasting glass. If each wine judging event was allowed to use their own glasses shaped to get the most enjoyment out of specific varietals of wine, it would be extremely difficult to judge wines consistently. It is like judging one marathon runner's time against another when the two runners have run over two different courses with different elevation rises and different wind conditions. We can still review the times, subject to what we know about race and course conditions to determine if the result was a great, good or poor one. While environments and conditions may be different, there exists a scientific basis and techniques to normalize them.

For each of the items mentioned as an argument for the subjective nature of wine tasting, further practice, understanding and experience helps us become more objective in how we use our bodily senses. In agreement with Korsmeyer, I believe the bodily senses are underrated and viewed negatively to the point of prejudice. Historically, the bodily senses have been viewed as being more subjective than the cognitive senses, but this is a belief derived from the cognitive senses having better defined systematic frameworks. Visual and auditory senses can be accurately recorded and replayed. These were the first senses to be recorded in a systematic manner (via the invention of the camera and phonograph). Yet, there has been recent progress similarly with smells and tastes. The frameworks for smells and tastes are more complex and multi-dimensional than those for visual and auditory recording. The resulting computer files therefore are much larger, representing the complexity inherent in defining and recording smells and tastes. However, significant progress has been made in individual odor 'noses' and even more broadly in a comprehensive 'electronic nose' which can smell, record, describe and play back the smell with a realistic match to the original.

Each sense has a definitional framework to some degree of completeness. If I use music as an example, any musical score (the language in which the music is written) can be input, defined and replayed as MIDI (Musical Instrument Digital Interface). MIDI is a reasonably comprehensive definitional framework to define and consistently replay a piece of music. It has fields and codification for vibrato, trills, uplifting or falling off a note, etc. Music has been recorded and replayed with improving representation of live music starting in the last century and improving over time. Edison's phonograph to recording eight tracks on magnetic tape, to electronic wave files and

MP3 files has been an ongoing evolution. Each succession has provided a more realistic live experience while advances in technology and mathematical algorithms have provided reduced methods and requirements for storing ever-increasingly realistic recordings.

This is happening with all the senses, but the frameworks for smells, taste and feelings are less understood and structured than for sight and sound. Smells, tastes and feelings are still more challenging to define and record. Yet, good progress continues to be made with every sense. Still photography and moving video are now easily captured, recorded and replayed with great realism; smell and taste are not far behind. The reality of having an 'Orgasmatron' as in the 1973 Woody Allen movie *Sleeper* is not too far in the distant future!

It is the complexity and challenge of smelling and tasting in a systematic manner that makes wine so beguiling and intriguing. And with over a thousand varieties of wine grapes (white wine is not just Chardonnay and red wine is not just Merlot!), the different soils, climates and other regional characteristics where the grapes are grown, the different styles, techniques and processes used by thousands of winemakers and the differences that mother nature presents year-to-year that provides an infinite set of wine drinking experiences. Wine is a simple product, derived simply by fermenting grapes. Yet, through vineyard management techniques and winemaking processes, there are almost infinite different types of wine. Amerine and Roessler describe a typical wine to have more than 400 organic compounds, of which approximately 200 or more are more or less odorous, with at least 182 esters, 52 alcohols, 75 aldehydes and ketones, 22 acetals, 18 lactones, 6 secondary acetamides, 11 phenols, 29 nitrogen-containing compounds, 18 sulfur-containing compounds, 2 ethers, 11 furans, and 18 epoxides, as well as 30 miscellaneous compounds![28] And over time, many of these are changed in various ways via aging and cellar treatment. Peynaud presents chemical analysis showing over 500 wine component peaks on a chromatograph when analyzing wine, sixty of them discernible by the human senses of smell and taste.[29] Therefore, defining smells and tastes in a systematic manner is challenging, but is reliably occurring and improving.

Therefore, wine can be evaluated objectively, but our knowledge and experience are limiting factors in being able to do so. This book is intended to help remove those factors and teach you how to enjoy and appreciate wine more. In recent evaluation and debate of wine tasting being objective versus subjective, a number of more recent philosophical studies are using terms such as 'relativism' (objective, but relative to our capabilities and experience) as defined and defended by Todd[30] and sensing wine as both relative and objective by Deroy.[31] I use the term 'contextual objectivity' which is an objective framework contextualized to our capabilities, experience and environment. The growing consensus is that wine tasting and evaluation is more objective than subjective and when it appears subjective, that we often can resolve those differences by understanding and translating the differences in context.

Steve Charters, MW, explains a framework for tasting and evaluating wine which comprises sensory, cognitive and affective dimensions which integrates our wine drinking experiences and reactions.[32] This framework is useful in understanding all of the inputs we process, our reactions, and how we respond and judge. It integrates our senses, our brain, and our emotions into a single model for tasting and evaluating wine. Studies by Charters and Pettigrew show that individual responses to assessing wine are both objective and subjective simultaneously. Quality is assessed approximately 70% - 80% objectively and the remainder subjectively, often influenced mostly by personal preference.[33]

There are a number of books on wine and philosophy that dive more deeply into these topics. I have listed a few of them in *Chapter 20: Further Wine Education.* They provide excellent background to better understand the evolution and views around the importance and reliability of the senses and broader concepts in philosophy as it relates to wine. Hopefully you are convinced that:

- Our sense of smell and taste can objectively and accurately provide responses to gustatory pursuits such as wine drinking.
- Much of the negative response to the bodily senses is prejudiced, and that gustatory pursuits and pleasure are worth pursuing and permissible.
- With practice and more experience, we can improve our objectiveness and enhance our wine drinking experiences.

In my view, philosophers have overlooked two important issues:

1. Sensory inputs and responses make wine more

appealing, intriguing, and pleasurable than objects where the primary characteristics are defined distally.

2. With an ever increasing understanding and ability to define bodily senses in a systematic, consistent manner, these objects can be evaluated and discussed objectively.

Advances in technology for the recording and replaying of all senses, including smell, taste and feel support this view.

I have been pondering the question as to why so many people willingly accept that wine tasting is only a subjective exercise. I believe it is because they are not willing to put in the effort or concentration to improve their skills. It is easier to point to others as being fakes or pretentious and accepting the belief that there is nothing they can do about it. I am of the opinion there is nothing further from the truth; with the right attitude and approach, most of us can come to understand the balance of wine tasting as having strong objective components and being an objective exercise with some degree of variability and subjectivity which can be explained.

Wine lovers who are philosophers or enjoy philosophy are in consensus that wine can be pursued and evaluated objectively and accurately through the bodily senses. I highly recommend the books referenced in *Chapter 20: Further Wine Education*. I have read, enjoyed and learned a great deal from them. They will help you continue to increase your wine drinking enjoyment. But they are not necessary to significantly enhance your wine drinking beyond what is learned from this book. With the foundations gained in *Part Two* and *Part Three*, you should be able to benefit from and accumulate significant knowledge by partaking in more wine drinking, which is where all the fun is anyway!

Notes

14. Korsmeyer, *Making Sense of Taste*, 13.
15. Ibid., 13.
16. Robards, *Book of Wine*, 2.
17. Deroy, "The Power of Tastes," 101.
18. Korsmeyer, "The Meaning of Taste and the Taste of Meaning," chap. 3.
19. Todd, *Philosophy of Wine*, 11.
20. Ibid., 14.
21. Amerine and Roessler, *Wines: Their Sensory Evaluation*, 62-63.
22. Ibid., 28.
23. Ibid., 33.
24. Ibid., 33.
25. Todd, *Philospohy of Wine*, 120-1.
26. Smith, "The Objectivity of Tastes and Tasting," 47.
27. Ibid., 61.
28. Amerine and Roessler, *Wines: Their Sensory Evaluation*, 32-33.
29. Peynaud, *The Taste of Wine*, 49.
30. Todd, *Philosophy of Wine*, 77-134.
31. Deroy, "The Power of Tastes," 101-21.
32. Charters, "On the Evaluation of Wine," 168-72.
33. Ibid., 170.

Chapter 4
Wine as an Aesthetic Experience

The enjoyment and consumption of wine as part of my lifestyle has always been an important part of my experiences while tasting a multitude of wines over the years. Through these experiences my intent was to view wine (and food) as an aesthetic experience, possibly even an art form. These ideas started to form when contemplating why wine gave me so much pleasure. I noticed similarities to my appreciation of music and other performing arts, and identified similarities between my wine drinking experiences with sexual gratification and religious contemplation! My interests were piqued further by reading some books on wine and philosophy, most notably by Barry Smith, Cain Todd and Roger Scruton. Through this process, it became evident that gustatory pleasures had aesthetic elements and characteristics similar to 'consuming' the experience of viewing art or a live musical or theatrical experience.

I then looked into the field of aesthetics and in particular into the matter of tastes and gustatory aesthetics. These topics were initially pursued by Plato and Aristotle. Wine and food as art was also reviewed and discarded, at least in part, by German and English philosophers such as Kant, Hegel, Locke and Hume. But the topic has recently and credibly been studied by Frank Sibley, Carolyn Korsmeyer and Elizabeth Telfer.

Many have tried to justify that food and wine can be considered aesthetically and be viewed as an art form. Fanny Farmer, states in introducing her famous cookbook, "Cooking may be as much a means of self-expression as any of the arts." Andre Simon claims that chefs and winemakers are artists along with being scientists.[34] Philosopher D.W. Prall pushes the position further by stating, "Like all sense presentations, smells and tastes can be pleasant to perception, can be dwelt on in contemplation, have specific and interesting character, recognizable and rememberable and objective. They offer an object, that is, for sustained discriminatory attention." And Margaret Visser goes on to say, "A meal is an artistic construct, ordering the foodstuff which comprise it into a complex dramatic whole, as a play organizes actions and words into component parts such as acts, scenes, speeches, dialogs, entrances, and exits, all in a sequence designed for them. However humble it may be, a meal has a definite plot, the intention of which is to intrigue, stimulate, and satisfy."[35] Many seem intent on viewing food and wine as an art form and one that can be viewed aesthetically. However, is it really deserving of such merit?

I personally have participated in meals with wine which were truly magnificent experiences and will be remembered forever. Wine is mysterious, seductive and used to enhance life. Much of the language of wine is taken from music; we discuss a wine's 'floral notes' and 'the harmony between the fruit, the spice and the oak.' I have drunk wine that has made my chest quiver in a manner similar to when I am listening to music I enjoy. The sensory responses are similar; drinking a fine wine is a sensual experience for me. But can it be considered an aesthetic pursuit or art form? Why even consider this?

It is worth contemplating since we spend a lot of our time eating and drinking. This is often in a social context where the dialog is about the food and wine we are imbibing. It also helps us understand if we should be spending money on wine education and the act of drinking in the first place. Is our life enhanced by adding wine to it? Should we spend money and time on the pursuit of drinking wine? How does it benefit us? Is wine drinking merely a sensual experience that without control could possibly ruin life, or is it a matter of contemplation and reflection which when properly consumed can enhance life? Should government money or educational funds be spent on teaching wine appreciation?

Aesthetics is difficult to frame and its meaning varies when applied to different forms such as still art and performing art. The framework further changes when applied to such areas as solving eloquent mathematical proofs or cooking up a 'masterpiece' banquet. Telfer states, "it is not just a matter of what you like."[36] We may like or even greatly enjoy a ham sandwich, but does it really merit our reflection and criticism? Is it something sustainable through time and something that can be universally appreciated by others? Not all food and wine can be viewed aesthetically, but then similarly, a picture made via 'paint by numbers' does not warrant that type of appreciation either. Therefore, we are limiting our discussion to what can be defined as fine wine or great wines.

Beardsley defines three universal aspects required for something to warrant aesthetic appreciation:[37]

- unity (integrated whole)
- complexity
- intensity

Certainly a fine wine seems to address those definitional requirements. Denis Dutton defines aesthetic universals to comprise:[38]

- expertise or virtuosity
- non-utilitarian pleasure
- style
- criticism
- imitation
- special focus
- imaginative experience for both producers and audience

It can still be argued that fine wine addresses the aesthetic universals defined by Dutton. Yet, others argue that experiences such as eating and drinking, which rely upon the gustatory senses of smell and taste, cannot be viewed aesthetically. There appears to be prejudice against gustatory sense responses. Eating and drinking are considered 'low-brow,' not 'high-brow' experiences as those perceived through the cognitive senses of seeing and hearing.

Sibley and Korsmeyer outline a number of points[39][40][41] which philosophers have used over time to discredit the gustatory senses as appropriate receptors for aesthetic response. These include:

- Food and wine are consumed and disposed, not lasting like a piece of artwork, and therefore lack sustainability.
- Eating and drinking are utilitarian, necessary for survival, but not worthy of reflection or criticism.
- Most food and wine are 'simple fare.'
- Eating and drinking are driven by appetites which cannot be controlled like cognitive senses.
- Cognitive senses can be systematically categorized, while gustatory senses cannot.
- Bodily sense consumption must be removed through unpleasant means such as bowel movements, vomiting, and sexual release.

All of these points can be refuted to some degree. In the previous chapter, we discussed that the gustatory senses can be systematically defined, even though achieving a systematic framework of the gustatory senses is more recently understood and challenging; progress has been slower in recording smell and taste electronically. Significant progress has been made recently, at least proving the point that the gustatory senses of taste and smell can be systematically, or at least representatively, defined. While most food is 'simple fare,' so is most art and music. There is complexity and multiple dimensions to the taste of many fine wines that make them far more intriguing and worthy of consideration than many well-known and successful works of art or music (in my opinion). Therefore, by definition and scope, we are limiting our discussion to only fine or great wines.

The other points have gaps in terms of a holistic aesthetic argument for being treated equally with other art forms. Wine is consumed and disposed of; however, the memories (especially with practice) can be retained over long periods of time, if not indefinitely, similarly if not more so, than remembering what a painting looks like or how a musical performance sounded. Paintings tend to have a much longer life cycle than a bottle of wine. Wine is more akin to live musical performances. You can enjoy the same (not the identical) bottle of wine over and over again. It may change slightly over time, but then so does the same song performed by the same group over time, or by a different group.

Wine styles have longevity, and similar to art, both endure and evolve over time. Wine making has occurred for 8,000 years, has evolved over that period of time and has in general improved over that period of time. As with great art, wine styles and specific wine types are develop through experimentation and continued improvement over many years. While a specific bottle of wine is consumed, never to be experienced again, the wine style has a sustainable aspect similar to other things that are viewed aesthetically. Wine in this regard, demands the same type of reflection, review and criticism that other art forms are accorded.

Eating and drinking are necessary for survival and much imbibing is utilitarian. Yet, drinking wine (and haute cuisine) is not necessary for survival. It is a choice based on consideration and interest similar to the choice to visit an art gallery. The utilitarian part of eating and drinking could be done from a tube of paste (as astronauts do) with the right nutrient composition if nourishing ourselves was all we were interested in. We could just as easily nourish ourselves intravenously if we so desired. But there is a pleasure, one worthy of appreciation and reflection, in preparing a good meal, selecting the right wine, and treating a meal and wine drinking as an event that is aesthetically appealing. In groups, we discourse over wine similar to the way we discourse over art or live musical or theatrical performances.

Korsmeyer describes the concept of representational food.[42][43] The 'common' pretzel was first invented by a monk to represent folded arms and meditation as used as an award for boys successfully studying their catechism. The croissant represents the defense of Vienna against the Ottoman Turks and Christians defeating Islam. This is representationally re-enacted every time we eat a croissant. The bread and wine representing the Eucharist and the Body and Blood of Christ is repeated weekly by hundreds of millions of Christians around the world.

Eggnog and candy canes for Christmas, pumpkins at Halloween, etc. are all examples of representational foods that cause and facilitate reflection of matters more important than merely eating food or drinking wine. When eating the blood and drinking wine during Holy Communion, I dive deep into reflection and contemplation of things far more important than the mere taste of the bread and wine; I encounter and become one with all they represent.

The foods we eat and the wine and other items we drink also are representative of our social class and our intimacy of the relationships of the people with whom we associate. We want to match the quality of food and wine to the people, events and experiences in which we are partaking.

A number of philosophers have argued that the bodily senses (smell, taste and feel) are appetite-driven and therefore cannot be trusted or controlled. They view the responses to bodily functions as being distractions to 'more important' cognitive senses. There is some truth to that, but also a lot of falsity. These issues tend to get entwined in moral and ethical viewpoints. It is easy to blame the bodily senses for our behavior. But I have found that our appetites are not driven by our sensual needs and responses as much as they are by our mental health and emotional states. The woman who drank ten liters of Coke each day until she died.[44] was not fueling a requirement to satisfy a sensual response that demanded satisfaction. Often, after over-imbibing, we are less satisfied and even disgusted with our behavior. It is our cognitive senses at work in allowing or restricting appetite more than our bodily senses. It is easier though to blame our bodily senses instead of admitting we are of 'weak mind.'

I dispute that the bodily senses are less accurate and objective than the cognitive ones. In fact, our eyes are capable of deceiving as much as or more so than other senses. Our sense of sight is so developed and trained from birth as to be prejudiced and override responses from the other senses. In research from Brochet (discussed in more detail elsewhere in the book), he shows just how far our eyes go to deceive when we put a red dye in white wine, or put an iconic brand label on a table wine.

Animals have other senses such as smell which are far more developed than sight in dogs and hearing which is far more developed than sight in bats. A friend of mine was at the dog park and his dog was playing with another dog. They seemed like two normal dogs having a romp, and my friend thanked the other dog owner for the play time. It was only at that point that my friend learned the other dog was blind. Yet, he was able to fully engage in playing through his sense of smell. With practice we can train our bodily senses to be as accurate and as objective as we can our cognitive senses. The scientific basis for this is explained in *Part Two: How Wine Interacts with the Senses*.

One of the key features exhibited in objects that are perceived to be worthy of aesthetic appreciation is that of balance or proportion. Art and architecture have proportions which often adhere to the Golden Ratio, defined as $[(a + b) / a] = a / b = \varphi$ (Greek letter phi). This ratio is considered to be in perfect harmony and proportion, and is often represented in architecture and the composition of paintings. In addition, it is highly visible in nature as viewed in the dimensions of the human body and face, galaxies and hurricane patterns, sunflowers and snail shells which follow Fibonacci ratios which asymptotically approach the Golden Ratio.[45]

Similarly, wine is judged on its balance, and its integration. Winemakers work hard to achieve the right combination of flavors, grape blends, alcohol levels, and many other characteristics to provide a beautiful taste and mouthfeel. One of the key characteristics that distinguish a great wine from a good wine is balance.

Telfer and Korsmeyer differ slightly on the smaller points representing a view of wine and food as art or an aesthetic. Telfer concludes that gustatory pursuits such as winemaking and the creation of haute cuisine can be considered a minor and simple art form, sharing many aesthetic considerations as major and more complex art forms, whereas Korsmeyer categorizes some food as being decorative art.

The prominent view is that haute cuisine and winemaking are more a craft, and winemakers and chefs are artisans, not quite artists in the traditional sense, even if they do possess genius in what they do. Wine and haute cuisine are capable of provoking aesthetic reactions. Much of the appreciation we get from haute cuisine and fine wine has to do with our aesthetic appreciation (and response) to it. We think and reflect on how wine was made, the influences that made this wine taste similar or different to other fine wines, and the benefits of this wine to our experiences. We use our cognitive senses, especially sight in enjoying and appreciating wine. Telfer states that not everything that provokes an aesthetic reaction can be considered art, but that works of art are created to produce an aesthetic reaction.[46] Not all wine that is produced is meant to provoke an aesthetic reaction, but I would assert that most fine wines are created with this intent.

The ability of fine wine to provoke an aesthetic reaction means it is provoking a sensual response and pleasure. A tuna fish sandwich (enjoyable as it may be!) does not do this, nor do other foods or drinks. Wine does. There are several additional elements as to why wine provokes aesthetic reactions greater than art and music. For art, only our cognitive senses are used. Art is primarily, almost solely, appreciated through our sense of sight; music, through our hearing sense. Wine and haute cuisine are experienced cross-modally, using our senses of sight, smell, taste, feel and even to some extent, hearing. This cross-modal dimension provides depth and complexity of experience that demands reflection, review and criticism. Inexperienced wine drinkers can possibly pick up on if a wine tastes good and with a little experience start to determine the grape from which the wine was made. They may also be able to determine if it has fruity or oak flavors. Wine drinkers can spend their lifetime enhancing their ability to smell and taste wine, and the infinitely different types of wine and flavors induced by focusing on one sense first and then another sense in sequence. And with continued practice, a wine enthusiast with a great deal of practice and experience can quickly pick up most of a wine's primary and secondary characteristics almost immediately. Wine is a cross-modal sensory experience, whereas art and music are appreciated through a single dominant cognitive sense.

Is it just a matter of boundaries in terms of defining what a craft versus art is, and what is sensual versus aesthetic? I think this is true and one person's sensual pursuit is another's aesthetic appreciation. Again I ask why the question is important. Cannot we just drink and enjoy without thinking about if a wine provokes an aesthetic reaction or not? That is a question for each of us to answer individually. However, governments and investment committees are providing funds and establishing policy based on these definitions. Large funds may be allocated to the arts, but not the crafts, for example in certain communities. Additionally, are certain groups prohibiting only hard (40% or more alcohol content) liquor, or anything with any level of alcohol content? Our ability to understand and even possibly influence these debates and decisions may provide or eliminate our ability to drink and appreciate wine the way we want.

On a more personal level, we need to become comfortable on what we spend on wine, how much we value it and how much we drink. Being comfortable with why we are drinking wine and being able to assess the value we get from it is important in helping us become comfortable about what we spend on wine and how we consume it. This topic is covered in detail in *Chapter 17: Buying and Storing Wine*. I have rarely paid more than $100 for a bottle of wine, and in the few occasions that I have done so, it has been for a special occasion or as a gift for another. Yet, many other people have spent tens of thousands and even more than $100,000 for a single bottle. I find it impossible to consider spending so much as it is my intent to consume the wine I buy. Spending so much must satisfy some other type of need (other than just to drink a good bottle) and its possession must trigger some type of aesthetic response, or emotional response similar to those who buy extremely expensive handbags, luggage, or other iconic brands when many suitable (at least functionally suitable) similar alternatives are available for far less money.

Therefore, I think each of us owe ourselves some time to reflect on why we enjoy wine and what it means to us. We need to think about how we take in the world around us through our senses. I have always been a bit of a high-brow, reading hundreds of books, enjoying music and art, and studying philosophy and mathematics. These were pursuits for aesthetic reasons and for no other purpose, except to fulfill and excite the soul. My cognitive senses have served me well in these pursuits.

Over the last few decades, I have started to experience and appreciate life more through my bodily senses. I never had a massage until after I turned fifty years old. Now I enjoy regular massages and it helps my health, but also pleases my sense of feel. I have learned to enjoy and appreciate gustatory pleasures also.

Scruton describes drinking wine as an intoxicating experience, one that is a sensory, not aesthetic experience. He compares it to reading poetry which he claims is aesthetic through and through. His definition of intoxication is not derived from the imbibing of alcohol, but rather the experience of drinking it: "The intoxication I feel is not just the effect caused by the wine: it feeds back into my experience of the wine, so as to become part of its taste. It is a way of relishing the wine."[47] The wine drinking experience is enhanced (and the wine seemingly tastes better) just through the experience of drinking it.

I think we often pursue intellectual or cognitively-derived activities, sometimes as an escape from the hard realities of life, or as an alternative to our otherwise routine and mundane existence. I certainly did. Then things changed for me and my view of life. My father had a massive stroke and for months could not do the most basic things. He had to be retrained to comb his hair and feed himself. Holding a fork full of food and getting it to his mouth under his own power was not possible. He could not dress himself, clean himself, or get himself into or out of bed on his own. Slowly, and with therapy and great personal desire, he was able to start doing these things again. His enjoyment of life and his dignity returned. Watching him struggle with these basic activities in the occupation of life, I came to appreciate and realize how important (and joyous) performing basic activities could be.

I started to relish being able to do the dishes, vacuum the floor, do the laundry, take care of my personal hygiene, and be able to feed myself. I learned to cook, I learned to feel and I learned to value and appreciate the interaction I was having with my bodily senses. The fundamental aspects of smelling, tasting, and feeling became far more important to me than they had been previously. I now understand and greatly value experiencing the world through my bodily senses as much as or more than through my cognitive ones. I have learned to aesthetically appreciate my gustatory experiences and my social interactions that result from or are facilitated by these pursuits as an important part of life. That is why I reflect, assess and evaluate how to improve them.

I agree with Korsmeyer, Sibley and Telfer that wine is not (or stops short of being) a fully aesthetic activity, but it does provoke significant aesthetic reactions. It does not qualify fully as an art form, but certainly shares many characteristics with other art forms that make it worthy of contemplation and appreciation, and most importantly, justifies the time and money we put into it. And that is more than enough for me. I have learned to appreciate experiencing the world through my smell and taste senses as much as the other ones.

Notes

34. Neil and Ridley, *Arguing About Art*, part 1.
35. Telfer, "Food as Art, chap. 2.
36. Telfer, "Food as Art," chap. 2.
37. Charters, "On the Evaluation of Wine," 166.
38. Dutton, "Aesthetic Universals," 286-8.
39. Sibley, *Approach to Aesthetics*, chap. 15.
40. Korsmeyer, "The Meaning of Taste and the Taste of Meaning," chap. 3.
41. Korsmeyer, *Making Sense of Taste*, 2-10.
42. Korsmeyer, "The Meaning of Taste and the Taste of Meaning," chap. 3,
43. Korsmeyer, *Making Sense of Taste*, 7.
44. "Woman dies after drinking 10 liters of Coke a day."
45. Wikipedia, s.v. "Golden ratio."
46. Telfer, "Food as Art," chap. 2.
47. Scruton, *I Drink Therefore I am*, 122-3.

Chapter 5
The Role of Language in Wine Appreciation

     Becoming comfortable with wine language helps us communicate more clearly with others, and heightens and makes more pleasurable the wine drinking experience by sharing it. As importantly, assimilating wine descriptors improves our wine drinking abilities by capturing and correlating wine terms with wine styles and flavors. This process reconditions and rewires the brain over time. Learning wine language plays an important role in enhancing our ability to taste and appreciate wine.

     Unfortunately, all language is abused, misinterpreted and butchered repeatedly. This applies to wine language also. Ken Bach finds it an interesting linguistic fact that whereas we have numerous words for specific shades of color, our vocabulary is sorely lacking when it comes to tastes, smells, and feeling.[48] It has only been recently (last two centuries) that semantics for wine have been more thoroughly developed. A large reason people have the perception that drinking wine is a subjective experience is that two (or more) people will describe their reaction to the same wine differently. This is as likely caused by poor language as it is our senses ability to respond accurately. Two people may drink and think similarly about wines characteristics, but one person may say the wine is bitter and another astringent, without truly understanding what the terms mean.

As individuals it is difficult to commit our wine tasting experiences to memory if we have not associated those experiences with words. Jancis Robinson, MW, discusses the importance of 'trigger words' to help remember wine taste and recall that taste later when it is associated with the wine we are now tasting. Robinson says that you can evolve your own vocabulary and if a wine tastes like clean sheets or a tennis ball to you, then make that association.[49] It will help you identify flavors and wines later on. And while not essential, it is beneficial to develop consistent terminology when discussing wine if you want to share your experiences with others. This requirement becomes critical if you write about wine and is essential if you want to pursue a Masters of Wine (MW), one of the wine industry's highest honors. You may have a personal trigger word of meaning, but that trigger word is useless in describing wine to others unless they understand and are using similar triggers.

One interesting example is Riesling. One person may describe certain Rieslings, like those made with grapes from Polish Hill vineyards in the Clare Valley region of South Australia, in one manner and others using different terminology. Polish Hill is known as a 'super-premium wine-growing district,' and has some of the world's most iconic Riesling producers residing there.[50] The soil comprises shale and clay, and is acidic. Some people have described these Rieslings to have strong mineral tastes, while others have said the wine tastes like battery acid! While the descriptions are different - one positive, the other negative - it is likely both parties had similar physiological responses to the chemical composition of the wine. Both may even say they really enjoy the wine, even though they describe the wine differently. Riesling was a poor selling varietal before the marketing department realized they needed to position Riesling as having intense mineral flavors (often compared to Evian as a bottled water with similar characteristics) instead of describing it as battery acid!

This chapter expands and clarifies several important topics of wine language:

- Help us understand the importance of wine language and requirement to be more pedantic about its use.
- Clarify some particular terms (like taste) used inconsistently when discussing wine.
- Discuss how wine language improves the wine drinking experiences.

Adrienne Lehrer, more than anyone else in the field, has advanced the concept and importance of wine language. Lehrer is Professor Emerita in Linguistics at The University of Arizona and has been writing on wine language for nearly half a century. Lehrer's classic text is *Wine and Conversation* (2nd edition, 2009). In this text, she provides a large wine vocabulary and taxonomy to help use correct wine words in a more consistent manner. She provides 'word scales' to relate terms positionally to each other (dry, off-dry, semi-dry, etc.) when discussing wine. Lehrer has conducted a number of experiments on wine language use and has concluded that with some education, and continued experience, people can assess and describe wine in a more consistent manner.

Consistency is highest when describing wines in technical terms, less so for evaluative terms. Some recent wine terminology goes beyond being useful, but is often used in social circles to impress. These are words like 'brawny,' 'joyous' or 'pretentious.' These terms may be fun to use in social circles, but are less useful when judging and scoring wines. A great deal of the development and consistency in wine language has been forged through the definition of structure in wine scoring systems such as the UC Davis 20-point system, the Australian Roseworthy 20-point system (modified UC Davis system), and the Parker 100-point system. While each system encapsulates different value judgments and terminology, they achieve consistency and authority that 'standard wine consumers' can use and believe in when purchasing wine. Reviews using consistent wine terminology provide confidence that the wine purchased is a good or excellent wine, even if the buyer cannot evaluate or describe what they like about the wine.

Amerine and Roessler mention how less experienced wine judges, and by implications most wine enthusiasts, confuse a number of wine characteristics, using incorrectly such terms as sourness, bitterness, and astringency.[51] Both in terms of the chemical composition and the flavors produced, these terms are different, yet have some overlapping dimensions of the underlying characteristics and definition of terms. Lehrer provides a detailed taxonomy for most common wine terms in *Wine and Conversation.* I highly recommend reading her book.

In Lehrer's essay *Can Wines be Brawny?: Reflections on Wine Vocabulary,*[52] she presents that there exists implied classes of expertize and authority. Oenologists (winemakers) can most accurately describe wines in technical terms. And wine reviewers and judges have been trained and can be counted on to describe wines according to the frameworks of the judging and scoring systems used. All of us, as wine enthusiasts, can improve and become more knowledgeable in assessing and describing wine accurately. Lehrer's book, *Wine and Conversation*, provides a great starting point for assembling trigger words and other descriptive words for defining wine's characteristics. Wine vocabulary also improves when drinking and discussing wine in the presence of others. Lehrer's experiments conclude that through wine discourse, each party gains in knowledge and consistency when discussing wine. This is particularly beneficial if we are in the presence of others with more expertise. In *Chapter 18: Wine Drinking Practice and Experience*, I present one of the quickest ways to improve your knowledge of wine and enhance your wine drinking experience is to drink and discuss wine in the presence of others who possess more expertise.

While Lehrer's essay or book is well worth reading, you may also refer to *Wine Folly's chart of wine terminology* for a quick introduction to wine terms.

This book is about 'tasting' wine. Yet, the term taste is used in many different ways. The term taste when referring to our senses is limited to mouth taste (excluding smells), others use this to mean 'flavors' (coming from taste buds only), while others mean flavors and mouthfeel or the tactile sensations involved. More broadly, tasting is used as the entire experience of evaluating and assessing the wine we drink. Finally, philosophers have hijacked the use of taste to represent the aesthetic response we have in terms of use in our taste for good clothes, our taste in music, etc. Hence taste has been used in five different ways!

In this book, taste is used all five ways as is best suited to explain various concepts. I have attempted to be as clear as possible when using the word taste. In *Chapter 9: Wine and Taste*, I refer to it as 'mouth taste' limited to flavors, in *Chapter 10: Wine and Feel*, I use it more broadly to describe the mouthfeel and tactile sensations experienced when drinking wine. In *Chapter 12: Improving Smell and Taste Sensations*, since most of the practical suggestions provided improve both smell and (mouth) taste together, I use it more broadly again.

I use a structure for taste terminology similar to Robinson in *How to Taste Wine* and Jackson in *Wine Science*.[53] The structure used (in this book) follows:

- taste (inclusive of odors and mouth taste)
- odors
- aroma
    - bouquet
- mouth taste (flavor)
    - flavors (coming from the taste buds)
    - mouthfeel (tactile, often defined as 'finish')
    - balance

However, the term 'taste' varies throughout the book when covering philosophical and aesthetic topics, the experience of tasting itself, and the physiological response as described in our sense of taste. As often as possible, I use the term 'taste' in its most common vernacular instead of being overly pedantic.

Jamie Goode uses a slightly different taxonomy and states in *Wine and the Brain*: "You can't taste wine without smelling it. Much of the sensory information when wine is in our mouth comes from the senses of olfaction and touch, which can't therefore be disassociated from the sensations coming from our taste buds. Thus I prefer to use the term 'flavor' to define this multiple sensing of wine in the mouth which results in a seamless, unified perception of wine."[54] This definition also starts to explain the cross-modal (multiple, different use of senses in wine tasting) experience that makes wine so pleasurable and worthy of reflection.

We drink milk or soda, and have some physiological taste response, but for the most part, it is a matter of ingesting liquid. This is what I describe as drinking. Some people drink wine as a means to consume alcohol and possibly get high or drunk from it. This again is drinking. When tasting wine, you take the additional steps of assessing, reflecting and evaluating what you are experiencing. The act of reflection and description then commits the experience to memory. This book is about tasting wine. Many liquids can be drunk, but it is almost the unique domain of wine as a liquid and more broadly a food product, that it merits being tasted. I will often use the term 'wine drinking' throughout the book as it is a standard English convention. But when I do use the term wine drinking, I am always implying tasting!

Todd makes the point that the language used can actually undermine people from trying good wines and believing that wine appreciation and expertise stems from the exotic and flowery use of an apparently straightforward sensory object.[55] By calling wines 'pretentious' or flirtatious,' we take away the seriousness of wine. Using metaphorical descriptions without presenting descriptive and evaluative judgments discourages wine drinking as a worthwhile pursuit.

Use of allegory can be descriptive, especially when articulating smells and tastes for evaluative judgment of wine. Todd uses comparisons to architecture in terms of a wine's structure and balance / proportion.[56] Even allegory such as a wine being smoky or smelling of wet grass or leather can be useful in providing triggers to other smells we have experienced which share the same underlying chemical characteristics as those smells. Using wine language allegorically helps us describe a wine's quality and access what we like about the wine.

As Robinson mentioned, it is not essential to be able to describe wine to enjoy it, but it certainly helps us enjoy it more and be able to discuss it with others. We learn more quickly when tasting wine in the presence of others. Using wine language helps rewire our brains and ability to access wine properly, regardless if we are alone or in the company of others. When tasting wine alone, I am mentally describing the wine and taking notes to reinforce my learning. Schuster believes we need clear wine language to study and appreciate wine effectively.[57] Schuster reinforces the concept of learning more quickly when experts are around to articulate language for our benefit. He is of the opinion that words help us notice things and remember them. Bach states: "Vivid verbal description can create the illusion of revealing an unnoticed quality without actually doing so. Perhaps all it does is put into words what you already sensed but weren't able to articulate. The question boils down to this: does the wine taste different now that its qualities are singled out and labeled, or does the description ring true because it captures the experience one was already having? I'm inclined to opt for the latter answer: the descriptions ring true not because it reveals something new but because one's experience already fits it."[58] This is why drinking among qualified wine tasters is important. They articulate while the rest of us learn to identify particular qualities we missed previously.

There are various wine glossaries and dictionaries that have evolved over time with regard to wine. Some of these have been used to encapsulate terms involved in winemaking and vineyard management. They are technical and scientific in nature. Some have evolved to include terms for tasting and appreciation, but not necessarily in a holistic or consistent manner. Peynaud captures recent efforts to describe wine tasting through various dictionaries:[59]

- Maupin, 41 words, 1779
- Chaptal, 60 words, 1807
- Féret, 180 words, 1896
- Norbert Got, 250 words, 1955
- Le Magnen, 150 words, 1962
- Féret, 450 words, 1962
- Vedel, 900 words, 1972 (of which about 470 referred to taste terms)

Peynaud also claims his own book *The Taste of Wine: The Art and Science of Wine Appreciation* has over 1,000 wine terms in it, of which 200 or so are used just to describe a wine's appearance. Wine language has also become more prominently used in literature and fiction to help visualize scene descriptions. We all know that James Bond drinks Bollinger Champagne!

More recently and to address Generation X and Y wine drinkers, wine brands have taken on the language of social media! Such brands as LOL Chardonnay, GR8 Cabernet, and others are on the market. This type of wine language is useless in terms of helping us understand wine better, but is of used to make a brand more approachable to the younger generation.

Our ability to systematically categorize and record smells and tastes is more difficult and multi-dimensional than for sight and hearing. As Scruton explains it, colors belong to a spectrum and vary along recognizable dimensions such as brightness and saturation.[60] Colors can be ordered and described in how they stand in relation to other colors. Taste exhibits order in several dimensions, but the process of discriminating and comparing tastes has no clear order and is best done by association.

Lehrer uses terms on a 'scale' with each scale ordering the words used to define a wine's attribute (be it sweetness, acidity, etc.) from Negative (too much or too little) to Positive (what most people would enjoy and appreciate) to Negative (the other extreme now being too little or too much). For example if a wine has too much sweetness, Lehrer uses words such as Syrupy, Cloying, or Sugary to describe the wine (in a Negative manner) and then uses Sweet, Semisweet, to Off-Dry to Dry to describe a wine's sweetness level in the generally acceptable range of tolerance. One of the challenges is that each scale does not easily segment from other scales nor run in the same linear manner. Lehrer does an excellent job of providing a framework and categorizing wine terminology for us to use in a consistent manner.

When describing the chemical make-up of wine, we have a more definitive and consistent dictionary of terms, but when we define how a wine smells and tastes, we use technical terms, and introduce allegory to relate what we experience and our physiological reaction to trigger words. This more easily defines and allows us to remember how wine tastes. Our evaluative description of wine often becomes verbose and even nonsensical. But through the efforts over the last several centuries and especially attributable to the work by Lehrer, we now have a framework for describing, in a relatively consistent manner, wine and our wine drinking experiences.

The act of discoursing wine with others is an affective experience which adds to our wine drinking pleasure. Discussing wine and doing so with an ability to share experiences and evaluations makes life and wine drinking more enjoyable. It also makes us more knowledgeable through the process. As Peynaud explains: "Great wine has that marvellous quality of immediately establishing communication between those who are drinking it. Tasting it at a table should not be a solitary activity and fine wine should not be drunk without comment. This would be a serious omission and practically an insult, as much to the guest and to the wine itself."[61]

Notes

48. Bach, "Knowledge, Wine and Taste," 36.
49. Robinson, *How To Taste Wine*, 35,77.
50. Wikipedia, s.v. "Polish Hill River, South Australia."
51. Amerine and Roessler, *Wines: Their Sensory Evaluation*, 47-49.
52. Lehrer, "Can Wines be Brawny?," chap. 6.
53. Jackson, *Wine Science*, 662.
54. Goode, "Wine and the Brain," 80.
55. Todd, *Philosophy of Wine*, 55-56.
56. Todd, *Philosophy of Wine*, 59.
57. Schuster, *Essential Winetasting*, 17.
58. Bach, "Knowledge, Wine and Taste," 26.
59. Peynaud, *The Taste of Wine*, 163-7.
60. Scruton, *I Drink Therefore I am*, 134.
61. Peynaud, *The Taste of Wine*, 164.

Part Two
How Wine Interacts with the Senses

Chapter 6
Overview of Wine & Sense Interaction

Much material exists on how our senses work. At the simplest level, almost everyone experiences:

- Sight, via eyes
- Sound, via ears
- Smell, via nose
- Taste, via mouth
- Feel, via skin

But we command our senses with different degrees of ability and consciousness. Peynaud claims: "Obviously you can taste without understanding the physiological mechanisms involved. But the taster is enabled to avoid errors of perception and the influence of suggestion if he or she has some knowledge of the functioning of taste and odor receptors and of the central mechanism of interpretation, and is aware of the internal and external factors which can affect judgment."[62] Therefore, being more knowledgeable on how our senses work helps us to taste and appreciate wine more. Amerine and Roessler point out, "Everything we learn about the world around us we learn through our senses. This is, of course, true for wines and our value judgments of them. Our appreciation of a wine depends, at least initially, on our sensory impressions."[63] It is therefore important to understand how our senses work, and keep them in relatively good working order if we want to enjoy and appreciate fine wine.

This is particularly true for smell and taste, the most important senses when it comes to enjoying wine. Estimates vary on how many taste buds an average person has, but the statistical mean is about 10,000. Some of us have far fewer and some of us a great deal more. There is an acknowledged segment of the population called "super tasters' who have 25% - 50% more taste buds than normal, usually combined with greater sensitivity to individual tastes.

This means some people taste the strong acidity in select Rieslings while others cannot; some individuals find a particular wine sweet while others do not. These variances make it appear that people disagree on wine tastes and claim tasting is subjective. We all have different abilities for being able to discern a wine's characteristics. Fortunately with training and practice, almost everyone can significantly improve their capabilities and different response caused by our physiological differences. Experience and knowledge in this area outweigh our inbred capabilities.

Can we really determine a wine's characteristics as true of the wine, or is it relative based on our different abilities and therefore, a useless exercise to even try?

My premise is that if you can taste different wines and foods and determine if you like them or not, then you have ample capabilities to be able to improve tasting through more practice; to greatly enjoy wine more; and share those experiences among others with confidence and consistency.

Philosophers and scientists in general agree that smell and taste are not as objective in interpretation and definition as the characteristics we can discern from our senses of seeing or hearing. Smell and taste are not part of the object, but rather part of the characteristics outside the object, and therefore, subjective and relative to our ability to discern them. This degree of relativity (of our ability and perception in discerning smell and taste) provides a vast set of experiences with regard to wine drinking and with little practice and even less knowledge, we are able to enjoy more pleasurable wine drinking experiences and reduce the number of unpleasant ones. Therefore, it is worth learning more about the topic. Having read *Chapter 3* and *Chapter 4*, hopefully you are convinced that you can experience the world in general, and wine drinking in particular, through your senses with clarity and enjoyment, and by understanding how your sense response works, you will be able to improve tasting significantly. Peynaud reminds us that: "The nose and tongue perceive certain properties in the chemical bodies which they encounter, and for this reason smell and taste are known as the chemical senses. They react to the molecules in chemical signals, whereas sight reacts to light waves, hearing to sound waves and touch to physical properties."[64] We all (unless we have a congenital defect or accident) possess the physiological foundation to enjoy and appreciate wine.

Ken Bach questions, "Why ask this question? Many people untutored in wine seem to be intimidated by it. They think they know nothing about wine and therefore can't appreciate it."[65] What Bach is saying is that most people are intimidated by wine experts - the writers, collectors, sommeliers, and snobs. My premise is that by learning a little more about how our senses work in response to drinking wine, we will develop an enhanced awareness of different styles of wine, the range of aromas involved, and what we like or don't like in certain wines, providing us the confidence to drink better wines and enjoy them more. We do this, as Peynaud says, through the: "twofold aspects to educating our senses: on the one hand on improving sensitivity and accuracy, on the other developing critical faculties."[66]

Over time, the human population has lost sensitivity, becoming used to the odors around us. We are no longer consciously aware of strong odors perceptible by others. If a person from a rural area comes into the city or a city person goes into the country, they will immediately be able to detect odors which are new and different because their nose is more sensitive to them. These odors have not been desensitized as have odors in their usual habitat. With simple conscious effort and practice, we are able to greatly reverse this, becoming far better tasters by understanding how our senses work.

To become a Master of Wine (MW), you must be able to taste and describe various wines in a consistent manner. There are less than 400 MWs world-wide, and most of them have drunk in excess of $200,000 worth of wine to get certified. This is the epitome of being a wine expert. MWs are expected to be able to describe wines in a similar manner. Being less trained, we can describe wines in a similar manner to a MW for some wine characteristics, but may miss some of the minor nuances in fine wine.

It appears difficult to become an expert when drinking wine, but it is not. There are limited impediments to us becoming a more experienced wine drinker. There are three dimensions which influence our ability to increase wine appreciation:

1. our natural abilities
2. experience
3. knowledge

We are all provided with different gifts and natural abilities. Most of us have the physiological capability to enjoy wine. Don't worry if you are not a super-smeller or super-taster as it can be a two-edged sword. (It means you can discern bad smells and tastes more vividly as well as pleasurable ones!)

The key to being able to better appreciate wine is through experience. Our reaction to wine is first one of perception. A wine's quality may be grasped, understood and appreciated without us understanding why. By drinking a variety of different wines, you are able to determine which ones you like and why. It is possible to improve your ability to appreciate fine wine through experience. This is further supported by understanding a wine's underlying chemical structure. With knowledge and experience, you much more quickly and with more certainty can assess the wine's style and quality. Peynaud likes to compare wine tasting to reading in that the well-read reader will be able to quickly size up a book by its title or a phrase describing the book.[67] Similarly, someone who has developed an understanding of what makes up a wine's odors and tastes can quickly 'read' the wine and assess if it is worthy to drink and understand why. We learn about wine tasting through our senses and by understanding how our senses work in responding to the wine. Doing so repeatedly continues to improve our senses in that regard.

Becoming more knowledgeable improves wine drinking in a cognitive manner. It also improves the sensory pleasure derived from drinking the wine as your senses become more attuned and trained. Knowledge enhances your ability and confidence to describe the wine and share those experiences with others. Many of us enjoy both the sensory and cognitive aspects wine drinking. Experience alone is sufficient to enjoy wine; cognitive knowledge is not necessary. It will, however, enhance your wine drinking experiences and social interactions by helping to articulate what you have experienced.

As with anything, if you over-analyze wine drinking, you may decrease your enjoyment. You may focus too much on the faults or negative aspects of the wine and become disappointed with more wines. Too much knowledge can be a bad thing if used improperly. However, this risk is extremely low for most of us and with the right attitude can be easily overcome. I have never worried about the disadvantages of having too much knowledge or experience!

Normal smellers and tasters can usually tell if a wine is sweet or dry, but may vary to some degree as to how sweet or dry the wine is when describing it to others. A group of MWs will be able to describe this with a narrower degree of variance. Occasionally MWs will disagree on how much they enjoy or would rate a wine on the 20-point scale described previously. They may describe and define the wine similarly in terms of the wines characteristics, but still differ on how much they enjoy the wine. Therefore, two MWs or wine judges may describe a wine similarly, but one could rate the wine an 18.5 while another rate the same wine a 15. These experts are not disagreeing on the wines characteristics, only about how much they personally enjoy the wine.

This is what makes wine so fascinating and alluring! When I first started to think about why I enjoyed wine drinking, it became clear that it was the many and various ways in which wine interacted with and fulfilled my senses. Surveys, for which senses we consider most important and which sense we would be willing to lose if we had to lose one, are consistent in rating the most important senses as follows (from most important to least important):

1. sight
2. sound
3. touch
4. taste
5. smell

Yet, I rate the senses in terms of importance for wine drinking as follows (again from most important to least important):

1. taste
2. smell
3. touch
4. sight
5. sound

Only 7% would be willing to give up their sense of sight or sound, while 73% would be willing to give up the three most important senses required for wine appreciation, those being taste, smell and touch.[68] When ask the question several years ago of which sense I would be willing to lose, my answer came easily. My response was sight. I enjoy my sensual pleasures far too much to give up the other senses. While I would lose my ability to view and appreciate most good art work by not being able to see, I could still feel much art work in terms of the form of sculptures or brush strokes and materials used in paintings. My love of reading and continuous learning could still be fulfilled through audio books and having others read to me.

However, without sound, I could not listen to and enjoy music, or hear my loved one talking to me. Without smell and taste, I could not enjoy food or wine or other gustatory pleasures, and without touch, I would not be able to caress or enjoy sexual gratification. My body has shaken uncontrollably when smelling (Château d'Yquem) and touching (when I rubbed the great racehorse, Empire Rose), so I know the power of sensory pleasure.

Philosophers and scientists generally agree the cognitive senses of sight and sound are more important and easier to quantify in a systematic and realistic manner, but it is the other three senses that make wine drinking and many other sensual pleasures fulfill our passions. Additionally, the cross-modal interaction of the senses when drinking wine provides enhanced experiences and nuances. We may not have been able to pick up a particular characteristic with only our sense of smell or taste, but we can through the two working together, or similarly we may experience additional pleasure from a wine through the tactile sensation provided.

It is this complexity and holistic use of senses that makes wine drinking so enjoyable and alluring. And with a little more experience and knowledge, we can greatly increase our enjoyment of fine wines. The rest of the book focuses on how to achieve this.

Notes

62. Peynaud, *The Taste of Wine*, 22.
63. Amerine and Roessler, *Wines: Their Sensory Evaluation*, 25.
64. Peynaud, *The Taste of Wine*, 45.
65. Bach, "Knowledge, Wine and Taste," 23.
66. Peynaud, *The Taste of Wine*, 26.
67. Peynaud, *The Taste of Wine*, 29.
68. Poll, "Which of the five senses would you give up?"

Chapter 7
Wine and Sight

Sight is the first sense invoked enjoying wine. The sense of sight creates anticipation as to how good the wine may be. It also provides important clues regarding the quality of the wine.

Our first interaction with sight is viewing the bottle and label. This gives us some insight into the creative nature of the winemaker. The bottle shape and quality provides insights. Different bottle standards are often used for Riesling, sparkling wines, Pinot Noir and other varietals providing an indication of grape used. Many producers use the bottle shape commonly used by Cabernet Sauvignon for Shiraz, Semillon, and many other grapes. Riesling and Gewürztraminer wines typically come in long slender bottles with a finely tapered neck; some Merlot or regional Cabernet Sauvignon, in a taller and heavier bottle.

Shape is not a definitive indicator of grape used; and it is certainly not an indicator of quality. One of the very best Barossa Valley Shiraz I have ever tasted comes in a bottle similar to the ones used for Port wine from several centuries ago.

For the most part, bottle shape does not matter, but there are four areas sight provides insight (and possibly pleasure) with regard to bottle:

- glass opaqueness
- wine opaqueness

- headroom
- type of sealer used (cork or screw cap)

A lot can be learned from looking at the bottle other than the winemaker's creativity with regard to label. An inordinate amount of research has gone into wine marketing and the importance of label design in wine sales. We are all attracted to a nicely produced label and as mentioned, it is a potential indicator of the winemaker's creativity. But creativity, on its own, is not an indication of quality. More importantly, you should check the glass color and opaqueness. Sampling my cellar reveals over 95% of bottles has tinted glass. There is good reason for this: prolonged light on a bottle can cause damage to wine. This can be avoided by storing wine properly and out of the light. However, not everyone has this luxury, especially when wine is displayed prominently in a bottle shop to entice you to buy it. Therefore, the winemaker can minimize damage from prolonged exposure to light by using a bottle with green, brown or black tint.

The only wine bottles I have seen (which have been bottled recently) with clear glass have been for Sauternes, Sauvignon Blanc, Rose and Moscato. Sauternes have been built to last a long time, and most sellers and buyers know enough to store great Sauternes properly. Additionally, the clear glass of Sauternes provides the ability to check on the color of the Sauternes wine to ensure it is ready for drinking. Rose styles vary a great deal based on the grapes used and how long the grape skins are in contact with the juice. Therefore, an indication to the style and taste of a Rose can often be determined by viewing the color of Rose. You can often determine if Rose wine was made from Merlot or Shiraz skins just by looking at it. Rose, Moscato and Sauvignon Blanc are also usually drunk within a year of purchase, so it is unlikely that exposure to light will cause deterioration. Clear bottles for these four styles of wine are sensible; for other wines, they are not. If you see wine in a clear bottle, it may be an indication the winemaker does not know what he is doing, or cutting corners and about to go out of business. In both cases, these wines should not be purchased.

While the actual color of the wine is somewhat camouflaged when viewed through tinted glass, there is still a lot you can discern about the wine by looking at it, including if it is clear or cloudy (indicating a fault). All wines should be clear without cloudy sediment throughout. Based on how a wine has been stored, you may find some tannin which has settled in the bottle and this is not a cause for concern. But a cloudy wine is a wine with fault.

The next thing to sight when looking at a bottle of wine is how much headroom (or ullage) there is. Compare it with comparable bottles. If there is an excessive amount of air at the top of the bottle, it is probably caused by leakage or evaporation through the cork. This should never occur for wine sealed with screw cap. For 20 – 30 year old wine, the excessive air space should be minor. If it is more excessive, it may be an indication the wine has a problem of becoming over-oxidized (turned to vinegar). However, never toss out a bottle due to excessive airspace without trying it first. I have had some truly outstanding bottles of vintage wine where the airspace has been large, but the tasting experience incredible. Always give an old bottle a chance!

For recently released bottles of wine sealed with screw cap, there should never be any excessive airspace unless the bottle filling machine was set to the wrong level. (And if that is the case, you would be short-changed and should be buying the bottle at a significant discount. (I once purchased some bottles filled to 747 ml [instead of the correct 750 ml] for one-third the normal price.)

A normal amount of ullage means the bottle will mature at the typical rate for that variety of grape and style of wine. If there is excessive airspace and the bottle has been recently bottled, then the wine will mature at a quicker than normal rate and should be cellared less time than normal. If it is an older bottle of wine with excessive ullage, it means the wine is already mature (or possibly ruined) and should be tasted immediately.

Noticing the amount of airspace helps determine if the wine should be cellared a normal amount of time or should be consumed earlier. For an older bottle with excessive ullage, make sure to decant and give the wine a chance to reveal itself. Excessive ullage does not mean that the wine has spoiled; in fact, it could be a unique and incredibly good bottle of wine. I have had some older wines with up to an inch of excessive headroom which have been outstanding. However, if the ullage is in excess of three inches, there is a larger chance it is no longer drinkable.

The next use and interaction of sight when drinking wine is the process used to open and serve it. I take great joy in viewing wine to check for further indications of the wine's health in anticipation of drinking it. Viewing a wine provides an indication of its health or faults. However, it is difficult to determine a wine's quality only by viewing it, but you can determine if it is faulty. Viewing the wine will build anticipation or trepidation of what to expect when smelling and tasting the wine in short order.

The process of opening and serving wine has strong visual appeal, and our sense of sight has a later impact on our smell and taste senses. Viewing the process (instead of just being handed a glass) enhances the drinking experience.

The major steps of serving wine that have visual impact include:

- opening the bottle (especially if a cork is involved);
- decanting and possibly aerating wine;
- pouring wine into a glass to taste and respond, proclaiming the wine suitable or not;
- the aesthetic use of the decanter and glassware used; and
- the pouring ritual into individual glasses.

I believe screw caps save far more wine from going bad than limit wines from becoming great. Screw caps save us from bad wine and wasted investments. Yet, there is great visual ceremony in removing cork that is not possible with screw cap. Additionally, the anticipation and excitement of relief caused by the proclamation that the cork did its job and the bottle is worth drinking is not available without the 'risk' of a cork.

With screw cap, the ritual of removing the cork is unfortunately eliminated. The process of selecting which corkscrew (some purely functional; others a work of art) to use always sets my heart beating faster. For a newer bottle under cork, I will use the type of corkscrew sommeliers use in a restaurant (referred to as sommelier's corkscrew).

If opening multiple bottles of wine and in a hurry, I use the Screwpull (this generic type of corkscrew is called "lever-style corkscrew"). The Screwpull is expensive ($200 - $400 based on model), but cheaper imitations can be acquired for $30 - $100. The lever-style corkscrew allows you to open many bottles in a short period of time. The quality and engineering of the Screwpull is exquisite and admirable in its own right. You can easily insert the Screwpull into cork, remove the cork from the bottle and remove the cork from the Screwpull in less than five seconds. It is a sight to behold when opening many bottles sequentially.

Wine Sense : The Art of Appreciating Wine

If required to remove a cork which has been in bottle for less than ten years, I use a Twisting Pull Cork or Winged corkscrew which has a circular base and rests on top of the bottle and is drilled straight through the center. I do this to ensure the alignment of screw into the cork is perfectly centered and imbedded. This provides the maximum opportunity to remove a slightly saturated cork without breaking it.

My favorite corkscrew in terms of removing extremely delicate and fragile older corks (more than 15 years old) is the Ah So (other generics brands are referred to as "two-prong" corkscrews). This type of corkscrew has two prongs which are wiggled back and forth down the outside of the cork with the blades sitting between the cork and the bottle neck. Then with pressure on the cork, squeezing it inward (so it won't burst apart), you first twist the Ah So (to break any seal caused by sugar crystallization between the cork and bottle neck), and then twist back and forth slowly while removing the cork from the bottle. Again, the visual dimension of removing a challenging cork without getting any cork in the wine, provides appreciation and relief, adding to the wine drinking experience.

Removing cork from bottle provides several minutes of visual pleasure, building anticipation for the tasting to follow. I afford slightly more time for vintage wines to make sure the right corkscrew is used, and cork removal is without error. If the wine bottle is sealed with screw cap, then I just twist off the top as quickly as possible to be able to move onto the decanting process. There is little visual

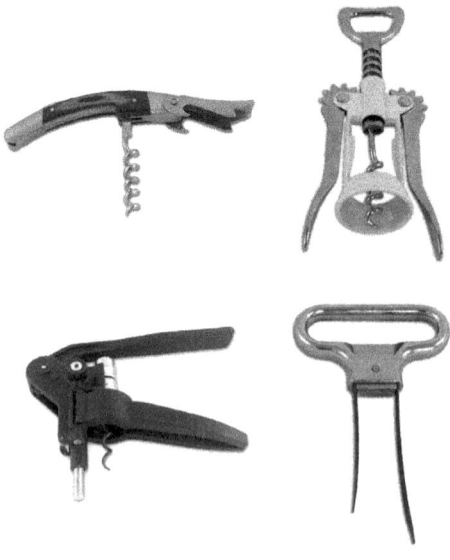

excitement in removing a screw cap, so get it over and done with as quickly as possible.

The filtering and aerating process disperses the wine, allowing maximum interaction with air and oxidation to occur more quickly, and provides a beautiful effect as the wine splays the side of the decanter, flowing in a uniform manner before collecting at the base. The display of color and movement, and seeing and knowing the wine is improving with each passing second, is a joy to behold. Even the residual tannins collected in the filter is a thing of beauty, both in terms of seeing the removal of harsh (only in its residual concentrated solid state), granular tannins, which usually possess a rich, brick-red color. You also are witness to the wine's history by viewing and studying the tannins which provide much of the wine's structure and flavor.

I usually decant using a filter and aerator, but occasionally do not. If a wine is 25 years or older, I will not filter nor aerate it. I will decant pouring slowly to ensure that any residual tannins stay at the bottom of the bottle and do not make their way into the decanter. The reason not to filter or aerate older wine is that the juice structure of the wine is far more fragile and prone to break apart if filtered or aerated. This wine does not require nor benefit from an aerator – in fact, it could be harmed by using one. If you have some cork you need to remove, then remove it with a spoon after pouring it into the glass, or use a filter with a loose mesh which captures small cork fragments, but will not fracture the already-fragile wine structure.

Once decanted, you can view the color of the wine. Many experts can tell immediately from the wine's color if the wine has strength or faults. While you may not be able to determine from viewing the color if the wine is a good or great wine, you can determine if the wine is healthy or with fault.

Many white wines, when just bottled will have a slight green tint. This is a sign that it may be too early to drink the white wine. As white wine matures, it turns more yellow or golden (signifying it is in its optimal drinking period), before finally turning brown from over-oxidation. However, some bronze-colored white wines, especially great Sauternes, will still be an outstanding drink.

Red wines are generally lighter red when younger, maturing to more intense brick red, then turning brown if over-oxidized. Seeing a brownish red wine usually means the wine is far past its optimal drinking age. When viewing wine, you can determine and anticipate if it is ready to drink or too young or past due. The darkness of red wines must be viewed in context of the grape from which the wine was made. An Australian Shiraz should appear darker than Cabernet Sauvignon which is still darker than a Pinot Noir or Zinfandel of the same age.

Michael Schuster looks at wine color with regard to brightness, hue and depth. He looks to the wine's clarity and for signs of the wines CO_2 content, sediment, and viscosity.[69] Brightness and depth of color reveals strength of flavor, but not wine quality. If a wine is cloudy, it will be a sign that a fault is present. Clear, bright wines are the signs of healthy wines. Dull wines are an indication of fault.

Having drunk many wines over the years, I know and can get excited (or worried!) immediately upon pouring the wine into a decanter. Sometimes I am surprised to find the wine drinks better or worse than it looks, but the color of the wine is a good indication as to if the wine is healthy or not. And just seeing the color can provide sensory pleasure before ever taking a sip from the glass! Ultimately, you need to smell and taste wine to determine its quality. Having sight of the decanting and glass pouring process can provide visual stimulation for what is to come.

One color wine should never be is creamy chocolate brown. This is a sign of a wine way past its due regardless if it is a white or a red wine. However, some very old white dessert wines from Sauternes may take on a bronze color and still be a glorious bottle of wine. I once bought a bottle of 1971 Château d'Yquem for my wife's birth-year celebration and was concerned that the dark bronze color showed signs of oxidation. Fortunately, the wine was spectacular and had aged well.

I am a great fan of Riedel glasses as they greatly improve the smell and taste experience of wine. They cannot improve the wine, but they do improve the way the wine interacts with the senses. And viewing fine wine in Riedel glasses provides an aesthetically appealing experience. Knowing the wine will provide an optimal nosing and tasting experience builds anticipation. The primary purpose of good glassware is to smell and taste wine, but they improve the visual experience also.

When it comes to decanters, there is no need to use one decanter over another – a milk jug or bowl will do just as well as an expensive decanter for improving smelling and tasting wine. I have invested heavily into my Riedel glassware, but I have never spent more than $20 for decanters. When doing tastings and having to use five or six decanters, it would appear foolish to use decanters that cost more than the wines they store.

I have been given a few nice decanters as gifts which I now use when we have a dinner party, and enjoy the visual pleasure from using these decanters. The decanter itself takes on an aesthetic role and is a piece of art in itself. Therefore, you may want to invest in nice decanters for the visual pleasure they can provide.

Some 'arty' and aesthetic decanters are close to useless though. If they do not have an even top, it becomes difficult to use a filter and aerator. And the massive size and unusual shapes of some decanters make them difficult, if not downright risky, for pouring. While a nicely shaped and functional decanter can add to the visual experience when drinking wine, an artistic, non-functional decanter detracts from the experience. Therefore, I am hesitant to invest in beautiful decanters, but do have several that are used on occasion to enhance the visual experience.

Once the wine is in the glass, you should swirl it to continue the oxidation process and raise the molecules to improve smelling. Swirling also adds to the visual experience of drinking wine. It makes the wine come to life, providing vibrancy. (Be careful not to swirl above the top of the glass or you will have to clean wine spills and have an unhappy host!)

After swirling, look at the glass and see if the wine has 'tears' (also called 'legs'). Tears are seen as clear liquid streaks on the side of the glass above where the wine has settled in the bottom of the glass. If there are none (or they quickly recede), the wine you are about to drink is likely thin and low in alcohol, while if there are tears, then the wine is likely heavier and higher in alcohol and will feel thicker on your palate. Seeing tears can help to build further anticipation and provide an indicator as to how the wine will taste. Tears are more viscous creating heavier mouthfeel (due to higher alcohol content).

Also, check the edge of the wine (touching the glass). It will be slightly lighter than the color of wine in the middle of the glass. If the lighter edge is thin, the wine is younger and tighter, and it may be too early to drink the wine. It may not be completely balanced yet. (However, many wines are now designed to be drunk early, so this in itself is not an indication of readiness, but usually is for fine, long-cellaring wines.) If the lighter edge is wide, you likely have a much older, more fragile wine. This wine will feel softer in your mouth. It should also be drunk soon as it will deteriorate and lose flavor quickly once exposed to air. (I don't mean for you to guzzle the wine; but it should be consumed in the next few hours.)

The sense of sight is far greater developed in humans than our other senses. I have previously discussed how our sense of sight can create anticipation and heighten what we expect is coming next. Since our sight plays such a predominant effect on our experiences, it can be deceiving as well. Our sense of sight will often prejudice us to the actual smell and taste of wine.

Brochet in his wine tasting dissertation of 2001, *Chemical Object Representation in the Field of Consciousness*, discusses an experiment where he had a large group of people taste and describe what they thought of a white and a red wine. One of his conclusions was there exists well-developed, yet quite different vocabularies used when describing white wine and red wine. Then a week later, using the exact same wines as the week before, he uses only the white wine for comparison, but in one glass he placed the white wine as is and in the other glass the same white wine, but with an odorless red dye added to it. The participants think they are drinking the same two wines as the previous week, but in fact are only drinking the white wine twice. Yet their descriptions of the wines followed the same pattern from a week earlier, and the white wine containing the red dye was described similarly in terms of characteristics as the red wine from a week earlier![70]

Multiple other studies show that even distinctive tasting white wine grapes such as Sauvignon Blanc or Riesling when colored with a red dye are described and 'guessed' to be a red wine by over 60% of participants. When these experiments are conducted with more sophisticated drinkers such as sommeliers and wine judges and critics, the percentage of those being misled is reduced, but is still high enough to show how predominant our sense of sight is in deceiving us. Brochet concludes that our perception of smell and taste conforms to color and that the sense of sight has more impact on wine tasting than most wine drinkers are willing to admit to!

There are some scientific reasons for this. Some white wines taste very full bodied and dry such as White Burgundy, big Chardonnays, and Semillons, while some red wines taste very 'white' if they have less weight to them such as Pinot Noir, according to Robinson.[71] This complicates our ability to determine red from white, let alone determine the varietal when doing a blind tasting. And when you add to that a 'trick of sight' such as using a red dye in the wine, you have preconditioned most people to have the confidence they are drinking red wine.

Brochet conducted another experiment using a table wine and grand cru wine in their original bottles and then when tested again, put the table wine in its original bottle and put the same table wine in the grand cru bottle (with label). The descriptions used for the table wine in the grand cru bottle were described similarly in terms of characteristics as if it was an actual grand cru wine. Again, our predominant sense of sight has played a role in deceiving us.[72]

You may claim this deception is good in that it improves the wine drinking experience for many involved by providing us a false sense of reality, but we all know the let down when finding out later we have been deceived! The point to emphasize is that our sense of sight overpowers other senses, and it is through improving our other senses such as smell, taste and feel, that we can really improve our wine drinking experiences. Sight is important in that it indirectly influences our ability to smell. We smell better in well-lit rooms. This is sometimes used by wine sellers or sommeliers to cover a wine fault by having us taste in a beautiful, yet dark private tasting room, the wine cellar or a 'lights out' room in a restaurant. The mood and the darkness make a wine's faults less distinguishable to us. I have had several instances of this happening to entice me to buy (or overpay for) wine that when later tasted in other conditions, I realized was not a very good wine. This topic is discussed further in *Chapter 17: Buying and Storing Wine*.

Our sense of sight is so strong and prejudicial that we must consciously be aware and attempt to overcome the bias if we want to be able to appreciate fine wine. We are constantly faced (without realizing it) with many situations where sight stimulus errors deceive us. We will often over-evaluate and judge a wine based on the bottle having an exotic and 'old world' label. And we will under-evaluate or negatively judge a wine which is sealed with screw cap instead of cork without giving the fine wine inside the bottle a chance to prove it. When researching topics for this book, I was shocked to see how many wine courses and advanced research papers had to do with wine label design. There is a significant correlation between the quality of a wine's label and our perception of the quality of the wine inside the bottle. This is one of the many reasons we overpay for wine of mediocre quality.

Another sight stimulus error that we confront is tears. Tears are the clear crawling or creeping thin liquid layers that appear on the side of the wine glass after swirling. They are caused by the alcohol being more volatile than water. People often admire the tears and think this is a sign of a good quality wine. But the tears have nothing to do with quality; they represent the alcoholic content of wine.

Remember the failed experiments of launching clear diet sodas, 'Pepsi Crystal' and 'Tab Clear?' Both products were withdrawn from market within months, if not weeks. It is also the reason red dye is added to meat. It certainly does not improve the taste of the meat, but rather our perception of the health and taste of the meat. We expect our food and our wine to look good, and if we think it looks good, we will likely think it tastes good!

To show how strong the color bias is in our perception of quality, Peynaud conducted an experiment on judging the quality of six wines. When judged on color alone and then the color being visible when tasting, the results in ranking the six wines was almost identical. But when tasting the wines on their own without the color being visible, the almost exact reverse order in ranking occurred! If a wine looks attractive, we are more forgiving of its flavor.[73]

Peynaud's Experiments on Six Wines

Test/Ranking	1st	2nd	3rd	4th	5th	6th
Based on color alone	F	E	B	C	A	D
On tasting, color visible	E	F	B	C	A	D
On tasting, color invisible	C	B	D	A	E	F

Rose wine has a very large variance of color based the type of grape skin used and the amount of time the skin is in contact with the wine. Studies have shown that we pay more attention and buy according to the color instead of the taste of Rose.

Just from having used your sense of sight, you can learn a great deal about the wine you are about to smell and taste. Clearly the sight of good food and wine has an appeal on its own. Peynaud uses the expression "to devour with one's eye" to reflect how our imagination starts working in anticipation of what is to follow. You connect with wine through sight and start to make it one with yourself, building anticipation and excitement as to how the wine will smell and taste. If in company, you have assessed and shared your views with others to open and make more comfortable the social experience.

And all of this has come from just looking at wine. Imagine how good it will be to smell and taste it properly!

Notes

69. Schuster, *Essential Winetasting*, 8-11.
70. Brochet, "Tasting: Chemical Object Representation in the Field of Consciousness."
71. Robinson, *How To Taste Wine*, 12.
72. Brochet, "Tasting: Chemical Object Representation in the Field of Consciousness."
73. Peynaud, *The Taste of Wine*, 33.

Chapter 8
Wine and Smell

Our sensory appreciation of wine is primarily due to odor claims Amerine and Roessler.[74] Schuster reminds us: "smell is a cerebral prelude to the palate's carnal gratification, conjuring up intensely vivid memories of people, places, occasions and emotions. It is, by a long way, the most important of our senses for both wine tasting and wine drinking."[75]

I have a Hindu friend who does not drink alcohol. However, he loves partaking in our wine tastings. He enjoys the visual stimulation described in the previous chapter, and he enjoys smelling wine. He is intoxicated by the experience without tasting or drinking alcohol. Both the sense of sight and smell play a large part in the wine drinking experience. For my Hindu friend, it is sufficient.

The sense of smell comes through our nose and mouth. The initial ceremony of smelling wine tells us a great deal about wine while providing pleasure. Then when tasting the wine, we again invoke the sense of smell through our olfactory glands, providing new smells as the wine molecules have been warmed and change the odors emitted.

This also explains why food and wine matching is so interesting. I have had wines taste one way on their own, but quite differently when combined with various food types. The smell of wine changes positively or negatively based on what food I am ingesting and how the smell is experienced through the mouth retronasally.

Smell is considered a characteristic of objects 'outside' of the object itself. It is also considered to be a characteristic that is most often described as a comparison to other objects with similar smells. We know when smelling a wine and stating it smells like blackberry or plum, that there is no blackberry or plum in the wine. The wine odors have evoked smells that are similar to the odor we think of as blackberries or plums. This is due to the wine having some components with molecular structures similar to blackberries or plums.

Some smells are inherent in the actual wine itself. For example, based on the soil in which the vines are planted, and if the soil is over limestone or other rocky surfaces, the wine may smell of minerals. When we describe wines to smell like an old saddle, smoky, citrus-like, or even cat's pee (a term sometimes used to describe Sauvignon Blanc), we know the wine does not contain these ingredients, but we sense odors similar to what we know those objects emit. Therefore, we often describe wines relationally to other smells we have previously encountered. As Léglise in his studies of wine language states on smelling wine, we would not say: "It smells of isoamyl acetate, alpha-ionone, glycerhysine, and benzaldehydecyanhydrine, but more simply say that it smells of acid drops, violets, liquorice and cherries!"[76]

Complexity of Smell Sense versus Sight and Sound

The color or shape and size of an object are integral parts of an object and easy to define. Therefore, when viewing an object, most people (other than those with color blindness, or having depth perception issues) can easily assess and define visually an object's characteristics. This is because the sense of sight benefits from these characteristics as being part of the object, and an object's sight characteristics being easy to describe in a systematic manner.

Sound is similar to smell in terms of sounds being apart from the object as smells are apart from the object. However, it is more like sight in terms of being easy to define in a systematic manner. Therefore, less people (unless trained properly) can accurately assess and describe sounds as they can visual aspects of an object. But many more people can do that for sounds than they can for smells. This is because smells are apart or outside the object (like sounds, but not sight), and are difficult to categorize and define in a systematic manner (unlike both sights and sounds).

With some training, many more people can become accomplished at assessing and describing sights and sounds (think piano tuner) than can assess and describe smells. However, similarly through training, many people can get better at assessing and describing smells (I have and so can you), even though the training to discern and categorize smells is more difficult and requires more comparative experiences. Studying wine language can also help one more easily recognize smells and tastes.

The simpler characteristics of sight and sound compared to smell are evident when looking at advances in technology to record sight and sound electronically. Both are easily achieved with high degrees of accuracy using current technology, and can be stored in relatively small files. Smells, tastes and feelings require much larger files at this point in time to record them.

Both sight and sound have been recorded for over a hundred years with the invention of the camera and phonograph and have evolved since then. We evolve the recording of sight from black and white still images to moving images to moving color images. Sight and sound senses have also achieved far greater resolution. The recording of sounds has improved from a single-track to multiple-track recording and from Wave to MP3 formats. The digital storing of both sights and sounds are easy, inexpensive and realistic, and continues to improve.

The recording and replaying of smells is in its relative infancy. Significant progress has been made in the last decade, even though the complexities for smell are greater than for sight or sound. One problem is that there is no universally-agreed system for defining and indexing smells. While sights and sounds can be accurately recorded using only several dimensions for defining them, smells are categorized using anywhere from several to 15 - 20 different dimensions and there is no universally-accepted standard today which has been manifested in a reliable mechanical or electronic form.[77] However, exciting new work by Jason Castro et al has recently been published which provides an interesting framework for categorizing smells in a reductionist, relationship manner to other smells we can easily identify and experience.[78]

Progress has been made analyzing an object's molecular structure volatility and its impact on smell. We know a wine will smell quite differently when the temperature of the wine changes by several degrees (and therefore, the molecule's volatility has increased). The other challenge is that sight and sound characteristics can be mathematically compared with precision to other sights and sounds, while smells are more based on experience and recognizing similar smells. It is easier to define sights and sounds using fundamental mathematical principles which can be recorded electronically, while we tend to describe smells by relating them to other smells.

Studies vary on how many different colors people can visualize (some claim up to 10 million).[79] By comparison, people generally agree we can only determine five different tastes. For smells, it is claimed (and based on how you try to systematically categorize smells) that there may exist between 2,000 and 10,000 smells. A major problem with smell is that there is no clear cut and consistent method to systematize smell. Researchers agree on a few common dimensions for describing smells such as the molecular structure and the molecular activity. This is why a wine can smell (and taste) so differently at different temperatures. The recent work by Castro provides a framework for ten fundamental smell descriptors, each with ten different vectors (dimensions which differentiate one smell from another) and is presented in *Appendix A: Castro's Categories of Wine Odors*.

Much research and ongoing work is being done by Dr. Noam Sobel and the team at the Weizmann Institute in Israel. This work is recent and cutting-edge and has led to the invention of an electronic nose that shows there are methods and technology available to assess, categorize and replay smells. However, smell files are much larger than comparable sight or sound files, which is evidence of the challenges still faced. Current prototypes of the nose can record and replay approximately 1,500 named smells. There are a number of commercial electronic noses available today, but they are sniffers for specific odors such as toxins. Devices to identify methane or carbon dioxide in mines have been in use for a long time. A general purpose electronic nose capable of describing, categorizing, recording and replaying identifiable smells with precision, however, is still a work in progress.

Multiplying each dimension means that theoretically there could exist many millions of different smells. Yet, as humans we do not have a well-developed enough sense of smell to determine or differentiate them with that degree of precision. Like the categorization and recording of sounds, we can use a significant reduction algorithm to represent a realistic representation for smells. This is the foundation of the approach Castro used in his research.

Food scientists are making great progress in providing smells to food without using the actual ingredients to evoke those smells. It is far cheaper, yet realistic (enough) to create orange, cherry, and onion odors without using real orange, cherry or onions. By understanding the basic molecular structure of various foods and their smells, food scientists are able to use a fraction of the overall chemical structure to emit realistic odors. By approaching it using reductionism and only focusing on several of the most prominent molecules to represent similar smells (to orange or cherry, for example), food processors can create a number of odor variants much less expensively than by using real flavor additives.

Most people can only identify up to four smells at any given time according to studies by Goode.[80] And a fine wine will have many more smells than that. Peynaud claims there are over 500 elements in wine that can be recorded on a chromatogram, but only 60 or so can be picked up as a distinct smell by the human nose.[81] Our sense of smell can be highly trained, but each of us has different sensitivities to individual smells. As a group we can often agree on what we all smell, but there will be certain compounds that some of us can smell that are nonexistent to others. Each of us has our own sensitivity scale to various smells and at the extreme, one person may be able to detect odors that another cannot.

There is no reason that through more experience and some study, that we cannot greatly improve our ability and enjoyment when smelling and tasting wine. Kent Bach in his chapter entitled *Knowledge, Wine and Taste: What good is knowledge (in enjoying wine)?* in the book *Questions of Taste: The Philosophy of Wine* edited by Barry C. Smith, asks the question on if we are enjoying the actual smell and taste of the wine, or are we getting further enjoyment from understanding and being able to assess, categorize and discuss the smells and taste. He claims that pleasure probably comes from both, but knowledge on its own is not sufficient to obtain the pleasure from drinking wine as nobody seems to enjoy assessing, categorizing or discussing liquid medicines or insect repellents! Therefore, further knowledge of smelling and tasting wine can enhance our experience, but it starts with the enjoyment of wine itself!

Describing how a wine smells and the classifications of a wine's odors are difficult as odors are derived from complicated sounding chemical names as Leglise points out. Therefore, we use word association to categorize and relate wine odors when smelling. While there are a number of different ways to classify smells, there are many similarities. Using consistent language to describe odors helps all of us better understand the wine we are drinking and why we are enjoying it (or not). One such classification which is a modification of the earlier classification by Leglise is used by Peynaud. I think this is as good as any in being able to start to describe and remember wine odors. Peynaud categorizes wine odors as follow:[82]

- animal
- balsamic
- woody
- chemical
- spicy
- empyreumatic (burnt organic matter)
- estery (fragrant organic matter)
- floral
- fruity
- vegetal

These ten categories are broken into individual odors which we recognize in daily life. By starting with these broad categorizations, and with more practice and experience, you will be able to more accurately discern what you like in a wine and be able to share that with others. The list of ten descriptors by Castro (in *Appendix A: Castro's Categories of Wine Odors*) is similar, but is two-dimensional and an attempt to be more precisely descriptive.

Where Wine Smell Comes From

We smell both orthonasally (initial smells through our nose into the nasal cavity) and retronasally (as wine in our mouth is picked up from the palate and pushed up to our olfactory glands at the back of the mouth). What is often called taste actually comes through retronasally smelling wine.

It is the dual path from smelling that make it so intriguing. As Kent Bach states, it is not just the sense of smelling, but the smelling of wine that is so special. Wine is almost unique (along with some fine spirits) where the link between smelling and tasting is so strong. For example, we often smell very strong odors when brewing tea, but are then presented with a weak taste as follow-up. If a wine smells flavorful, it is likely to taste flavorful.

Our ability to smell odors is extremely high, but varies person by person. Some people are ten or more times more sensitive than others and dogs are 100 times more sensitive than humans.[83] Women are slightly better than men at identifying odors and we all lose a little of our ability to smell as we age. Having said all that, our ability to smell is great. What most of us lack is the ability to describe what we smell and to categorize it and remember it. This is the domain of so-called 'wine experts' of great ability and experience. But there is no reason most of us cannot achieve that level with some further practice, experience and knowledge.

According to Peynaud, the smell of wine will depend on the grape variety, where it comes from, on its age and how it has been kept.[84] The smell from fine wines is one of its most distinctive aspects. Wine smells are made up of aroma and bouquet. While these may seem like synonymous words, they have a different meaning in terms of wine odors. Some confuse the terminology and describe aroma to be odors ingested through the nose, while bouquet is odor ingested retronasally. But the common use is that aroma is the sum of odors designated with young wines (deemed more natural to the odors found directly created from the grape and soil and initial fermentation process), while bouquet is the sum of the odors found in older wines and created more from the long-term aging process. Primary odors are directly derived from the grape and its skin, the soil in which the grapes are grown, and manner of care of the vines. They tend to be the dominant aromas and with the proper combination of grape and its growing region, a wine's primary aromas can be remarkable in terms of its distinctness of smell.

The relations between grape varietal and type of soil and region grown cannot be over emphasized. Some grapes such as Merlot and Pinot Noir with a less rigid flesh and skin structure have been transformed to the point of being unrecognizable when transplanted elsewhere. Other stronger grape structures such as Riesling, Sauvignon Blanc and Cabernet Sauvignon are less influenced based on where they are grown as long as the climatic conditions are suitable to bring out the characteristics of the particular varietal during the growing season.

Secondary, harder to identify aromas come from the yeast used in the fermentation process and the temperature of the room (and therefore the wine's respective volatility), and the use of other techniques such as using sulfur dioxide during the manufacturing process. The secondary aromas dissipate over time and take on the complexities through aging to become bouquet. The wonderful odors from bouquet exhibited in an older wine come from the maturing of the tannin giving rise to new odors such as apple, nuts, quince, and leather. Some oxygen (as stored in the headroom of the bottle and to a very minor extent through oxygen exchange passed through cork) is necessary for this aging to occur and to promote the aldehyde compounds responsible for those odors.

There are several young wines I enjoy drinking including some Semillons. More fine wines are being crafted to be drunk earlier. But for the most part, people drink good wine far too early when it would benefit from aging and developing pronounced bouquet. Therefore, I drink most of my wines with some age on them to allow the bouquet to develop fully. My wife follows one simple rule when drinking wine and that is to drink wine from a different decade than we are living in. In other words, her favorite wines are usually ten or more years in the bottle before we open them.

How We Smell Wine During the Drinking Process

There are four main aspects involved when smelling wine:

- decanting
- using proper glassware
- swirling
- achieving proper wine temperature

Decanting mainly impacts the taste and feel senses, but also enhances the smell sense. Based on the age of the wine; yeast and other chemicals such as sulfur dioxide used; and the quality of the cork and storage conditions; sometimes a bottle of wine will contain an 'off" odor upon opening. This does not mean the wine is bad; only that a residual odor existed during winemaking, secondary fermentation (in the bottle), or storage processes. These processes create wine bouquet, but sometimes create a residual odor in the headroom. It should quickly (in less than minutes) dissipate when opened or decanted. If you serve this wine immediately, you will smell the bad odor and think the wine is bad. By letting it breathe, the odor will dissipate. However, if after several minutes, there is still an unpleasant odor, then the wine likely has a fault and may not be drinkable.

Much like learning good smells through association, it is important to learn smells associated with wine faults. This provides you the ability to smell a bad wine, know it is bad and why. Then you can pour the wine away with confidence to avoid drinking bad wine.

There are kits from Le Nez Du Vin you can buy which provide a variety of typical wine odors and wine faults (the kit includes twelve common faults) which allow you to practice and relate various smells, good and bad. These can be useful to learn to sniff for typical fault conditions.

A critical component to smelling wine properly is the type of glassware used. All glasses should have the top close in slightly towards center. If the glass continues to open outward, the wine will smell tepid or flat. The molecules released from swirling will too quickly dissipate before you can inhale them. The glass needs to close in slightly to enclose the airborne molecules when in a vibrant state to release maximum odor. Never use a wine glass that is shaped like a "V' or a 'U' with the top points veering outward. The next chapter describes more fully the importance of proper glassware as it affects a wine's taste. However, to get the most out of smelling wine, it is critical to have a tulip-shaped glass.

Based on grape used, differently shaped glasses exist to accommodate the individual wine characteristics fully. This is most important to enhance taste, but also significantly influences smell. Different grapes have different structures and density impacting smell. In general, this is why most white wines (with the exception of great aged Chardonnays) are usually served in a glass with a smaller bowl and narrower opening than red wines. But there exist large structural differences within white and red wine ranges also. Some specialty glassware companies make you believe you need 40 – 50 different types of glasses to accommodate the more than 1,000 grape varieties in existence. Yet, most of us drink 95% of our wines from only five to ten different types of grapes and blends. And some grape varieties only have limited differences to other popular grapes. Therefore, I suggest that five to seven different glass types is sufficient, even for the most discerning wine drinkers.

Sniffing or smelling wine is usually done in three phases. The first is to smell the wine from the glass prior to agitating it. This provides the opportunity to smell the most delicate and natural odors provided directly from the grape. It also provides an opportunity to pick up on any obvious faults the wine may have. People have different levels of sensitivity to wine with some people picking up faults while others cannot. But with training or by using the smelling kit mentioned earlier, you can improve your sensitivity and accuracies to faults.

The second phase is to swirl the wine to increase the wine's volatility. It is recommended that right handers swirl counter-clockwise, while left handers swirl clockwise. (This will occur naturally for most of us due to the way are wrists are structured.) We discussed the beautiful visual effect of swirling in the previous chapter. But swirling is not done just to show off the color of the wine or the steadfastness of the swirler. Swirling makes the surface of the wine larger, releasing more wine molecules into the air above the wine, yet still contained within the glass. Therefore, if you put your nose to the glass (in the opening, not next to the side of the glass!), you will be treated with inhaling and enjoying thousands of wine molecules and the odor contained within. It is important to bring your nose to the wine glass within seconds of finishing swirling, or the majority of the molecules will recede back into the wine or escape into the room. Therefore, if you get interrupted and stop swirling for a period of time, restart the swirling and then immediately nose the wine for maximum enjoyment.

Most people do not consider wine temperature when drinking. Wine smell and taste vary greatly with only a few degrees change in temperature. I found out recently that I had been drinking my very good Chardonnays far too cold. For boxed Chardonnay or a medium quality bottle of Chardonnay, the more chilled the wine is, the better. The cooling temperature is what is most pleasant about this type of wine, not the odors or flavors. But with a better quality Chardonnay, the complexity of secondary and tertiary smells and flavors are released with a few degrees warmer temperature. I love warming a good Chardonnay (or any other grape varietal) in my mouth where the body temperature quickly warms the wine and releases a cacophony of smells and flavors within a very short period of time.

We will discuss a number of helpful suggestions *Chapter 12: Improving Smell and Taste* for serving wine at the right temperature. For now, it is just important to know that various temperatures make wines smell and taste differently.

Over the last decade, I have put more concentration into smelling both food and wine and observing primary and secondary smells. This has significantly increased my ability to smell and identify more aromas. As a by-product of this, I enjoy wine and food more. In some instances, it is now second nature to identify smells quickly. This has helped me cook better by being able to pick out key ingredients in meals that I would have previously missed. That means I can more easily and closely reproduce meals without the recipe. It also means I can tweak and improve recipes since I know what ingredients to add to make the recipes more suited to my tastes. This means I can also improve my food and wine matching.

There is some dispute among wine tasters on the value of the 'strong sniff.' Some people believe it provides a more powerful and enhanced sense of odor. However, it tires our sniffing apparatus which must then be rested before effectively using it again. Others believe it is best to sniff normally, inhaling and exhaling to pass the wine molecules over the smelling apparatus. My personal experience has shown that with improved capabilities I more easily discern smells further away and do not require a strong sniff. However, if you are just beginning to become more conscious of how wine smells, you may consider using a strong sniff. This will provide the optimal amount of odor to your olfactory system. Just make sure to let your 'snifter' rest for 15 - 30 seconds before attempting another strong sniff.

If you require more volatility to release odor, agitate it by violently shaking the wine. This is done with your hand over the top of the wine glass to prevent spillage (make sure to wash your hand immediately afterward so as not to drop any wine to the carpet below!) This provides the maximum ability to smell various odors. However, if you need to do this, it may be a sign that this wine is not worth drinking. I have never considered doing this, nor do I recommend it to you other than as an experiment, or in a situation where you feel you must evaluate a potentially mediocre wine.

When the wine is in our mouth, we then start to smell retronasally as the molecules are pushed up through our internal olfactory system. This provides a different set of odors as the wine temperature increases due to our body temperature. At the point of swallowing, we have the taste, the mouthfeel and the retronasal smells integrated into a single sensation. All three senses are working to provide an almost religious experience.

Our ability to smell odors decreases with age. By the time we are 80, we may have approximately one-third the ability to smell (in terms of our physiological capabilities) that we did when younger. Fortunately, with practice and experience, we continue to become better at smelling as we grow older. Through continued smelling and discussing smells with others in accordance with wine language for smells, you will continue to become better at it. I certainly have. The gaining of experience should more than compensate for the loss of physiological capabilities.

I recognize the secondary and tertiary smells of wine and better appreciate the use of oak and other winemaking and storage techniques which make a wine smoky, of leather or wet grass, and if the berry smells are really one of blackberry or boysenberry, which allows me to better match wine to food.

On a negative side when not nosing a fine wine, it also means, I pick up garbage and urine smells when walking the street. I pick up body odors and bad breathe more easily. While this has helped me keep on top of my body hygiene, it means I am more sensitive to those who are not aware of their own poor hygiene! This has changed where I walk and where I sit on public transportation. I have now trained myself to shut down this capability when out in public and turn it back on when around fine food and wine.

Notes

74. Amerine and Roessler, *Wines: Their Sensory Evaluation*, 31.
75. Schuster, *Essential Winetasting*, 12.
76. Peynaud, *The Taste of Wine*, 163.
77. Bach, "Knowledge, Wine and Taste," 31.
78. Castro, Ramanathan and Chennubhotla, Categorical Dimensions of Human Odor Descriptor Space."
79. Bach, "Knowledge, Wine and Taste," 31.
80. Todd, *Philospohy of Wine*, 28.
81. Peynaud, *The Taste of Wine*, 49.
82. Peynaud, *The Taste of Wine*, 48.
83. Jackson, *Wine Science*, 657-660.
84. Peynaud, *The Taste of Wine*, 53-64.

Chapter 9
Wine and Taste

Tasting wine is what we do. We use our mouth and we drink. Therefore, it should not be surprising that Taste comprises 60% of the 20-point Davis scoring system. Taste becomes more prominent, being further influenced by our sense of smell and feel. It is possible to smell without tasting, but not possible to taste without smelling or feeling. Smell, taste and feel are all sensed together and often defined singly as taste. This cross-modal evaluation across smell, taste, and feel is one of the factors which cause discrepancies when describing wine. Our various physiological abilities differ from person to person which supports the argument that tasting wine is a subjective experience. While there is some truth to that, it has also been proven that wine experts such as sommeliers, wine judges and critics agree more consistently; and brain scans have shown that they have clearly different brain wave activity when tasting than less experienced tasters.

Research by Goode[85], [86] suggests that results of brain scans do not undermine the possibility of expertise, rather it reinforces it, implying that people with the same background experience, expectations and knowledge may well have the same kinds of experiences when confronted by the same wine. Similarly, brain scans when listening to music shows trained musicians have different and more active brain scans than casual listeners do. We have evidence that the experience of the novice wine drinker and the experienced wine drinker are different. We know the novice can learn from more experienced wine drinkers by being around them. Over time, and subject to our inherent ability, each of us can become far better trained in tasting wine.

People use their mouth to drink wine same as they do water and other alcoholic beverages, but they usually do it differently. Water is drunk quickly to ingest fluids into our body for re-hydration. Alcoholic beverages are often drunk quickly with inebriation the goal. Wine drinking is usually savored, a sip at a time, taking minutes, if not longer, between swallows to appreciate the multi-dimensional characteristics using every sense in the process. Wine is tasted and revered like few other beverages. While there are connoisseurs of fine whiskeys and cognacs, these alcoholic beverages are much higher in alcohol, lacking the multi-dimensionality of taste characteristics. Wine drinking is different from eating other foods or drinking other beverages, being more volatile with flavor elements exploding into the air repeatedly.[87] Physiologically, wine drinking is far more interesting and rewarding than eating bread or drinking a soda.

Before continuing, I want to define tasting and drinking. Tasting is what wine judges do when evaluating and scoring wine. They do so in a considered and systematic manner requiring sensing, evaluation, and reflection. Drinking is what those of us do who want to enjoy wine. I use the terms interchangeably. The intent of this book is to help you improve your wine drinking experiences. To do so, you should think and behave like a taster - sensing, evaluating and reflecting. The skills and characteristics of wine tasting are easy to acquire, and they further enhance the wine drinking experience. This book is not aimed to train you to become a wine judge; it is aimed at helping you enjoy and appreciate wine more. I reference several books in *Chapter 20: Further Wine Education* which can help you become a wine judge or more critical taster if you like.

Emile Peynaud states: "What distinguishes the considered act of tasting from the simple reflex act of drinking is that in tasting one's approach is systematic, and one's impressions must be coordinated. Wine tasting is the rationalization of an epicurean activity. To be appreciated, wine demands attention and contemplation; and the appeal of tasting enhanced if one can analyze it. Countless pleasures are wasted through ignorance and a want of skill and attention".[88]

For discussion within this chapter, I am limiting the definition of taste to be 'mouth taste.' These are tastes experienced by the tongue's taste buds. As mentioned throughout, the overall tasting experience is one that involves also the senses of smell and feel.

Tastes are difficult to quantify, categorize and describe. They fall into four basic categories:

1. sweet
2. salty
3. sour
4. bitter

A fifth taste called umami has been added recently and is often found in Asian foods. Therefore, you would think that tastes would be easy to categorize and describe, but once you get outside of trying to describe tastes as various combinations of intensities of sweet, salty, sour and bitter, it becomes very difficult. People often describe flavors as relative to other flavors they have experienced such as lemon, honey, plum, etc. The actual ingredients in wine can only come from three areas, being the grapes themselves; the factors which influence the grape's taste such as soil, climate or other factors; or from other additive factors (yeasts, other chemicals, filtering or storage [oak or steel] processes) that the winemaker has introduced. Robinson claims that people can detect over 1,000 different flavors, many that are found in wine, so we are well equipped and have the tasting mechanism to deal with and detect flavors in wine.[89]

When people describe wine having flavors of honey, lemon, wet grass, leather, or even cat's pee as is used sometimes to describe Sauvignon Blanc, we know that these ingredients are not present in the wine. They are used to describe wine because people tasting wine have remembered and related the taste of the ingredients to similar tastes. If a wine is highly acidic (a position on the sourness scale), it may taste like lemon, lime, or possibly other citrus fruits, even though neither lemon nor lime are present. The association with flavors outside the wine's chemical composition is due to the wine having similar molecular composition to other foods which make us think of those flavors.

Most people have approximately 10,000 tasted buds, all located on their tongue and distributed in a fairly consistent manner. Tongue taste maps are quite consistently presented as follows for all taste types:

- Sweet taste buds are on front of tongue.
- Salty taste buds are on the sides, behind tip of tongue.

- Sour taste buds are on the sides, further back and behind the salty taste buds.
- Bitter taste buds are far back on the tongue.

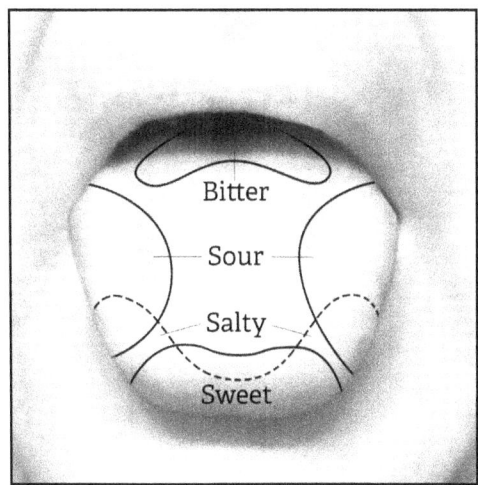

Many believe the center of the tongue contains relatively few taste buds. With regard to umami, there are drastically varying opinions as to how this taste is sensed. Some believe it is a tactile sensation intermingled with other tastes. Others believe it is sensed across the other four taste bud categories. And a number of people believe it comes from different types of taste buds in the center of the tongue. With this variance in opinions, you can understand why there is the view that taste is both relative and subjective.

I make the claim throughout that wine tasting, with practice and experience, can be considered objectively. We can train our senses to react to tastes in a consistent manner. Yet, as individuals we have different thresholds of sensitivity. This is no more apparent than with our ability to detect sweetness. Studies by Amerine and Roessler, and Peynaud have shown that people, to an enormous degree, differ in their preference for or aversion to sweetness.[90] One person may describe a wine as nearly dry while another person will describe the same wine as sweet. Similarly some people feel a sweet wine offers a pleasant mouthfeel while others find the same wine to have a cloy or sickly feel within the mouth if they consider it too sweet. Therefore, it is important to build up your own experience and determine what tastes (and the vocabulary you assign to those tastes) to be meaningful for you. You should not completely trust in others making judgments (in their entirety) for you.

Seven things will impact how wine tastes:

1. decanting and preparation before drinking
2. shape of the glass
3. temperature
4. tasting process used in mouth
5. impediments and distractions
6. foods we eat before and while drinking
7. mood / attitudes

The actual wine taste (chemically) changes through decanting and with changes of temperature. The wine itself does not change based on the glass used (unless it is soapy or has some other impediments), but the perception of taste changes greatly based on how the shape guides the wine into the mouth and onto the tongue. The perception will also change significantly based on impediments or the food you are eating while drinking. (It is not a good idea to have a breath mint just before sipping wine, for example!)

This chapter focuses on what is physiologically going on with our sense of taste. *In Chapter 12: Improving Smell and Taste Sensations,* you will be provided with practical advice as to how to improve the tasting experience in each of these areas.

Decanting

There are two primary reasons for decanting wine. The first is to remove sediment that may be in older or non-filtered wine; the second, to let the wine mix with air and soften it. Most wines today have been filtered and are more approachable for drink earlier (having less tannin), so the issue of removing sediment has been reduced. Yet, it still occurs and the mouthfeel of a wine is usually improved by removing the sediment.

One school of thought is that wine rarely benefits from decanting and any exposure to air will only cause the deterioration more quickly from being left exposed. It is believed that for young wines, or wines that have mediocre quality that there is no benefit from decanting. Similarly for older wines, that are already mature and softened, they are at risk of quickly losing flavor if left opened too long prior to drinking. It is important not to let aged wine sit too long or its remaining live fruit flavors may weaken.

However, I find most wines improve from some decanting and you are in a position to monitor if the wine is improving or deteriorating throughout the decanting process. With a little experience, you will be able to know for how long to decant wine before re-bottling it. I am convinced that almost all aged fine wines are better when decanted. I also find there is a group of fine wines which are coming to the proper age of being drunk that benefit significantly from (up to) several hours of decanting. And there are red blends including three or four different grape varieties that benefit from being exposed to air for even longer.

Young to medium aged wines may not benefit from decanting, but they often benefit from aeration. The high degree of agitation intensifies immediate exposure to air and increases volatility. This super-oxygenation of the wine will improve the perception of wine quality.

The previous chapter discussed how decanting will quickly release any off-odor that may have built up during the bottling and storage process. This occurs within minutes and will improve the smell of the wine. The main reason we decant though, is to reintroduce the grapes to oxygen. During the storage process wine ages almost imperceptibly as its only exposure to air is through the air in the headroom. That small amount of air is just enough to allow wines to achieve optimal bouquet. Based on the grape and the winemaking process used, this may take several years or much longer, such as for robust Shiraz or great Sauternes.

The Sauvignon Blanc grape usually lasts for several years in bottle before going off, but other grapes, especially steeped in tannins, will last much longer. One reason different grapes are blended together is to provide some structure to prolong aging. If you blend Sauvignon Blanc and Semillon, the structure of the Semillon will make this blend last five to seven years instead of the few years you would get with 100% Sauvignon Blanc. The intent is that secondary characteristics and flavors will develop, improving the overall taste.

It is important to learn about various grapes and understand for how long you should cellar wines made from those grapes. If you drink them too early, they will be tight and harsh, and if you wait too long, the fruit may have 'died,' or worse, the wine has turned to vinegar. There are many sources in books, online services and reviews, and through vintage notes from winemakers to provide this information. Make sure you have some understanding of this, or you will not be drinking the wine when it is at its best.

Regardless of how long you should cellar a wine and if you are drinking it during its peak drinking time frame, the wine should improve by decanting it for 30 minutes to several hours. Oxidation softens wine (which provides a smoother texture to your palate), and activates the molecules which release more flavor. A wine which may taste tight or harsh just after opening will taste better in a very short period of time. The amount of time to decant a wine varies based on the grapes involved, the age of the wine, and the type of decanter. In general, a decanting time up to one hour should be sufficient for most wines and they will not improve from further decanting. A few older and more complex wines may benefit from decanting for several hours. I have had some older blends which included Malbec and Cabernet Franc (along with Cabernet Sauvignon and sometimes Merlot) which continue to improve through eight hours of decanting. Some wines will taste better the day after opening them than they did the day they were opened. For fragile older wines (which you can determine by looking at the rim of the wine and by smelling it), you may deaden it by decanting; very fragile wines should not be decanted.

I find almost all good wine in the young to medium age range benefits from decanting and provides a softer, smoother taste than you would otherwise achieve without decanting. With some practice you will be able to determine how long to decant wine. For safety (and enjoyment!), I test a sip every ten minutes or so for the first 30 minutes to ensure the wine benefits from further decanting. If it has not changed or is weakening, you should serve the wine immediately and then re-bottle the remainder. While the wine lasted many years in the bottle, once opened and in contact with air, wine will only be good to drink for several days (or maybe only several hours if it is an old, fragile wine). If you plan to drink it over several days, you should definitely cap the bottle again or it will go off. There are several techniques for doing this which are described in *Chapter 12: Improving Smell and Taste Sensations*.

Glassware

Some people refuse to believe Riedel and other manufacturers of custom-shaped wine glassware promote credible products. They believe these manufacturers are 'playing us' to buy multiple glasses when one - any one - glass will do. My response is those people's reluctance to believe is compromising their wine drinking experience. Properly shaped glassware for grape varietal and wine style is critically important to enjoying fine wine fully.

Neither the wine's inherent flavor nor quality changes based on which glass is used. The tasting (and smelling) experience however may change dramatically. The curvature of the glass bulb and tightness of bulb opening determines how the wine flows into our mouth, first hitting different points on the tongue, determining which taste buds are first used. It also channels the liquid flow differently based on shape which impacts how quickly or fully our retronasal capacities are invoked. Our physiological response to wine differs by the shape of the wine glass.

Fifteen years ago, I bought about $400 worth of fine wine, ranging between $25 and $50 per bottle. Most of the wines were Cabernet Sauvignon or Shiraz and of good quality. Having noticed that I was buying some decent wine, the store clerk asked if I would like to sample some similar wines from glasses specifically made for those grapes.

My immediate thought was that there could be no possible difference that the glass could make in the way the wine tasted. Since I was certain I would prove the clerk wrong, I took him up on his challenge. At this point in my wine drinking life, I was just starting to appreciate finer wines. I was able to discern some differences between a good and a great wine, but I had limited knowledge or experience to be able to understand what those differences were.

The clerk stood up two Riedel Cabernet Sauvignon glasses and two Shiraz glasses and poured some Cabernet Sauvignon and some Shiraz into one of each different glass type. I would have a comparison tasting each wine in the glass designed for it and in a glass designed for the other wine varietal. I noticed what appeared to be minute differences in the shape of the glasses (they both looked like typical red wine glasses to me at the time), I thought this would be one of the easiest things I had ever done to prove someone else wrong.

Wine Sense : The Art of Appreciating Wine

Without knowledge of which glass should be used for which grape (but knowing the Cabernet Sauvignon was in the two glasses to the left and the Shiraz in the two glasses to the right), I tasted each of the four wine samples. My first surprise was that for each wine, I could tell a clear difference in how the wine tasted, and my second surprise was that I easily knew which glass was designed for the Cabernet Sauvignon and which for the Shiraz. While I did not know why

and was not able to describe what the differences were, I was able to easily determine which samples provided a more pleasurable drinking experience!

I know some people will refuse to spend several hundred dollars on getting good glassware; they would rather spend it on the wine. I bought most of my Riedel glasses 12 – 15 years ago and have used each hundreds, if not thousands, of times. I am spending less than one cent per drink for the glassware and if I have $3 dollars of wine in the glass that is now tasting like $5 dollars instead of $2, then there is a great business case for spending a few dollars to get the right shape of glassware.

Peynaud uses five pages in his classic book, *The Taste of Wine: The Art and Science of Wine Appreciation*, to describe what proper glassware should look like and how it works.[91] Peynaud is one of the greatest wine tasters of all time and if he believes and can explain why properly-shaped glassware is important, we need to listen! How to select and use glassware optimally is discussed in *Chapter 12: Improving Smell and Taste Sensations*.

Wine Temperature

Without a trained palate, most people can still distinguish how wine flavors change as the temperature changes. This occurs slowly over time after the wine has been removed from the cellar or the refrigerator. And it changes quickly when the wine enters our mouth, continuing to warm to our body temperature. A chilled sparkling wine or white wine may go through six to eight changes and reveal different flavors over temperature change of a few degrees. Winemakers and wine experts can chart the different flavors released almost degree by degree. The reason for storing sparkling wines at a lower temperature (such as in the refrigerator) prior to opening them is that the cold sensation is intrinsically pleasant when drinking a sparkling wine due to carbon dioxide maintaining optimal volatility.[92]

Wine drinkers usually notice a wine tastes better as the temperature rises. With a rise in temperature, the wine's molecules become more active, releasing more flavor, and revealing new secondary and tertiary flavors not previously detected when the wine was cooler.

One of the reasons cheap white wine (usually served out of the box) is kept refrigerated is that the chill of white wine provides more pleasure to the tasting experience than the actual flavor of mediocre grapes. By contrast, drinking a great aged Chardonnay can only be appreciated as the temperature warms, revealing the wine's complex flavors. I had been drinking my better white wines too cold for much of my life and now truly appreciate drinking excellent white wines at a warmer temperature.

For example, the taste of vanilla may be realized in different ways, coming from different molecules, either by vanilline, ethyl vanillate, or vanilla acid. The vanilla taste we experience may come from being aged in oak, or from grape stems being crushed into the wine and released when aging. The various different ways in which vanilla is released is due to changes in the wine's temperature. Small rises in temperature increase volatility, releasing different vanilla flavors at different temperature points.

In general, it is the amount of tannin that determines what temperature the wine should be served at. Simple white wines are devoid of tannin and should be served cold, whereas red wines made for aging are high in tannin and should be served at room temperature. How to achieve and maintain the proper temperature for wine while serving and consuming are presented in *Chapter 12: Improving Smell and Taste Sensations*.

Tasting Wine in the Mouth

Taking wine into the mouth almost immediately starts to change our perception of wine. Our saliva will diminish acid taste and if kept in the mouth too long, the wine generates excess saliva diluting the flavor of the wine. Additionally, different tastes occur over different time periods and with different intensities based on time in mouth. This has to do with the positioning of different taste buds on different parts of the tongue, but mostly it has to do with the time it takes for the different taste buds to identify and react to the taste.

Peynaud and others recommend a three-phase approach to tasting which involves a first phase called 'Attack' which lasts for two to three seconds, followed by 'Evolution' which lasts for five to twelve seconds, and then 'Final Impression' which may last for up to two minutes or beyond.[93] Attack is meant to provide a quick overall impression and quickly identify sweetness (or lack of it), vinosity and other immediate responses. Evolution searches for other tastes further back on your tongue such as bitterness and acidity, plus mellowness and overall mouthfeel, and if the wine is integrated and well balanced. You also may identify secondary flavors released by the rising temperature of the wine in your mouth. Final Impression is really a matter of how well the wine finished, and how balanced it was.

The sense of balance was one of the first things I learned to appreciate about better wines. It means that all parts of the drinking process are integrated and in harmony. The wine is not too sweet nor too acidic - all components are working in harmony and without any one causing discord.

Do not keep wine in your mouth too long as it reduces acid and dilutes flavor. Approximately ten seconds is sufficient to move the liquid over all your taste buds and to provide evaluation and judgment. If necessary, you can repeat the process with another mouthful.

During each mouthful, have several small swallows as swallowing forces retronasal breathing and combines your smell, taste and mouthfeel at its most intense period. You must swallow to get the most out of wine enjoyment.

Impediments

Impediments greatly and negatively influence wine drinking. Sometimes they are visual as when cork or residual tannin flakes are present. Other times they may not be noticeable through sight, but they are picked up when tasting. This occurs too commonly when wine decanters and wine glasses are not cleaned properly and have a soapy residue or even worse, built up smells from drying the glasses with well-used drying towels which have food particles in them.

But the biggest problem with impediments occurs with what is in your mouth or close by when tasting. Women in particular who wear heavy perfume or lipstick are introducing impediments which may taint their and others drinking experiences. Since we usually drink in a social environment, many of us will have brushed our teeth before drinking wine. If this has occurred just before wine drinking and we have not cleansed our mouth prior to drinking, the wine may taste minty and unpleasant. You should make sure your mouth and palate are clean by rinsing them repeatedly with water or having a small sorbet which cleanses your mouth and then quickly dissipates. Using a strong toothpaste or mouthwash prior to wine tasting introduces impediments which worsen the wine tasting experience.

Even taking vitamins can leave a mineral or metallic taste inside your mouth. As an experiment today, I had a cup of coffee about an hour after brushing my teeth and rinsing my mouth with water. The coffee tasted the way I expected it to taste. Then I took two Vitamin C tablets and had another coffee. This time the coffee tasted more acidic and metallic and was not pleasant. Others will appreciate you showing up with fresh breath at a public function, but do not introduce other minty or metallic impediments to your drinking experience! And keep away from lipstick, perfume, cologne and hairspray.

The worst impediment of all is a head cold. It is just not possible to taste wine with a cold. Lacking the ability to initially smell or retronasally smell, you cannot pick up the primary, let alone secondary tastes of wine. A fine wine is wasted by attempting to drink it through a head cold.

Interestingly, smoking does not seem to impair our ability to evaluate as long as we have not smoked for at least an hour before tasting. Some of the best winemakers throughout history have been heavy smokers. (Max Schubert, the creator of Penfolds Grange was a heavy smoker.) Our taste buds recover quickly from smoking. Studies have shown that thresholds to sensitivity of tastes are similar for smokers and non-smokers.[94]

A larger and more concerning impediment is that of palate fatigue. Sampling wine too quickly or continuously causes your palate to become fatigued and appear damaged. Fortunately, there are things you can do to restore it and these will be covered in *Chapter 12: Improving Smell and Taste Sensations*. But it is important to understand how this occurs, how to identify and avoid it, and how to restore your palate if it happens. Both the olfactory bulb and your taste buds are very sensitive. Tannins can build up on your palate and interfere with your ability to taste much of anything. I had a period over ten days where I was doing a lot of tasting of a lot of similar wines and from day six onward, I did not rate any wine highly. The all tasted the same and they all tasted average. It was only upon tasting some of the same wines several months later that I realized my palate was previously damaged. Some of the wines I thought were average when sampled with palate fatigue, but with a fresh palate, were superb! If your mouth is feeling gritty and your tongue heavy, and if you can notice that your ability to sense has declined (easy to miss as it occurs without noticeable change), then take the time to stop tasting, drink some water, and maybe eat a piece of bread or a biscuit to help absorb and remove wine residue from your mouth.

Be aware that our ability to taste also drops off with age. Fortunately, through gaining more experience we can often compensate for the drop-off. Most of us taste better later in life because of practice and knowledge gained through regular wine tasting. In general, we lose our acute sensitivity to sweet, bitter and salty tastes. By the time we are 80, we will likely have about one-third the taste buds we had as a young adult and they will be less sensitive. Most professional tasters and wine judges consider retirement around 60 - 65 years of age, even though they still will have a great palate to taste. As with brain cells, we fortunately can get by on using very few of them! As you get older, you can still greatly enjoy fine wine. Just beware your physiological abilities are slowly changing and your taste in wine may change also.

Combining Food and Wine

One of the great joys in life is eating good food while drinking good wine. The two go hand-in-hand and are enhanced further with good friends. We ingest many different types of food. Some are oily, some thick, some hot, others bland, and some must be chewed heavily before swallowing. These various differences explain why different styles of wines and grape varietals go better with certain foods instead of others. Your physiological response to wine changes based on the food you eat. Peynaud states: "For example, eating meat prior to drinking wine raises the sensation threshold for sweetness and acidity while lowering that for saltiness and bitterness. Green salad has the opposite effect. Cheese and lemon also alter sensitivity to the four basic tastes."[95]

When pairing food and wine, many people start and end with 'white wine with chicken and fish: red wine with red meat.' But it is so easy to improve upon that: Riesling with crab and prawns; Semillon with scallops; Sauvignon Blanc with certain types of fish; Pinot Noir with other fish; and an aged Chardonnay with lobster or a crustacean platter makes for a far better match than 'any' white wine. And having an Iced Riesling with an apple pie for dessert goes better than other iced wines using different grapes.

Jeannie Cho Lee, MW, in her great book entitled *Asian Palate: Savoring Asian Cuisine and Wine*, presents three potential objectives of wine when served with Asian food.[96] These are to have the wine:

- complement;
- contrast; or
- accompany.

the Asian food being served. I believe this is a good framework and set of objectives to have when matching wine to any type of food and provides for a variety of different culinary experiences using a far greater variety of food and wine.

Based on your taste buds, you may have different preferences, but for most of us, there are common food and wine combinations that work better than others and improve our gustatory pleasure. When considering what wines to drink with food, the wine choice should not just be based only on the main ingredient (beef, chicken, lamb, pork, etc.), but also on the sauces and spices used and the type of side dishes. One of the benefits of larger groups is that you have more wines to choose from and switch between wines as you switch between courses.

Cheese for example is not just cheese. There are many different forms of cheese, textures and densities to the same type of cheese and often other ingredients such as pepper, jalapenos, or nut flavoring blended in. There are entire books on wine and cheese matching, and based on the type of cheeses selected, a variety of white and red wines work better with some cheeses rather than others.

Chocolate and wine tasting is another pleasurable experience. I have attended several chocolate and wine matching events and greatly enjoyed sampling different combinations. I will use the example of wines matched to chocolates to illustrate the point of the importance of food and wine matching as it is easy to understand the principals involved.

When looking to match wine with food, you want to make sure that one does not outperform or overwhelm the other. Robust food demands robust wine and bland food usually requires softer, less complex wines. Pure chocolate is sold with varying degrees of cocoa in it. Milk chocolate has less cocoa than dark chocolate. A Pinot Noir goes very well with milk chocolate as it is smoother, and less bitter than dark chocolate. They both are in balance. A Cabernet Sauvignon goes well with a dark chocolate like the Lindt 70% cocoa chocolate bar.

Other chocolates are infused with secondary flavors such as an orange or chili flavor or filling. This changes the taste dramatically and therefore should change the wine you are drinking with it. A spicy, peppery Shiraz goes well with chili-infused chocolate and a Muscat with orange-flavored chocolate.

It makes sense that red wine and 'brown' chocolate work well together in the simple combinations mentioned above (Pinot Noir with milk chocolate and Cabernet Sauvignon with dark chocolate). Consider how the nature of the chocolate changes and therefore, how a different wine should be selected (such as the afore-mentioned example of Shiraz with chili-infused chocolate and Muscat with orange-flavored chocolate).

Notice the primary matching ingredient above was chocolate, but it varied by cocoa concentration with different levels of cocoa demanding different grapes for the best pairings. Infusing chocolate with secondary flavors such as chili or orange often leads to a different wine being more appropriate. This is due to the compatibility or conflict of the actual ingredients and if they can coexist compatibly on your palate or not.

When looking to match wine across an entire sit-down meal, it becomes more complex as it is difficult to pace the food with wine at each point in the meal. Things to consider include:

- main ingredient used (beef, lamb, pork, chicken, fish);
- how many courses and how are they paced;
- the purity or fattiness involved based on what part of the animal the meat came from;
- the feel of the meat – dense, marbleized, oily, etc.;
- other secondary flavorings – chili, paprika, basil, etc.;
- other sides such as salads, potatoes, vegetables; and
- the flavoring of the sides

This makes it almost impossible to select one wine to go with a meal. When doing larger dinner parties, you have the ability to open several bottles and 'go with the flow,' making it easier to match good wines with good food.

This is not a book on matching wine with food. There are plenty of other good resources for that. What I wish to emphasize is there is not a solitary issue (main ingredient) to consider, but many things that dictate more precisely what type of wine you should use. Our sense of taste has a physiological reaction, positively or negatively to wine when combined with food and various combinations can change that drastically.

Most people will drink a white wine with fish. However, if I am having swordfish which is denser and gamier than other fish and it is being served with tomato-based sauce, then I may choose a Pinot Noir over Sauvignon Blanc. The heavier fish meat and tomato means a light red works better than white wine. I have considered it is not just fish I am eating, but have also considered the mouthfeel and sauce being consumed.

Fortunately most good chefs will consider all the ingredients and create an integrated and well balanced meal for you. Or if you are cooking at home and using a cookbook written by a good chef, you should have the same results. All the ingredients and the proportions should be considered when selecting the wine to go with a meal.

This means that when having the same main ingredient, but with different flavorings, you could choose a wine to match the flavorings. By adding mushrooms into a beef meal and creating a creamier sauce from the mushrooms, I might switch from a red wine to an aged Chardonnay because the sauce is now playing a different and more prominent part than the meat. And if the meat is sliced into smaller portions and covered with the sauce, then an aged Chardonnay tends to be a better choice than if the meat is still served in a whole piece and then sliced and dipped into the sauce. In that case, the meat is still the main feature, sauce less-so, so red wine would usually work better.

There are three avenues available to gain experience and make it easier to match food and wine:

- Open a few slightly different bottles of wine with a meal to taste and compare which ones go better and why (practice).
- Make friends with chefs and winemakers to discuss and understand what makes food and wine combinations work (education).
- Start cooking (experience).

Wine drinking pleasure is derived from a combination of capabilities, education and experience. Learning more about food and cooking helps gain experience and improve wine drinking experiences. For me, it also has improved my tasting abilities. Another side benefit is that I have a healthier lifestyle than I did previously. My palate is fresher, my taste buds more sensitive, and nasal passages cleaner. We cannot change the inbred capabilities we have been provided, but we can live a life that improves and keeps them in the best working order possible.

When it is just my wife and myself eating and drinking together, I have a bottle or two open at the same time. If stoppered properly, the wine will last for several days before deteriorating. The wine changes slightly each day, and observing these changes is educational. One common trait is that a wine will soften over a day or two; another is the fruit flavors lessen. For some wines, this may actually improve the wine, but usually with each passing day, exposure to air spoils the wine further.

The experience of tasting several wines with the same food is a great way to learn what works for you. This is easy to do with cheeses and chocolates as described above and you can quickly learn from those experiences and apply that to a broader set of food items.

Wine and Taste

My wife and I are introverts, but sharing common food and wine interests with others has made it easier to approach others and learn from them. We have done this with a number of people in the wine and wine-related industries and also a number of great chefs. Several have become good friends and we now share food and wine together, providing an ongoing education and many varied experiences from which to learn.

Another good way to improve food and wine matching is to attend winery member dinners. One of our favorite wineries has an afternoon tasting each vintage. The winemakers host this tasting and compare newly launched wines. That is then followed by a four-course dinner with food and matching wines. Each table has a member of the winery at each table to be able to describe and discuss the wines and why that wine was selected for that course. They also answer questions and provide insights. Then the owners or employees of the winery switch tables from course to course to share their knowledge with others. In several hours, you have learned a lot about matching food and wine from multiple sources.

Over the last two years, I have taken several cooking lessons. I am cooking a lot more at home. This has saved us a great deal of money, both in terms of spending less on food and avoiding the restaurant mark-up on the wine. That money can then be used to buy better quality wines, or to attend the type of annual vintage meals I have mentioned above.

More importantly, I have learned a great deal about how to select and use ingredients when cooking a meal. I can now distinguish between different spices and why and how much is used to change the flavoring of a meal. This helps me to determine, for example, if I want to go with a fruitier or spicier Shiraz, or a sweeter or dryer Riesling. A little orange or lemon zest in the meal can significantly change the acidity of the food and therefore the choice of which specific Riesling to select. And the amount of seasoning in a red meat dish and sauces will influence if you go with a fruity or spicy Shiraz.

The wonder and complexity of fine food combined with fine wine can be a sensory, even hedonistic gustatory experience. We have been blessed with multiple senses involved in tasting to be able to enjoy so many different types of food flavors. This is further enhanced by matching it with the right wines. Doing so is not just a matter of 'meat or fish," but by considering all of the components of the meal mentioned above, you have the ability to choose an optimal wine with food and enhance the pleasure of ingesting both.

Asian food in general warrants a special mention as it would appear more challenging to find matching wines to go with the variety of dishes and flavors presented. Most Asian cuisines use small amounts of the primary ingredients such as fish, meat, poultry, etc. and use a lot of different vegetables and spices. A typical Asian meal may consist of six to ten dishes providing great variety of tastes. Lee mentions the importance of versatility when it comes to wines to go with Asian food to be able to cover the multitude of different flavors involved during the course of a meal.[97] She provides a good guide in thinking through the types of Asian foods served to be able to select the best wines. Asian foods typically fall into five categories which she describes as the "5 S's:"

- spicy (use a refreshing, fruity wine)
- sweet (use a wine to match or contrast sweetness)
- sour (wine with high acidity or contrast with a sweet wine)
- salty (white wine or low tannin reds)
- smoky (fruity, flavorful wine)

This book cannot cover all of the possible matches of food and wine. What I have attempted to explain is how the physiological response through our senses is altered significantly when wine is served with food, and to illustrate that with cheese, chocolate and Asian food.

Wine drinking is important to me and I have a book on how to match food to wine, not the other way around! I sometimes know and am in the mood to drink a particular wine and need to figure out what food to serve with it. Learn, even a little bit, how to match wine with food and you will enjoy your meals more. Some references to good books on the topic are presented in *Chapter 20: Further Wine Education*.

Your Mood

Your mood (and attitude), like the shape of a wine glass, does not change the way a wine tastes or its quality. It does however, change the way you perceive the experience and how much you are likely to enjoy it.

I enjoy wine and drink regularly, but also responsibly. I have my RSA (Responsible Service of Alcohol) certification and make sure others around me drink responsibly also. (I also have an inexpensive breathalyzer for people to use to ensure they are not consuming too much alcohol.) There are far cheaper alternatives to drinking wine if you want to consume alcohol. I do not drink wine for the alcohol, I drink it for flavor and experience. Wine is unique as a beverage, and even unique as an alcoholic beverage. Alcohol is a part of the wine drinking experience and an important part of the wine, but it has a supporting role, not the predominant one. Wine is not just alcohol, but other dimensions including terroir, annual renewal, celebration, quality, community, process, craftsmanship, risk, and many more components which comprise the wine drinking experience. Wine can have a great effect on our mood and our mood on our enjoyment of wine.

Mood also impacts what wine to select and how enjoyable it will be. If it is a normal day, I may choose a well-tested wine consistent with my mood. The wine helps me transition from work to home, from work to relaxation and starts the daily renewal and rejuvenation process. The wine might be a Riesling, Chardonnay, Cabernet Sauvignon, Sangiovese, or Pinot Noir of reasonable quality. These grapes are not dull, nor are they over the top. This is my normal drinking experience. I like a glass of wine when returning home from work.

If I have had a bad day (or couple of them), I tend not to drink wine or any alcohol at all. But if I am coming out of a bad day, understand the path forward, and am feeling strong and committed to a course of action, then I want to be inspired by my wine choice. I then may select a more expensive Cabernet Sauvignon or a robust Shiraz. And if am celebrating a personal or work success (like selling our house or closing a large deal we worked on for months), then I want to reward myself and usually will pick out a special bottle, often an import, or a wine made from a more exotic grape or a top-end Australian Shiraz.

If I am troubled or distracted and have lost the ability to focus, I avoid drinking more expensive and complex wines. Similar to the impact of impediments mentioned earlier in the book, our attitude and mood can be a large impediment to enjoying wine. If we are not focusing and using the proper areas of our brain to connect with our taste buds and do not take the time to properly assess the wine, we are wasting the wine drinking experience. When in a bad mood, we are likely to miss many nuances of a fine wine. We will not pick up on secondary characteristics or take the time to enjoy the retronasal odors or long finish. When in a bad mood, we tend to make eating and drinking a functional activity, not an aesthetic one. Your wine may act as a digestive, but it will not be a gustatory experience.

Your mood can be an impediment, similar to any physical impediment, and compromise your wine drinking experience. Wine can also be a cause for celebration and if you are in a celebratory mood, then an average wine can taste great! It works both ways. Be conscious of mood and your drinking choices. Like good food, your wine and mood choices should match.

Notes

85. Goode, "Wine and the Brain, 88-89.
86. Todd, *Philosophy of Wine*, 33.
87. Robinson, *How To Taste Wine*, 14.
88. Peynaud, *The Taste of Wine*, 14.
89. Robinson, *How To Taste Wine*, 9.
90. Amerine and Roessler, *Wines: Their Sensory Evaluation*, 46.
91. Peynaud, *The Taste of Wine*, 97-101.
92. Amerine and Roessler, *Wines: Their Sensory Evaluation*, 54.
93. Peynaud, *The Taste of Wine*, 70.
94. Amerine and Roessler, *Wines: Their Sensory Evaluation*, 58.
95. Peynaud, *The Taste of Wine*, 107.
96. Lee, *Asian Palate*, 4.
97. Ibid., 3-5.

Chapter 10
Wine and Feel

This chapter is about mouthfeel, defined as feeling wine within the mouth. However, the wine drinking experience also involves the sense of feel from initial bottle touch when lifting it at the cellar door or bottle shop to feel its weight and balance.

Wine is a living object and continues to go through chemical changes after being bottled. This is particularly true of sparkling wines, but is also true for non-sparkling ones. The bottle needs to be strong enough to hold the wine through fermentation, transportation and cellaring. While it is difficult to determine if the bottle is thick enough, we can feel its weight to get an indication if the bottle feels like we would expect it to feel.

When my father produced wine at home, due to bottle quality and mistakes in the fermentation process, we had a number of bottles explode days or weeks after bottling. You would expect all commercial wine producers would be bottling their wine in bottles of sufficient bottle strength. However, you occasionally run across one who has cut corners on their bottles. I bought a couple dozen nice Semillon wines from a producer who went bankrupt shortly thereafter. While none of the bottles exploded, I had a large number where the opening chipped when using a sommelier corkscrew (which places more pressure on one side of the opening than the other). I quickly figured out the only way to open these bottles without damage was to use a center-drilled corkscrew which uniformly distributed the pressure across the opening.

When I purchased these bottles, I did not lift the bottle to see if it felt right. The cellar door staff poured my tasting drinks and then I had the wine shipped to me. After the chipping occurred, I held the bottle and compared it to other bottles of the same shape and could feel the lightness of the one that was frequently chipping. I was disappointed in having been sold wine in bottles inadequate to handle their basic requirements, but there was nothing I could do now as the producer was no longer in business. It may seem unnecessary to have to lift a bottle to test its weight, but you can feel the difference in how a bottle should feel and if it feels light or different from similar bottles, you should be hesitant to purchase this wine. I do this now when buying from a producer I have never heard of before. For the larger wine producers, this should not be an issue.

We primarily taste wine; our senses of smell and taste are the most important senses used when appreciating wine. We have previously discussed how important smell is for tasting; similarly mouthfeel is an integral component of taste. When asked how a wine tastes, many times we will reply by responding how the wine feels; we describe it as heavy (high alcohol) or light (low alcohol) on our palate, or being gritty or chewy (high in tannins or containing crushed stems).

I have developed the ability to determine wine flavors such as honey, vanilla, orange, lemon, freshly cut grass, etc. in white wines and berry, plum, cherry, tobacco, and leather in red wines. But far earlier in my wine drinking maturity, I first noticed how wine felt on my palate. This was a key aspect in my evaluating wine as being good or great. Great wines feel right on the palate, being perfectly balanced, and creating pleasant sensations on the tongue and cheeks. Great wines have a long finish and the feel of the wine still pleasantly resides in the mouth long after swallowing it. Most of us learn to feel wine before we learn to taste it thoroughly.

Feeling provides great sensory pleasure and is an important part of our overall perception of taste. The sense of touch enhancing our wine drinking experience starts well before we ever swallow the wine though. It comes from holding the bottle and the glassware before the wine reaches our mouth. We feel the bottle shape and balance when lifting it. Holding and feeling the bottle can provide a clue as to the wine being sparkling or not, and if the grape is Riesling, Pinot Noir, or a Bordeaux blend.

You also feel the temperature of the bottle and sense if it requires time to warm after removing it from the cellar or the refrig-

Wine and Feel

erator. You feel through touch if the wine is at or approaching the right temperature. When the wine is in our glass, our sense of feeling plays an even more important role. Since we will likely be holding the glass during the entire drinking experience (unless we are seated at a table), it is important that the glass feels right. When using good glassware such as Riedel, the glass of wine feels balanced in our hand. In later chapters we will discuss the use of glassware and how much wine is in a glass to enhance the smelling and tasting experience, but it also plays an important role in how we feel wine.

I believe strongly in the value of bottling wine sealed with screw cap. It greatly reduces ruin-age and provides a more consistent aging result bottle to bottle. You will be pouring much less wine down the drain with screw caps than you will if the bottle is stored with cork. I have been fortunate in not having had much of a problem with this. By far the worst situation I had was losing 75 bottles of good New Zealand wine from the early 1990s when moving. The movers did not know better and stored the wine straight up. I was living overseas at the time and did not get back to the wine for several years by which time they had all turned to vinegar. This would not have happened had the bottles been sealed with screw cap.

I still love the feeling of removing cork from a bottle. It is a slower and far more sensual process than twisting off the cap. Based on the age of the cork, there is the mental stimulation of determining the best way to remove the cork. Then there is the slow and careful physical exertion of removing the cork by first breaking the seal and then twisting ever so slightly while pulling the cork without breaking it. The feeling of doing this is stimulating and creates excitement about the wine we will soon be drinking.

Using proper glassware is important. I enjoy frequenting BYOW (Bring Your Own Wine) eating establishments. Not only do they save you substantial money, they allow you to bring exactly what you wish to drink, without being limited to what is on their wine list. Some of these finer establishments provide excellent glassware which allows your senses to fully interact with and enjoy the wine you have brought along.

Riedel provides a wine glass carrying case with cushioning that allows you to BYOWG (Bring Your Own Wine Glassware). I do this unless I am absolutely certain the eating establishment has good glassware. You can usually fit four or possibly five glasses with stems into the case. This limits (unless you pack more than one case) you to only two white and two red glasses which is sufficient when there are only two of you.

To make it easier to carry more glasses and also to reduce the risk of breaking the stem, Riedel has introduced a set of glasses called 'O Series' glassware. The wine glass bowl (where the wine is held) of the glass is shaped like other Riedel styles customized to maximize the smelling and tasting pleasure. However, the glass does not have a stem, making the height of the glass about half of what it would be with stem. This allows you to bring as many as eight different glasses along unless you are trying to carry both the Montrachet and Pinot glasses which are significantly larger.

In using the O Series glasses, I found that while I was still able to enjoy the improved smelling and tasting aspects of drinking wine, that the visual aesthetics of using the O glasses was far less pleasing. More importantly, I found it difficult to lift the O Series Montrachet or Pinot glasses holding only the bowl with one hand. To be certain of not dropping the glass, I often used two hands, but found the feeling to be quite awkward and uncomfortable. I also lost the sense of balance when holding the glass with both hands and was more focused on not dropping the glass than I was on enjoying the wine. Therefore, I quit using O glasses because they do not feel right (to me). I insist on wine glasses with stems. They provide both an improved visual and touch experience.

Overall, there is a physical interaction through feeling which improves the wine drinking experience before we smell or taste wine. Once the wine is in our mouth, we experience tactile sensations or mouthfeel. Mouthfeel plays an important part in the overall perception of taste. We cannot truly judge wine until it is in our mouth and has been swallowed. While we can smell and taste flavors, certain judgments such as overall balance and finish can only be rendered from feeling and swallowing wine. A wine should feel the proper weight, not too heavy or light. You should also note its viscosity. Is it gritty or does it flow around your mouth with ease? Is it thick or thin? How astringent is it? Astringency comes from tannins and if high in tannins, will make your cheeks pucker. The feeling of wine in your mouth is the combination of three things:[98]

- viscosity (alcohol related)
- pain (does any component of the wine overstimulate your nerve endings?)
- astringency (puckerness and grittiness caused by tannins)

Balance, as experienced through mouthfeel, includes many dimensions:

- totality of its constituent parts
- taste to smell
- feel to flavor
- weight and viscosity to elegance and refinement
- balance of flavor: sweet and sugary to bitter and astringent
- good tannins playing off softness against astringency
- aroma and bouquet

Balance is not measurable, but can be easily detected by mouthfeel. Let wine linger in mouth for a short period before swallowing. Determine and enjoy the heaviness of the wine as it rests on the tongue. Feel the sensations the tannins make on the inside of your cheeks. Feel the wine warming and then discern the different flavors released as temperature rises.

I enjoy a reasonable amount of astringency from tannins, but if a wine built to last is opened too early, and the tannins have not yet fully integrated, the astringency is overbearing and unpleasant. Too much tannin absorbed too quickly also causes palate fatigue. Peynaud describes the different reactions we experience from 'Noble' tannin and other tannins as follows: "Noble tannin, flavorsome and developed, comes from ripe fruit, good grape varieties and fine, old bottles; bitter tannin is found in certain ordinary varieties or sometimes in wines with very low acidity; sharp, acid tannin is that of thin, aggressive wines; rough, harsh tannin, with a marked astringency, is found in young wines and press wine; wood or oak tannin comes from barrels made of good quality oak, and vegetal tannin is the product of unripe grapes or wines from regions with undistinguished soil."[99] Therefore tannin is often a pleasurable experience, but if opened at the wrong point in the aging process or for wines that have not been classified as fine wines, tannin can be an unpleasant drinking experience with regard to mouthfeel.

The sensory pleasures derived from feeling wine enhance our sense of taste. It also makes wine unique as a liquid; sensory pleasures from feeling the liquid do not come from water, carrot juice, milk or with less intensity when drinking tea or coffee, even though some of the pleasure derived from feeling wine (such as tannins) is also inherent in drinking tea or coffee. A fine wine is judged so by its balance and finish which can only be achieved from feeling the wine inside your mouth.

Wine and food provide gustatory pleasures primarily achieved through our senses of smell and taste, but are completed by feel. This is why so many people love to eat and drink and spend a lot of money doing so. Philosophers and wine connoisseurs appreciate the unique pleasure of feeling wine (over other liquids). Wine does not need to be chewed prior to swallowing and does not 'drop to your gut' to undergo a further digestive process. One does not feel heavy or discomforted by wine as they would from eating too much or eating the wrong things. It is possible that you may have some sort of allergic reaction to the yeast or sulfites used in some wines, but wine fills every bodily crevice and feels like it is binding your body and psyche when swallowing. That is why wine is so pleasurable to drink on its own or to have with food. It enhances a meal not just by providing other flavors and taste combined with food, but also because the feeling of drinking wine is far more integrated with our body and its senses than eating food alone. Wine writers often describe the 'infusion' of wine into body and soul, becoming 'one' with both.

Notes

98. Amerine and Roessler, *Wines: Their Sensory Evaluation*, 52.
99. Peynaud, *The Taste of Wine*, 80.

Chapter 11
Wine and Sound

When I starting thinking about why I enjoyed wine so much, I realized it was because it interacted with most of my senses. I had clear examples of sensory reactions to sight, smell, taste and feel. Yet our hearing also plays a small role in wine drinking.

Sounds are created when decanting and swirling wine, and readies the other senses. Hearing bubbles released while visualizing what is happening to your glass of Champagne or other sparkling wine adds to the experience.

The sense of sound can enhance wine drinking, albeit in a small way.

The sound that really matters is the sound of friends in conversation. While it is questionable that discussing wine adds to the sensory pleasure of drinking wine, it does add to the cognitive pleasure. I enjoy drinking a glass alone while reading a good book or listening to music, but I greatly enjoy sharing my wine experiences with friends and other like-minded people. They enhance the overall experience and pleasure.

Part Three
Enhancing the Wine Drinking Experience

Part One and *Part Two* provided insights into the philosophical and physiological reasons why wine drinking can be an aesthetic, even hedonistic, pleasure. The remainder of the book provides a practical and pragmatic approach to improving and enhancing your wine drinking experiences.

We will review the wine drinking process to show how to improve each aspect when:

- Sighting wine
- Sniffing it
- Sipping it
- Reflecting and evaluating the wine
- After effects

Each chapter provides useful tips which can immediately and easily be put into use to enhance wine drinking. Many, if not most, of the tips can be implemented at no, or very little, cost. In some cases, an implied value assessment is made from my perspective which may or may not be similar to yours. An example of this, is the worth and money I have spent on Riedel glassware. A number of you may not believe it is worth the investment, or may choose an alternative subset of a competing brand to heighten your wine drinking, and spend less in terms of the number of different glasses and the cost per glass.

Similarly, I have not purchased nor do I believe in spending a lot on decanters, as decanting wine into a glass cooking tray or Corningware pot achieves the same result. However, you may value the aesthetic beauty of using a top-end Riedel or other decanter.

Therefore, evaluate and adjust accordingly, how much you spend and how best to implement some of the ideas presented in this part. I attempt to provide suggestions for an audience of wine drinkers who wish to improve their drinking experiences. Fortunately, most of these ideas will improve your wine drinking and appreciation without additional cost.

Chapter 12
Improving Smell and Taste Sensations

In *Part Two*, the subjects of smell and taste were treated separately to provide background on the physiological impacts of both and their differences. It was also a useful construct to explain the cross-modal interaction of how several senses work together when drinking wine.

Because smell and taste are so intertwined, many of the suggestions that enhance one sense enhance the other in regards to wine tasting; therefore, I have decided to treat them together.

Improving how to smell and taste will improve your overall wine drinking experiences more than through any other sense. Therefore, we cover this subject first. Many suggestions are self-explanatory and are explained simply. Once introduced and aware of a concept, you can immediately apply it to improve wine drinking.

In general, two broad areas influence your wine smelling and tasting: opening the bottle and exposing the wine to air, and the methods used when wine approaches the nose and mouth. The former optimizes last minute changes and improvements in the intrinsic characteristics and quality of the wine and the latter the manner in which the wine interacts with your sense of smell and taste.

Below, I present detailed processes for wine drinking from

removing wine from a cellar, decanting a bottle of wine, through to swallowing and reflection. A number of tips may appear trivial in their ability to improve wine drinking. For any one of them on its own, that may be true. But cumulatively they make a large difference. A number of them are 'insurance' policies which provides a solution if some other aspect is amiss. I have developed techniques over time that work and have become second nature. Some steps improve quality while others minimize or eliminate risks of the wine being inferior.

Robards states, "A great mystique has grown up over the years surrounding the way in which wine is served. Indeed, a certain ritual if often involved, and it is understandable that people who are unfamiliar with the ritual may be not only confused but repelled by it. Nevertheless, many of the procedures used in serving wine exist for sound reasons, and a thorough understanding of them will add to the total experience and make the difference between a routine occasion and an event of rich enjoyment."[100] Understanding and learning each of those 'trivial' procedures is the focus of this and subsequent chapters to ensure you have an event of rich enjoyment and not just a routine experience.

Removing Bottle from Storage

Bottles are usually stored at cooler temperatures than serving temperature and are usually stored horizontally. Therefore, it is important to remove the bottle from storage conditions at least thirty minutes prior to the time you want to serve it. If able, for red wine, remove the bottle from storage at least several hours and up to a day before you plan to use it. Stand it upright for sediment to settle to the bottom. For an older wine that should not be filtered, this reduces the possibility of residual tannin ending up in the glass.

If good white wine has been stored in the refrigerator, remove it 20 – 30 minutes prior to the time you intend to serve it. This is explained later in the section on temperature control; the main purpose is to warm white wine several degrees to release more flavor.

By standing the bottle upright, you improve the efficiency of filtering as all remaining tannins have settled at the bottle bottom and will not slow the filtering process. As mentioned earlier, not every bottle of aged red wine should be filtered. If the wine is old and fragile, it likely contains far less free-floating tannin if standing upright for at least several hours.

Tannin is necessary during the aging process to enhance wine's ability to improve over time. When wine matures, the tannins are (or should be) fully integrated (or adhesively stuck to the side of the bottle), providing a well-integrated and balanced wine. Wine at this stage has a smooth mouthfeel. But if the tannin has not settled and the wine not filtered, you may end up with residual sediment in the glass, providing a grittier mouthfeel and less pleasant drinking experience.

Wine, like food, is a living thing, or at least was made from living things. Meat needs to rest for a period of time after cooking it. This makes the meat easier to prepare, and less stressed when serving. The same is true with wine. Give it a chance to rest in the upright position, minimally for thirty minutes and ideally for a day before opening the bottle.

If the bottle is sealed with cork, remove the tin foil covering the cork and make sure there are no veins or other damage to the cork. If it looks like the possibility the cork has been damaged, retrieve another bottle as back-up. If there is cork damage, remove the cork immediately and test a small amount of wine. If the wine is bad, use the back-up bottle. If the wine is all right or in question, then keep the remainder in a glass, occasionally sipping over time to determine if it is improving or is, in fact, not drinkable. You should be able to determine immediately if it is tainted and not drinkable, but it sometimes may take several sips over a longer period of time to see if the wine is salvageable. Then you have the choice of drinking the wine or pouring it away. Which option you choose is a personal one based on your tastes and I have little guidance to offer here. The wine may be suitable and even appreciated by those you are serving. However, if you had high expectations for this wine or have had a better bottle, you may not be happy with it and may want to consider your back-up bottle instead.

Opening the Bottle

Wine ages and is constantly changing during its life in the bottle. Wine may still possess an odor in the head space due to ongoing fermentation in bottle, based on what type of yeast was used or if sulfur dioxide was introduced into the winemaking process. These are well acknowledged and standard activities in winemaking and

Improving Smell and Taste Sensations

the odor that may result is a common and natural occurrence.

When opening the bottle, it may still be present in the head space. The odor should dissipate in several minutes. After opening the bottle, let it sit for several minutes before doing anything else to ensure any odor dissipates. This can happen whether bottles are sealed with cork or screw cap. It is caused by ongoing chemical transformation of the wine after sealing.

After several minutes, smell the wine in the bottle. At this point, the smell should be pleasant. If not, then something else is possibly wrong and the wine needs to be examined further to determine if it is drinkable or not.

You should be able to tell immediately if wine has oxidized due to bad cork or from maturing well beyond its desired drinking period. The wine may even smell like vinegar. If so, it should be tossed.

Other wines may not smell at all or smell off when compared to similar wines. In this case, you should decant the wine to provide the opportunity for it to come right. After an hour or two of decanting, exposure to air may have helped it greatly. Pour a small amount into a glass and nose and taste it immediately after decanting to determine if it is improving or not. Some wines will benefit greatly from exposure to air and become drinkable after initially assessing the wine poorly.

There are various wine faults that may cause a bottle of wine to be undrinkable. Experience will help you determine if the wine is drinkable or not. There are also various smelling kits representing the smell of wine faults that you can buy to quickly learn what type of odors are associated with wine faults. Links to these resources are provided in *Part Four* of the book.

I attempt to do everything I can to save a bottle of wine once it has been opened! Especially if it is a bottle of fine wine that is somewhat past its due date. While the fruit may have deaden a bit and too much oxidation occurred (determined by smell and a brown tint to the color of the wine), it still may provide a beautiful drink since it was likely made from excellent grapes. But a wine in this condition needs to be finished off within hours after opening as it is fragile and will fall apart quickly once exposed to air.

However if a wine is bad, there is no reason to drink it unless you do not care about the taste. Dispose of it and go with your back-up bottle.

Decanting

There are two reasons to decant wine. The first is to remove sediment, the second to expose it to air to soften it and release more flavor. More and more, wines are being made to drink earlier and most are filtered, so the need for decanting has been decreasing. Yet, if you have a cellar of good, aging red wines, there are plenty of opportunities for you to decant wine. There is no difference if a wine has been bottled under screw cap or cork, the wine will benefit the same from decanting.

As a general rule, I usually decant most red wines and also decant a select few bottles of aged robust white wine. White and red winemaking processes differ, but have many similarities, so both white and red wine can benefit from decanting. However, the amount of change in white wine due to secondary fermentation is less than for red wine and the amount of tannin in white wine is typically less than in red wine. Therefore, decanting has far more impact on red wine.

Decanting exposes red wine to more air than has been introduced as headroom when bottled. Therefore, decanting changes wine quickly compared to the change in wine while in the bottle. It can change as much in an hour in the decanter as it has in the last five years in the bottle. This helps provide a longer duration when the wine is optimally drinkable. As an example, if a wine has been built to be drunk over a 15 — 25 year period, then we would expect the wine to change little year-on-year, during that time, before it starts to slowly deteriorate towards and beyond 20 – 25 years (or longer if stored in colder conditions which slows the maturation process).

Decanting provides the 'last stage' in the aging process and allows us to fine tune the wine to be optimally drinkable in a short amount of time. The 15-year-old version of this wine would be tighter, with sharper flavors. It would require several hours decanting to soften and open it up. When the same wine is 20-years old, we would only need to decant it for one hour to 90 minutes. And for the 25-year-old wine, we may only need to decant it for less than 30 minutes or not at all.

This means that the wine will taste generally the same when having a bottle after 15 years of aging and the same one after 25 years of aging. Decanting times can be used to control and normalize the way the wine tastes when drinking several bottles of the same wine over long periods of time. We tasted a twelve-year-old Henschke Hill of Grace and had to decant it for five hours to open it up and become approachable. This bottle will be smoother and more enjoyable to drink when it is twenty years old and would require far less decanting at that point in time.

Of course, other things are going on in terms of the additional secondary flavors and enhanced bouquet that may develop, and if the red wine is a blend of different grapes, they will mature at different rates and the integrated flavor will take on characteristics over 25 years that could not be achieved in under 15. No amount of decanting will alter that. This is one of the pleasures of drinking several of the same bottles of fine wine over a long period of time. It will generally and for the most part taste the same, but it will also change based on the aging time and other contextual conditions (such as your mood or what food you are eating).

I enjoy reds wines that could be defined as fine wines or better. These are wines that should be cellared for a decade or longer. They are complex and need the time to develop their characteristics and achieve balance. I almost always decant these wines and usually for a period of one to two hours.

Peynaud disputes the value of decanting and believes there is no benefit in decanting wine for any period of time beyond several minutes.[101] He claims there is minimal benefit and some risk in decanting wine for a longer period of time. While I have tremendous respect for Peynaud, my personal experience has shown wines having benefited from the increased oxidation that occurs over a thirty minute to several-hour period. (I also imagine that Peynaud was drinking far better and aged wines than I do which could account for the difference!) However, for old wines, a period of prolonged decanting may cause the wine to lose its remaining flavor quickly, so check the wine early and frequently. These wines may not require more than a few minutes decanting as Peynaud recommends. Robards says, "old wines tend to lose what remaining fruit they have within a matter of moments. It is possible to miss everything that a noble old bottle has to offer by waiting too long to drink it after uncorking it."[102]

There are two situations when you should bypass decanting. The first is when the wine is extremely old and close to or past the end of its optimal drinking period. In this case, pour a small amount of wine (15 – 20 ml) into a glass to observe the color and dispersion of color along the glass edge. If the color is a brownish-red, the wine is already over-oxidized and will not benefit from any more air; in fact, it will be hurt by it. Pour this wine directly into the glass and drink it (assuming it smells ok and in no other way exhibits any faults).

The second exception is when the red wine exhibits a large ban of dispersion where the color on the outside edge of the glass is lighter and only turns darker over 10 mm – 15 mm before getting to a richer, darker red color in the center. The wider the path of lighter dispersed red color, the more fragile the wine is. Decanting a fragile wine could destroy any remaining structure, making the wine less enjoyable to drink. You would have further separation of wine characteristics (losing integration and balance) and the mouthfeel would be more like dirty water than fine wine. If the wine has an outer lighter band of only 3 mm – 5 mm, then the wine is not fragile, can be decanted and is likely to be better for it.

Therefore, do not decant red wine with a brownish tint or fragile red wine (evidenced by a wide light rim in the glass). It would make the wine less drinkable and could even destroy any chance of drinkability. In any case, these wines should be drunk quickly as any further exposure to air deteriorates them quickly.

I use standard shaped decanters to provide maximum surface area exposure of wine to air. There are some extremely exotic decanters made of very thin glass tubes that are meant to present the wine as art. These decanters, in my opinion, are a waste of money. They cost about $4,000, are fragile and easy to break, and difficult to use for pouring wine into the glass. They also expose minimum wine surface area to air for oxidation. I know people who appreciate the visual aesthetics of this type of decanter, who go through the trouble of using a standard $20 decanter and aerator and then pouring the wine into the thin tube decanter for display! While I like to provide visual aesthetics to improve my wine drinking experience, I find this type of extra effort to be an intrusion to the wine drinking experience.

When bringing fine red wine to a BYO restaurant, decant it beforehand. Most BYOs do not have sufficient decanters to decant several bottles of fine red wine per table. Further, by decanting at home, you are able to ensure the wine is suitable to drink (or be able to open another bottle if required), and prepare the wine for immediate consumption when arriving at the restaurant.

When decanting a bottle for re-bottling and take out, rinse the bottle to remove any residual tannin. Fill the bottle with a small amount of water, cover the bottle opening, and shake it to remove the tannin possibly affixed to the bottle. Then pour the water and all sediment out. You may need to do this several times, but this is important to avoid any grit poured into your glass when drinking the

Improving Smell and Taste Sensations

wine later in the restaurant.

Then turn the bottle upside down and shake it a few more times to remove any residual water (so as not to dilute the wine when refilling) and let the bottle sit to return to room temperature. After decanting, place a funnel into the original wine bottle and refill. Stopper the bottle using a manual vacuum pump and rubber stopper. This will stop the wine from deteriorating further and prepare it for being transported to the restaurant. Just make sure while traveling that you store the wine bottles upright so as not to break the seal or spill any wine.

Many red wines are made today with the intent of being drinkable immediately or within several years of cellaring. When drinking a bottle of this type of wine (usually under $20 per bottle), I see no reason to decant, especially if the bottle has been sealed with screw cap. The wine has usually been manufactured so the wine is already oxidized and drinkable when opened. Aging will not improve this wine much, so decanting will not help either.

Younger medium quality red wines that have been made to drink immediately do not require decanting. However, I will use a Vinturi device which does a filter and 'super-charged' aeration in a matter of seconds. You pour the wine from the bottle through the Vinturi (by holding it above the glass) and it spins and disperses the wine in a super-charged state.

Often we are in a situation where we need to open and drink wine immediately. There are ways to speed the decanting process significantly. The decanting process occurs more quickly when more wine surface area is exposed to air. Therefore, aerating wine significantly shortens the time required to decant. An aerator splays (separates) the wine outward when pouring to increase the wine's surface area to air.

There is also a device by Vinturi which does the same thing and is used by pouring wine directly from the bottle to the glass without spending any time in a decanter. You can certainly hear the 'gurgling' through the Vinturi as proof the wine is being agitated.

It is claimed the Vinturi is equivalent to decanting for three hours. I believe this to be an exaggeration. If given the time, I would rather decant, keeping the wine more stable, and slowly exchanging air and wine in a decanter. A fine wine should only be poured through a Vinturi if you have not had time to decant the wine properly and if not in a fragile state as the Vinturi will likely destroy any remaining structure. If you need to serve fine wine immediately, then use a Vinturi. For newer, medium quality red wines, you can use a Vinturi for quick oxidation.

Only recently have I started to decant robust and aged white wines. If the white wine has a big golden color and is 5 – 15 years old, it can benefit from decanting. I usually decant a white wine for 15 – 45 minutes. White wines have less tannin and do not require as much time to decant. Decanting white wines is to release and enhance flavor, not to soften it. I only decant Montrachet and other older vintage Chardonnays and Semillons and some of the truly outstanding 'built to last' Verdelhos. Recent vintages of white wines (similar to recent vintages of red wines) will not benefit from decanting.

Temperature Control

Temperature control plays an important part in making and storing wine, and also when drinking it. Bringing the wine's temperature from storage to serving conditions has a major impact on a wine's taste and a difference of only several degrees can have significant effect. While you may not have total control over the surrounding ambient temperature, you can control and maintain the temperature of the wine in your decanter, open bottle, or glass to ensure you are drinking wine at the correct temperature.

Wine drinking, like a lot of other activity, is enjoyed within a normal temperature range for human activities. I never drink wine in extremely cold temperatures. If I need to wear gloves or outer garments, I would not enjoy drinking wine. The glass will be cold, the wine tight and flat and in general, an unpleasant experience. I would opt to drink hot tea or coffee instead or have a small shot of brandy or liqueur. Likewise, I would avoid drinking wine in extremely hot temperatures. In this situation, I would have cold beer, water, or juice. Wine is not pleasant to drink at extreme temperatures.

As mentioned in *Chapter 9: Wine and Taste*, wine reaches its

Improving Smell and Taste Sensations

maximum flavor when served at the right temperature. A quick and simple summary is as follows:

- Cheap, medium quality white wines – serve immediately from refrigerator and keep stored in refrigerator between serves
- Sparkling wines – serve immediately from refrigerator and keep stored in refrigerator between serves
- Decent to fine white wines – remove from refrigerator for five to ten minutes and place in ice bucket (with little ice) between serves
- Aged, robust white wines – removed from refrigerator for thirty minutes, then place in ice bucket (with no ice) between serves
- Red wines – remove from cellar and serve at room temperature
- Dessert wines – remove from refrigerator for five to ten minutes and place in ice bucket between serves. If finer Sauternes or other big 'stickies,' once opened, keep at room temperature assuming the wine will be drunk within 30 – 45 minutes

Drinking Temperature for Wine Varietals

Wine Category	Varietals	Fahrenheit	Celsius
Robust Reds	Shiraz, Cabernet Sauvignon, Merlot, Grenache, Tannat	63° - 65°	17° - 18°
Lighter Reds	Pinot Noir, Zinfandel, Sangiovese, Tempranillo	59° - 61°	15° - 16°
Most Whites / Others	Semillon, Sauternes, 'stickies,' Rose	50° - 54°	10° - 12°
Cooler Whites	Chardonnay, Riesling, Sauvignon Blanc	46° - 50°	8° - 10°
Sparkling	Champagne, Sparklings, Frizzante, Spumanti	43° - 46°	6° - 8°

It is relatively easy to maintain the wine's temperature when first served. The objective should be to maintain the wine at optimal serving temperature prolonging warming as long as possible during consumption. As a general rule, serve lower quality wines at lower temperatures, and for better wines, let the wine run through a broader temperature range to open and release the many and varied flavors and its complexity. You are then able to enjoy a variety of different tasting experiences recognizing primary aromas and flavors followed by the release of secondary flavors and other nuances as you move through a temperature range of several degrees.

The challenge is to prolong the wine at optimal temperature once it is in your glass. This can be controlled by how much wine you put in the glass and how often. There needs to be enough to give it a good swirl and then make sure that you can get a decent mouthful (approximately 6 - 10 ml). One major mistake is filling a wine glass too full. Doing so makes it difficult to swirl and nose properly. Additionally, it is easier to control and maintain constant wine temperature in the bottle than it is in the glass, as a bottle is easier to store in an ice bucket or refrigerator for white wine) and the bottle glass is thicker than the thickness of a drinking glass which will slow warming. You have far more control of maintaining a relatively constant temperature of the wine in your glass if you pour smaller amounts more frequently. I tend to fill my glass approximately one-third full and just below the point of maximum glass circumference.

Improving Smell and Taste Sensations

Sparkling and cheap white wines are best when served directly from the refrigerator. Ensure there is ample height on the refrigerator door tray to be able to stand a bottle upright. It is not a good idea to lay a bottle down if it has a rubber stopper in it. It can ruin the vacuum seal, or worse, spill wine throughout the refrigerator.

Another option to keep sparkling and cheap white wines cold is to use a cooler or wide ice bucket where you can submerge most of the bottle in ice. By covering most of the bottle in ice, you are providing a temperature just above freezing similar to being in a refrigerator. Coolers or large Champagne buckets work the best. Ensure there is enough water and ice to be able to easily remove and replace the bottle in between serves. For large groups, use a large cooler to store open bottles of white wine. A large cooler with lots of ice (and occasionally refilling with another bag of ice) is the best way to provide a refrigerated cooling experience over a long period of time if your refrigerator's space is limited.

For better white wines, after removal from the refrigerator for 30 minutes, place the wine in an ice bucket, but with only a layer of ice on the bottom. The width of the bucket should only be slightly wider than the width of the bottle. The intent is to maintain or minimally retard the wine warming. Once you have achieved the correct temperature for good white wine, this is the best method of keep the wine at a constant serving temperature.

When wine is in the glass, it warms toward ambient temperature. In general, this is suitable for good wine, as small increases in temperature activate the wine's molecular structure, releasing further flavors and nuances not experienced when the wine is cooler, tighter and more constrained. Once the wine is in the mouth, it warms to body temperature. I love to experience how the taste of a fine wine changes and releases more flavors as it is tossed around inside my mouth. It is worthwhile to savor a good wine on the palate for up to a minute before completely swallowing to experience the many changes in flavor.

While in the glass, wine just removed from the refrigerator will increase towards room temperature at the rate of about 1°C (2°F) every three or four minutes. Wine served warmer, but not at room temperature, will take about twice that long for the temperature to raise a similar amount. Sip small amounts frequently noticing the change in flavor. Each style of wine has its own temperature when it is best to drink and learning what that temperature is can significantly heighten your wine drinking experience without spending for better quality wine!

It is impossible to keep wine at the same temperature for a prolonged period unless you have a high-end temperature-controlled storage system for open bottles. These range in cost from approximately $500 to upwards of several thousand dollars. For most of us, this is not a viable solution. Our challenge when drinking several glasses of the same wine over a period of time is to control and minimize the change in temperature as best we can by following the guidance provided above. Part of the solution has been presented previously in terms of storage in the refrigerator or a wine bucket. The other part of the solution is what you should do with the wine in your glass.

The rate of change in the temperature of your wine in your glass is determined by the starting temperature of the wine, the shape of your glass, the surrounding ambient temperature and how quickly you drink the wine. As the shape and size of your glass should be determined by the type of wine you are drinking, the key factor you have control over is how much wine is put in the glass and how quickly the wine is drunk. I tend to drink a glass over a period of 10 – 20 minutes, including time to reflect on the wine.

During that time, the wine is warming according to the above formula and influenced mostly by the ambient temperature. Usually this occurs in a room where the ambient room temperature is similar to the ideal temperature for drinking red wine. Small changes in the wine's temperature provide interesting and usually pleasurable experiences. In general for white wines we are trying to retard and prolong the temperature from raising much above the ideal temperature for drinking since this temperature is going to be several degrees below the ambient temperature. For red wine, this is usually not a problem because the starting temperature for the wine is close to the ambient temperature.

One does not want to be rushed to drink a cool white wine too quickly. You can do one of two things to retard warming. The first is to refill your glass early (before finishing all wine in the glass) and more frequently. The cooler temperature of the wine in the ice bucket or refrigerator will balance out the warmer wine in the glass maintaining a few degrees variance during your entire drinking experience. This may occur several times while drinking wine. (Warning: Be careful not to think you are only drinking one glass of wine when in fact, you have had several using this method of refilling!)

The other technique used is a reusable ice cube. After about

5 – 10 minutes of drinking white wine, if the wine is warming too much, insert a reusable ice cube into the glass. If needed again 5 – 10 minutes later, replace with another one. This only works if you have reusable ice cubes around. I make it a point to have them for just such an occasion if required. Do not use real ice cubes as they melt into the wine diluting the flavor and intensity of the wine significantly.

By keeping wine at a cooler temperature in an ice bucket or the refrigerator, and using an early refill or reusable ice cube approach, you can keep the wine in your glass at a reasonably constant and correct temperature. I rarely need to do anything for red wine for the reasons mentioned just previously. However, if I am in an environment of high ambient temperature (such as outside on a hot summer day), I may elect to place a reusable ice cube in red wine to slightly reduce the wine's temperature.

There is very little effort that needs to go into controlling a wine's temperature, and the effort is worth it to manifest the wine's complexities and nuances.

Choosing Glassware

I hope you are convinced about the need and value of using glassware specifically designed to get the most out of the wine varietal being drunk. The logic and benefits have been described in *Chapter 8: Wine and Smell* and *Chapter 9: Wine and Taste*.

If drinking alone or with my wife, or if we have another couple for dinner that really enjoys their food and wine, we use the very best glassware on hand. That is the Riedel Sommelier line. The shape and feel of the glassware is brilliant and adds to the wine drinking experience immensely. Each glass is expensive, averaging approximately $100 per glass, so we have limited glasses from the Sommelier line. But, when drinking fine to great wines, the wine demands being served in Riedel Sommelier glasses.

We acquired more of the Riedel Vinum line of glassware which retails at about $40 per glass and acquired enough to cater for a group of eight. For tastings of up to thirty people, we use standard well-shaped white wine glasses and larger red wine glasses purchased in bulk. These glasses are tulip-shaped and cost about $5 per glass. When there are only several of us, we use the very best glassware we have, but cannot afford to do that when there are 25 or 30 people. That is why we have decent, yet very inexpensive glasses for larger functions. These types of glasses can be purchased easily at IKEA, or a local discount kitchen and restaurant company.

We mostly eat and entertain at home. This makes it easy to select the right glass for each occasion. When we go out, it is usually to a BYO restaurant. Some of these have adequate glassware, but many don't. Therefore, we bring our own and suggest that you do also as it can really make a difference to the overall dining experience. Riedel makes a glass carrying case which protects your glasses against small accidents or bumps. Or if you need to carry more, you could use a small roller suitcase. This may seem like an unusual and attention-attracting thing to do! However, when we arrive at the restaurant, we unload our glassware and set the carrying case or small suitcase off to the side. And when we are done, we load it up again and go home. If I am going to drink good wine, I am going to get the most out of it and use proper glassware!

Most restaurants appreciate this as they have learned the value of using good glassware and how that attracts customers. If everything else is considered equal, we choose the restaurant with good glassware – then we avoid the effort of packing and bringing our own. Restaurants understand that. They also appreciate that they do not need to bus or clean glassware, so it saves them labor. I keep large sealed baggies in my carrying case and suitcase to put the used glasses in so no drops fall into the fabric of the case. This keeps the case fresh and avoids the need to clean the case. Of course we rinse and clean the glasses when we return home.

If you drink fine wine regularly, it makes great financial sense to use good glassware. It comes down to pennies per serve while enhancing your wine drinking pleasure. I made this point previously, but it is worth repeating: why have a $5 glass of wine taste like a $2 glass when for pennies, you could have got the best from it?

As mentioned in the previous section, filling your glass to the right level helps to control and maintain constant wine temperature. I usually fill my glass about one-third full. Peynaud recommends filling a glass from one-third to two-fifths full.[103] This provides ample room for swirling and nosing a wine, and the right amount of pressure and flow when pouring the wine into your mouth.

Peynaud speaks derogatorily of common wine and common glassware and is greatly respectful of fine wine and appropriate glassware. He states "Drink ordinary table wine in any glass you like. However, a wine of some distinction cannot show at its best in just any old goblet, it needs a stemmed glass made of crystal; smooth, transparent, colorless, and without ornament or engraving. The glass should remain in the background, leaving the wine to be the center of attention...How many fine wines there must be which are ruined by poor glasses."[104]

Cleaning and Storing Glassware

Above all, ensure your glassware does not retain residual particles or odors. A simple process for cleaning and storing glassware can ensure they are without blemish and do not introduce impediments into wine drinking.

After using a wine glass or many wine glasses through the course of an evening, the glasses are usually set aside to be cleaned later. While they sit aside, air will dry them out leaving small deposits of wine crystals and residue at the bottom of the glass. While you may not see it, it is true for white wine as well as red. If only several glasses have been used and you have energy, clean them immediately. For a larger party and being devoid of energy from cooking and socializing with guests, then the glasses tend to be set aside to be cleaned the following day.

Minimally, introduce a little hot water into each glass to soak overnight. This quickly dissolves any residue, making it easy to clean later. Look for any lipstick, other stains or food particles that have hardened on the glass and remove them immediately so they do not harden to the glass overnight.

If you have a dishwasher and sturdy glassware, you can place the glassware in the dishwasher and run at normal cycle. Many dishwashers are now safe for even the finest glassware. Miele, however (as far as I know), is the only one who provides a guarantee that your Riedel glasses are safe. I personally hand-clean my glasses. I want to visually inspect they are dried properly without water spots or other blemishes. Most importantly, I want to make sure they have been rinsed multiple times to remove any possibility of soap residue. Other wine enthusiasts I know use a neutral (non-scented) soap and dishwasher to clean glasses.

Use mild detergent and scrubbing brush to clean glasses. Make sure to clean and dry the glasses before using the brush and drying towel to clean plates, silverware and other cooking items to avoid introducing food particles onto the glassware. Take ample time to rinse the glassware to make sure they are absolutely clean and void of soap. Then turn the glasses upside down for several minutes on a drying rack to let excess water drip off. If the drying rack is elevated and breathable, you may keep the glasses there until completely dry. If on a closed surface and towel, then turn over and dry with a clean towel to complete drying.

The same process should be used for decanters. Over time, cheaper decanters may build up a slight red film. Use a denture stain remover and fill the decanter with hot water, placing two denture stain remover tablets in the decanter. (I have personally found Polident to work the best.) The denture stain remover cleans the red film, but leaves a minty smell, so use soap and water to clean the decanter as you did the glasses.

I have never had to remove stains from my glassware as the glassware I use is much higher quality than the glass used in many of my decanters. Additionally, wine stays in the glass far less time than it does in the decanter. More expensive decanters made with good glassware should not build up a stain as quickly.

Glassware should be stored with the opening up. Many people think they should store glassware upside-down to keep dust from collecting. This makes sense in terms of limiting dust collection inside the glass bowl where the wine is poured. However, if you are placing the glasses upside down on a standard shelf, you will create a seal which traps any micro-biotic particles (left over from previous use or introduced by non-careful use of dirty washing or drying towel). This may build up a bad odor on the glass which has settled on the inside of the glass and potentially noticeable the next time you use the glass. This type of odor impediment should be avoided.

If you choose to store your glasses right-side-up, have them stored in cabinets with doors that keep the dust out. If you do not have doors on the cabinets or are storing your glasses on an open shelf, then cover the glasses with a drying towel. The towel itself is tight-grained enough to keep dust out, but porous enough to allow air through and remove the possibility of any foul odors developing. (However, if you use this approach, be very careful in placement and removal of the towel as you run the risk of knocking over and breaking your glassware!)

The ideal solution if you have the space under shelf or under cabinet storage racks to hang your glassware upside down, leaving the glass bowl uncovered, while keeping dust out. Or buy a porous shelf to store your glassware on which will allow the glass bowl to breathe while being upside down.

While I tend to clean my own glasses after use, guests or chefs (we sometimes hire a chef to cook a dinner party at home for us) try to be helpful and clean glasses for us. While appreciating their help, many do not know how to clean and dry a glass properly. Therefore, before every use, I will smell the glass to make sure it is without noticeable odors. If it is has odors, I will clean it if I have time or set it aside and use another glass.

I am pedantic about the cleanliness of my glassware, but it takes so little time and effort to ensure the glasses are clean and without odor. Why would you want to introduce soapy or minty odors and tastes when serving a fine wine? To monitor how good a job you do cleaning glasses, pick out several glasses and smell them. I expect most of you will find that some have odors and they all smell somewhat differently. If that is the case, you have not done a proper job cleaning them. These types of odors can create an impediment you should avoid introducing into wine drinking.

In general very little or no soap is necessary to clean glasses or decanters. Wine contains a self-cleaning ingredient in the alcohol to kill germs. I made a horrible, horrible mistake recently using a decanter that had not been rinsed properly the previous time used, The decanter looked fine, but had a soap residue not visible until I poured a $200 bottle of wine into the decanter. It was somewhat dark and it was only after noticing the wine was slightly cloudy and picking up some of soap residue from the decanter neck that I realized I had a problem and had made a very expensive mistake! While the soap introduced was minimal, it clearly impacted the taste of the wine. Since it was an excellent wine and a little soap, we drank it anyway. But the taste was a bit off from what should have been an otherwise, excellent wine drinking experience. Since then, I usually rinse decanters with warm water (and no soap) only.

After using a decanter many times with red wine, a decanter glass will have a red stain. The best way to rid the stain is to use Polident or some other denture cleansing solution. I leave the decanter sit overnight to completely dissolve the red stain. However, if you only rinse the solution out with hot water, you still may leave a minty taste on the inside glass walls of the decanter. Therefore, you need to wash the decanter out again with soap and water to get rid of the mint taste, and then rinse thoroughly with hot water to get rid of the soap.

You can also use an alcohol spray to clean glassware and then wipe with a polished cloth. Many restaurants do this to ensure the glasses are clean and without spots. This removes the possibility of soap taint entirely. You may buy a microfiber drying cloth from Riedel or others to really get your glass without blemish. Using a microfiber clothe to clean glassware provides the very best results and only takes a fraction of the time and effort using an ordinary drying towel would when cleaning glassware.

Swirling

Swirling is critical to improving the wine tasting process. Wine (or any other fluid or substance in a fluid solution) requires being in a volatile state to be able to produce odor. Volatility is critical for releasing smell. Swirling is the best way to agitate and release the wine molecules (and their respective odors) into the air above the glass and in perfect position to be able to smell the wine. This causes several effects, the first being that the glass is filled with the wine's bouquet and makes 'nosing' the wine easier and more appealing. The bouquet has risen to the top of the glass, at a point now easily ingested through the nose.

The activity of swirling also increases the wine's surface to air, to continue to warm the wine to room temperature (if not already there) and soften the wine, improving mouthfeel. The interaction and integration of liquid and air allows improved transfer of odors and taste to nose and mouth. This increased interplay (through swirling) continues to affect us even after swallowing as the wine is more active on the palate and therefore has a longer and more pleasant finish. (Swirling also provides visual enhancement to wine drinking, covered appropriately in the next chapter.)

Don't let anyone tell you that swirling is pretentious: far from it; it is a necessary part of drinking wine. Make sure to swirl properly so as not to spill any wine. Swirl vigorously enough to maximize agitation without creating a mess for you or your host. Make sure your glass is not over-filled with wine. The level of wine in the glass should never be higher than the one-third mark. This height will provide ample room for swirling without making a mess.

You may use a flat surface which is non-porous for swirling until more comfortable with it. Place the glass on the surface, holding the stem between the fingers and rotating the glass in a circular manner while keeping the glass flat and in contact with the surface. Do not tilt the glass. The centrifugal force of the rotation makes the wine rise in the glass giving it the same effect as tilting the glass slightly when rotating in air.

Rotate the glass continuously at about one rotation per second for about 5 – 7 seconds in total. Then raise the glass to your nose to smell the wine. This is the safest way to swirl without causing an accident. However, if a flat (non-porous) surface is not available, then hold the glass in front of you and rotate using a slight tilt of 5° or less. As with the glass being on a flat, non-porous surface, rotate about one revolution per second for 5 – 7 seconds. Right handers should swirl counter-clockwise and lefthanders, clockwise. This is the most natural movement for our wrists.

After swirling, you should immediately bring the glass to your nose. The bouquet will only be alive and above the glass for a short amount of time, no longer than thirty seconds or so before it recedes back towards the glass bottom. The ability to get a good nose of the wine's bouquet evaporates if you wait too long. This is an easy problem to fix as you just need to swirl again. I frequently, swirl and make sure to swirl (and nose the wine) before every taste.

Swirl carefully and avoid any chance of accident. If you are drinking (especially red wine) over an expensive carpet, you should consider removing yourself to a location standing above a non-porous floor surface such as tile or hard wood. Wine spills can be cleaned, but they should be attended to immediately to avoid damage. You should avoid wine spills at any cost. With a little practice, you will become much better and more confident. Also be careful when using different glasses as the weight and feeling is different and a swirl which may be appropriate for one glass may not be so for another.

Always be cautious when swirling to avoid accidents. Taking time to attend to a wine spill, especially if over a nice carpet, will ruin most wine drinking experiences. For tablecloths, I always try to avoid a spill, but it is less critical and it happens with both food and wine frequently dropping to a tablecloth. Unlike carpet, a tablecloth can be removed, bleached, washed and reused. A dark red wine spill over expensive carpet can be fixed, but is a dampening experience to the best party and often requires a professional to fix it.

Earlier in this chapter we have discussed the importance of using proper glassware and how that can enhance the wine drinking experience. The shape of the glass is an important factor on how the wine interacts with your nose and mouth (mostly tongue and taste buds). But if you are unwilling or unbelieving of the importance of glass shape, you can still improve the interaction of the wine with your nose and mouth by swirling. You should use proper glassware and then swirl to heighten the wine drinking experience to optimal levels, but swirling on its own may be used as a "poor man's substitute" for better-shaped glassware.

Swirling is not pretentious, but is a critical activity in the wine drinking experience. Practice and become comfortable doing it.

Sniffing and Smelling

To get the most from sniffing, your nose should be as close to the wine as possible. The active molecules releasing odors are strongest closest to the wine and significantly lessen the further away your nose is. Bring your glass to engulf your nose and possibly even come to touch parts of your face.

Be careful not to 'over-sniff' or overuse your sniffing mechanism (olfactory bulb) as it can fatigue quickly. There are various techniques (and some disagreement) on the best way to smell. Everyone agrees you should smell the wine immediately after swirling using a normal inhale. However, some experts believe this is the only step required in sniffing properly while others believe a two-step or three-step approach is more suitable to get the most from sniffing. In the two-step approach, you would first sniff the wine without swirling to understand the wine's potential and basic foundation of the wine's quality. (I am doubtful on the necessity of this as an indicator of quality; for young wines it may represent the wine's potential.) However, like changes in temperature, you may perceive differences in wine in its non-volatile and volatile states, providing a more complete review. I suggest you try both approaches to see what works best for you. For me, it is really the smelling after swirling that provides the best indication as to how the wine is going to taste. I have tried both and enjoy doing the comparison of the wine's odors in a non-volatile and volatile state, but it is smelling wine in its volatile (after swirling) state that is most useful.

Peynaud recommends three quick stages of 'nosing' a wine consisting of (1) smelling before agitation / swirling to detect the most diffusible odors which would otherwise be over-powered by the dominant ones released after swirling; (2) smelling the wine immediately after swirling to discern the wine basic characteristics; and (3) smelling specifically for any subtle wine faults.[105]

After swirling, there is also some disagreement on if a normal sniff or a 'big' sniff is a better technique. While I have achieved slightly more odor concentration with a big sniff, I find it unnatural and of little additional benefit. A big sniff tires your olfactory capabilities and requires at least thirty seconds of rest before another attempt. Amerine is in favor of using one big sniff, while Peynaud thinks it is a waste of time and effort. Regardless, you should not repetitively be using big sniffs for a prolonged period of time, or your smelling ability will be in a state of disrepair. I find using a considered and slightly more forceful (than normal breathing) sniff to work best and can be repeated as necessary without concern of (temporary) damage to the olfactory bulb.

Our natural smelling capabilities means that even wine drinking novices are capable of being able to smell most aspects of a wine. Yet a novice usually does not spend much time smelling as they do not appreciate the benefits of smelling and want to move onto tasting. Nor will a novice know what to seek during the smelling process. By being in the presence of more accomplished wine drinkers willing to point out what is happening with odors they smell, the novice will immediately be able to identify and remember those odors. And after several similar sessions, the novice is no longer so, and can start to discern and pick up on the various odors present in various wines.

Le Nez Du Vin provides various sets of wine odors typical in many wines and is a useful way to be able to learn to smell better. This will accelerate the process and more quickly enhance your ability to smell wine with confidence. Le Nez Du Vin has a total of 54 different wine samples at the time of writing, including twelve which are wine faults. By using their samples, you can quickly compare wine odors and be able to identify and describe them more quickly and accurately.

Additionally, take the time to practice smelling everything around you. My increasing desire and ability to cook has greatly improved my smelling sense. Taking time to notice odors when you are cooking or just walking down the street and passing other individuals (what cologne are they wearing?, have they been smoking?, etc.) greatly improves and makes more natural your ability to smell more and various odors. Unfortunately this provides opportunities to smell the bad with the good, but the practice will become second nature and certainly be put to good use when smelling wine!

Tasting

Tasting wine is what this book is all about! Tasting is defined as to what happens when wine is in the mouth. The traditional definition of taste refers to the sensation that occurs when your tongue's taste buds pick an object's sweetness, saltiness, bitterness, etc. Yet, the integrated and more holistic experience of tasting when it comes to wine involves smell and feel in almost equal proportions. Tasting wine is a truly-cross modal sensing experience that brings a number of senses together to experience and appreciate wine through multiple responses. These sensations heighten and enhance each other and do more than any one sense could to provide us with wine drinking enjoyment.

As mentioned previously, the use of proper glassware starts the process of getting wine into the mouth with proper flow, interacting with our taste buds appropriately. Always start the tasting process with proper glassware. The next thing to be aware of is how much wine is ingested. It depends on the size of the mouth, but for most people, a range of six to ten ml is sufficient. There should be enough wine to be able to coat every aspect of your tongue and inside the mouth, but not too much that you cannot move the wine around your mouth without spilling. You want enough to provide a few small swallows during the tasting process and enough room to be able to inhale some more air into your mouth if necessary.

Keep the wine in your mouth from thirty seconds to one minute. Anything longer will dilute the wine and its flavor as we generate saliva while tasting. Ultimately, you will swallow the wine, but there are a number of steps to perform while the wine is in your mouth. Use your tongue and cheek muscles to move the wine around your mouth, coating every taste bud and providing the maximum coverage possible. Inhale and exhale a few times to increase the retronasal smells. Continue to agitate the wine and increase its volatility (similar to what happens when swirling and then smelling) by pursing your lips to provide a thin opening, sucking in more air to mix with the wine. (You can only do this without dribbling if you did not overfill your mouth with wine in the first place.) This process provides continued volatility, releasing wine odors and flavors.

People have described swallowing fine wine as 'orgasmic!' While that may be an exaggeration, the act of swallowing does force more liquid to the back of your throat and pushes the odors into your retronasal passage, integrating again the senses of smell and taste. When swallowing, you also experience more taste using receptors in your throat. The act of swallowing is critically important for wine enjoyment. It extends the mouthfeel and taste while increasing the use of our smelling sense holistically. Therefore, make several small swallows before completely swallowing the remaining wine. Take several seconds to reflect upon and identify what you are experiencing and enjoy about the wine, be it the wine's flavors, the weight of the wine, or its balance. Upon your first small swallow, try to identify the most immediate and obvious effects and your reaction to the wine, and then with each subsequent swallow, try to identify other flavors and characteristics. If you are eating at the same time, try some of the wine on its own and some with food to determine how the food has changed the taste of the wine.

I consider drinking wine to be a fulfilling and worthwhile experience. Think of the math behind my sentiment: if you sip 7.5 ml of wine at a time and have three swallows per mouthful, which provides you about 100 sips of wine and 300 swallows per bottle. That is great value! It also can be a real education in terms of understanding and being able to appreciate what you like about a particular wine.

<u>Storing Wine after Opening Bottle</u>

Fine wine will age well over 10 – 20 years with modest changes year-after-year until it is in a range of time when it should drink beautifully. After opening a bottle of fine wine, the change in the taste of the wine over the next few hours to the next day or two are accelerated exponentially. This is due to massively more air coming in contact with the wine.

During time in the bottle, only about 25 ml of air space exists in a 750-ml bottle of wine for the wine to mature by interacting with air. With cork, a few more milliliters seep through each year to continue to help the wine mature. If there is a cork problem, though, and a lot of air is leaking into the bottle, the wine will mature far too quickly and not be drinkable if cellared too long. For this same reason, once opened and exposed to more air, the opened bottle becomes undrinkable after a few days.

Unless you are going to drink the entire bottle over several hours, you need to limit the amount of air in contact with the wine to prolong its life. This provides you more time to finish the bottle before it goes bad. There are several ways of doing this:

- Stick the original cork back in to stopper the wine bottle (keeps wine good for about a day unless the wine is already highly oxidized)
- Use a simple manual rubber stopper and vacuum pump to extract excess air from the bottle (keeps wine good for 2 – 3 days, again, unless already oxidized)
- Use a commercial pump and storage set (usually good for two bottles and can keep wine good for 4 – 6 days)
- Use a gas replacement system that is completely close-sealed (keeps wine good for several weeks)

After decanting wine for the right period of time, it is important to place the wine back into the bottle and seal it. While several minutes to several hours (in most cases) of decanting will improve the wine, anything after that causes the wine to deteriorate and turn to vinegar. To slow this process so you can finish the bottle of wine prior to it going off, you need to minimize its interaction with air once the bottle has been opened and decanted.

Every time you open the bottle to pour another glass, you are letting more air into the bottle, and as the bottle depletes, the amount of new air introduced increases, which quickens the pace of deterioration. Therefore, it is important to stopper the bottle immediately after each serve to minimize any excess air in bottle. This is why vacuuming air out and replacing it with a gaseous blend is the most effective way to keep wine fresh for several weeks.

If the cork is intact or you still have the screw cap after opening the bottle, you can use it to stopper the wine. While there is no expense to this method, the wine will worsen overnight and not be as drinkable the following day, and less drinkable after that (due to new air being introduced and not extracted). If the bottle has been left half empty overnight, you have introduced a lot of air into the wine which will quickly deteriorate it. This approach can be used successfully for keeping a bottle of wine fresh for several hours or maybe from afternoon until evening, but should never be used to store a half-empty bottle overnight. Only use this approach after decanting and refilling a bottle to bring to a restaurant immediately thereafter.

If you do not have a simple vacuum pump, Robinson suggests keeping several half-bottles or splits (quarter bottles) around to use for wine storage.[106] Instead of dealing with a lot of air trapped in the bottle after stoppering it, you have better matched the bottle size to the amount of wine which remains to reduce the amount of new air introduced. This will make the wine last longer.

The most cost-effective way to store wine and keep it drinkable for a few more days is to use a vacuum pump and rubber stopper set. These tend to cost around $20 - $25 for a pump and a few stoppers and you can buy more stoppers separately as required. This uses a special artificial stopper with small holes and one-way openings. The pump is used to extract as much air as possible and create a vacuum in the bottle. This significantly reduces the amount of air in contact with the wine and slows the deterioration process, extending the wine's drinkable life.

I use the vacuum pump for most bottles which are drunk over two days. For only $20 - $25, you will save many quarter- to half-bottles of wine for another day and over time this can mean keeping thousands of dollars of wine drinkable. Since it is usually just my wife and me at home for dinner, we may not drink more than a half-bottle per day. We will usually have two or three bottles opened at a time, as our mood changes or to be matched with a meal. Using the vacuum pump and stopper method keeps several bottles fresh and available to provide suitable choice of wines.

Additionally, when we have larger dinner parties, we will have eight or ten bottles of wine we want to serve upon arrival, with each food course, and after dinner. But you are never sure how many people are going to be drinking (one night a friend who we did not know was pregnant was not drinking, for example), and we may have already decanted several of the finer wines, so we might have three or four partial bottles left over at the end of the evening. By using the vacuum pump to store the wine, we can consume the rest over several days.

The vacuum pump set is a great option for the money. However, the technology is limited when compared to commercial models. Sometimes the rubber stopper seal is nudged (possibly even upon removal of the pump) and air re-enters the bottle. (You can tell if this has occurred when you open the bottle and there is no popping of the vacuum. If there is a definite vacuum breakage popping sound, then you know it was sealed properly.) If no popping occurs, you should make sure to drink the rest of the wine right away, or risk it going bad. If the seal has remained intact, you may be able to get another day of good drinking from the wine. Unfortunately, there is really nothing you can do to determine if the seal is intact or not until you open it again. Be careful when removing the pump from the stopper by lifting it straight up. The seal also may loosen during storage due to changes in temperature or humidity. Based on bottle type, there may be some small differences in the diameter of the bottle opening, causing the seal to be more susceptible to failure with wider bottle openings. Additionally, if there is residual wine on the bottle's neck, there may be some slippage and the seal breaks.

The next day or day after, you will have noticed some changes in the taste of the wine. It is usually smoother (which can be a pleasant improvement if it was tight when you first opened it), but you have usually lost the fullness of grape flavor. The wine might taste less powerful. After a couple of days, it may taste flat or 'dead.'

Sparkling wines have the additional challenge of staying fresh once they are opened. In addition to preserving the live fruit flavors, you also need to retain the carbonation which is more quickly and noticeably lost if not re-stoppered. Fortunately for about $10, you can buy wine stoppers designed for sparkling wines which will do the job for a day or two. They have a much larger insertion mechanism which creates a vacuum (less so than using a regular manual vacuum pump), but more importantly, pressurizes the remaining sparkling wine to keep the carbonation from fading.

The next (more expensive) option for wine storage comes as a small refrigerated unit with individual compartments to hold two bottles. Each bottle has a pumping and extraction capability and for most models, each bottle can be stored at a standard white wine or red wine temperature. Each compartment is set separately so you can either store two whites, two reds or one of each at the right temperature.

This commercial option cost $500 - $700 based on features and engineering, but they all function similarly. They also require an electric outlet. This technology provides a better seal and air extraction system than the manual vacuum pump so it provides several more days of storage with less noticeable change. I have considered buying such a system, but have not yet as I have very few bottles that require five or six days of storage. Additionally, I have not been entirely comfortable with the value point of the technology. I expect more competition in this field and the quality and durability to improve while the price drops in the near term. I am open to buying a system, but have not done so yet. I continue to monitor this type of device to see what is available and if it is reaching a value point where I am comfortable purchasing one. If you are constantly drinking fine wines over a longer period of time, this is a worthwhile option to consider.

The top of the line storage unit for open bottles costs several thousand dollars and can be configured to store as many bottles as you like. They typically come in a configuration to store four bottles, but can be customized to store more. Additionally, they can be provided as a counter top unit or built into the wall or cabinetry. Wine features such as this type of storage unit plus Vintec or other manufacturer's cellar units are now being featured as key aspects of kitchen renovations. I love things that are functional and stylish and this type of system fits both characteristics!

These systems are manufactured as closed systems where a tight seal is provided for each bottle. They provide temperature control to be able to adjust the temperature to be suitable for a certain type of wine (sparkling versus white versus red). They have much higher quality parts and are custom assembled to suit your needs. I am hopeful to get such a unit someday when I have the money and also know that I will be living in that house for a long, long time. They allow wine to be opened and drunk over several weeks. The reason they work so well is that they ensure air cannot creep into the space in the bottle as the air has been replaced with carbon dioxide, nitrogen and argon. By doing so, oxidation has been reduced drastically, preserving the quality of the wine for a far longer period of time. You can view these types of units by visiting a wine bar or searching for them online.

A new device which has been over a decade in testing is the Coravin. The Coravin uses a needle to pierce the foil and cork and remove as much wine as you like while replacing the air space with argon gas. This preserves the remainder of the wine over long periods of time. I have not used the Coravin personally, but the reviews are positive and one of my friends swears by it. They cost about $300 and the argon gas replacements cost under a dollar per glass of wine removed. But when you want to drink $100 bottle of wine over several months or even several years, it is well worth it. Additional advantages to using the Coravin are that you can sample an old bottle or bottle at risk to ensure it is suitable to drink, and you can determine when is the optimal time for aging and then opening a bottle to drink without having to sacrifice an entire bottle to make that determination. This looks to be an excellent option for those who like to drink (a little) very fine wine over long periods of time.

These are a number of suitable options to keep wine fresh once you have opened the bottle. They come at different value points and vary based on how long you would typically need to keep bottles opened before finishing them. The important thing is to always stopper the bottle with one method or another as soon as possible and to extract as much air as you can from the bottle. This will slow the rate of deterioration.

<u>Avoiding Impediments</u>

Impediments can significantly decrease your drinking wine pleasure. People are often unaware of impediments they introduce that may impede their drinking pleasure; or worse, the experience of others. There are some simple rules to follow to reduce impediments.

If you are sick or taking medication, your taste buds and olfactory glands will not be working properly. You are likely to have too much or too little mucus which will impede or change the ingestion of smells and tastes. Not only are you 'wine tasting handicapped,' you are also potentially putting yourself in a dangerous situation combining alcohol with medication and risk infecting others. Memories and collective experience are a large part of wine appreciation, and getting sick while tasting ruins memories.

Medications often contain Zinc, Vitamin C, and other ingredients which introduce metallic, citric or other dominant tastes making it difficult to assess or enjoy wine. Be careful not to ingest vitamins near a wine tasting experience as these tastes linger on your palate and in your digestive tract. The same is true for leaving a minty taste from brushing teeth or using mouthwash just prior to tasting.

Wearing perfume or cologne is also a problem, not just for you, but for others around you, as your scent is now filling the glasses of others, diminishing the wine's natural bouquet. The same is

Improving Smell and Taste Sensations

true of hair spray; or air freshener.

Others around us appreciate us not smelling bad, but by using items that cover up smells (like perfume or cologne), or improve our looks (hairspray), we are worsening the wine drinking experience for ourselves and others. Similarly, do not use mouthwash or lipstick which changes both the taste and texture of wine as it passes the lips.

Try to be as natural and unobtrusive with body odors as possible when drinking wine, and hope others around you feel the same. While I shower before I go out, if I am going for wine tasting, I take a little extra time to rinse off soap (especially if using a fragrant soap) and I do not use cologne. I brush and freshen my teeth, but then use a palate cleanser (like a mouthful of sorbet) to bring my mouth to a more naturally absorbent state. I want my body, especially around my head to be free from exterior odorants. I have dry skin and use three different types of moisturizers. The one I like the best is rose-scented. Another one I use which is stronger and applied to my driest spots has a medicinal smell. The third one is the most scent-neutral and is the one I apply if I am going to be drinking wine. I do not want to introduce rose or medicinal scents to wine tasting.

We have daily cleansing and make-up programs which are second nature to us and appropriate for being in public. We hardly think about what we are doing. However, some of these activities can introduce impediments to wine drinking. Develop awareness and be conscious not to introduce odors or flavors into the wine drinking experience. I would not eat Spam, Vegemite or Durian prior to kissing someone, and similarly, I would not use a minty breath spray before sipping a fine wine!

It is not a good idea to catch a last smoke just before tasting wine. Fortunately for smokers, their taste buds recover quickly from the effects of smoking. If you have brushed your teeth or had a smoke, leave yourself minimally one hour before tasting and your tastes buds and olfactory glands should work fine.

It is a pleasant experience to burn candles or incense or place scent enhancers around a room. However, these pleasantries should be avoided when drinking wine. They create flower, woody or other smells that confuse people when sniffing wine. Professional tastings go to great length to provide a sealed environment where it is difficult to introduce extraneous smells into the environment. While you do not need to go that far, avoid introducing any odors, even good smelling ones, into your wine drinking environments.

Avoiding Stimulus and Sequence Tasting Errors

When watching talent competitions such as *Britain's Got Talent* or *The X Factor*, I have often wondered how the sequencing of the contestants impacts how they are judged. I expect the impact is high, based on the order presented. Similarly, I know the positioning and sequencing of lanes when running a 400-meter race makes a difference in how well the runners do. While they are all running the exact same distance, the outside runners are initially ahead of the rest of the crowd based on where they are placed at the start (due to the wider circumference they need to traverse) and cannot see if the runners behind them are catching up to them or not. And the runner on the inside lane has a tighter curvature around the bends and traversing this requires the expenditure of more energy. Therefore the best positioning is to be in Lanes 2 or 3. The same is true in swimming where you are better off being positioned in the center lanes than in the outside lanes where you get less cross-movement of water interfering with your forward motion. While these runners and swimmers are all competing over the exact same race length, there position changes the outcome of their performance.

The same is true when tasting and drinking wine. There is a typical sequence of serving white wine first, followed by reds and within the whites and the reds, going from lighter to heavier wines. A Pinot Noir is typically served before Shiraz. If we had the Pinot Noir after drinking Shiraz, we would likely find the Pinot Noir to taste flatter and less flavorful due to having drunk the heavier wine first. If multiple wines are being served, it is important to get the order and sequencing of the wines correct. The general rule is to order your wines in the following sequence:

1. sparkling wines
2. lighter, more acidic whites
3. smoother, aged whites
4. lighter reds
5. heavier, more aged reds
6. 'sticky' wines and iced wines (dessert wines)

If you follow this order, you are generally enhancing the experience with each new bottle. Sometimes with a meal, it is not possible to follow this order based on the order in which the food is being served.

It is also important to vary the quality and intensity of the wines. For my 58th birthday party, we had an outstanding wine line-up. We were at a steak house and I decided to feature big, high-quality red wines. We started the celebration with a bottle of Pommery Champagne, and followed that with three outstanding red wines in this sequence: 1998 Tyrrell's Vat 9 Shiraz, the 2001 Yalumba Octavius Shiraz, and the 1981 Penfolds Grange. Any one of these three red wines could have been the finish wine for a big celebration, and I sequenced the wines properly in going from the lightest to the heaviest. Yet, drinking the 1998 Tyrrell's Vat 9 Shiraz after the great Champagne provided the perception that we were finished drinking wine for the evening. We were already satiated! The 'warm-up' wine would have served as almost any meal's 'finish' wine (before dessert wines). By the time we got to the 1981 Penfolds Grange, we could not experience any more pleasure. Our palates and emotional states were completely satiated. Looking back, I should never have placed three big, great wines together in sequence.

Comparing various wines to each other is a good and quick way to learn a lot about what you like and dislike about particular wines and why. Novices should only compare two wines when they are starting to be able to focus on a few identifiable differences. Then several more may be added over time. Even wine judges have a difficult time assessing and comparing more than five to fifteen wines at the same setting.[107]

In addition to sequencing errors and poor judgment in the ordering of wines served, there are a number of other stimulus errors that can occur. Unfortunately, many of them are so subtle we do not identify them. That is why we are going through the trouble of identifying them for you now; I missed many of these early on, but have learned over time. Once you are aware of them, it is much easier to avoid being deceived by them. Stimulus errors are events where we are stimulated by some aspect of the wine drinking experience that causes us to think more or less highly of the wine than it deserves. We are stimulated by something not related to the wine's quality. Most stimulus errors occur through our sight, such as viewing a label or seeing if a wine is sealed with cork or screw cap and assessing the wine's quality based on the image and not the wine itself. These will be discussed in the next chapter as they are more focused on our sense of sight. Most stimulus errors with regard to taste or smell are caused by:

1. smells introduced into the wine drinking environment;
2. fatigue or non-functioning of our smell, taste or feel senses, or
3. our general mood and attitude.

It is impossible to separate surrounding smells in the wine drinking environment from the odors and taste of the wine, if the surrounding smells are strong. That is why so much effort is put into providing the right environment when wine judging occurs. While we are more conscious of how our legs tire when running or our arms when lifting weights, we are less conscious that our olfactory bulb is tired, or our cheeks are coated with tannins from several days of drinking to be able to recognize it. I experienced two cups of coffee one morning that tasted overly astringent. I was confused by this as those cups of coffee were identical in every aspect to coffee I have had previously. At first, I thought I may have had a bad batch of beans, but after my second cup, I realized it had to do with the manner in which my palate was functioning at the time. Once I thought about it, I realized that it was the change in vitamins I had taken that morning which was likely causing the difference. The effect wore off in a few more hours and my coffee again tasted right.

Once you realize something may be different about the sensations you are picking up on your tongue or elsewhere within your mouth, you can do something to address the issue. Water on its own may rinse solid particulars out of your mouth, but is not a very good palate cleanser. Use something like a plain piece of bread or a dry cracker to help absorb and remove already existing coatings. A slice of cucumber or another raw vegetable can also quickly absorb and remove what may be on your palate, but some vegetables will introduce a different taste which may not be any better in the short term. And some influences may not be in your mouth directly, such as how your olfactory bulb, or surrounding mucus is affected by longer term medicines you may have been taking. In this case, there is nothing you can do except to drink copious amounts of water to flush out the effects as quickly as possible.

Mood and attitude are important in being able to perceive a wine's quality and in being able to appreciate fine wine. Fine wines are wasted on bad attitudes! Let me highlight this in an obvious and extreme case. There was a group of six of us who had been in a joyous mood, having been to a new restaurant and wine bar launch. We had a glorious time and everyone was in high spirits; several came from overseas and it was nice to be able to get the group together. Since it was only 7:30 pm and while we had consumed some nice canapés at the launch, since we were already together (which was a rare occasion on its own), we made reservations at a BYO restaurant close by where we lived, and stopped by our place to pick out some very nice wine to consume during dinner. This was a celebration of life and relationships and the wines needed to match. While picking out the wines, my wife realized that she had missed a call and checked her voice mail. In checking her voice mail, we found out that a dear friend had died unexpectedly. We then decided that we would cancel our meal, but overturned that and decided to go out to be together, but the purpose and the mood of the meal changed greatly. I selected some other 'middling' wines to go with the meal. There was no way we would be able to concentrate on or appreciate quality wine that evening. We wanted to drink, but could not concentrate on the flavor. Our mood changed everything about what wines were best suited to the situation.

Recognizing what mood we are in and why makes it much easier to determine if, why, and what we should be drinking. There are wines of celebration, wines of contemplation and wines to help bury our sorrows. Don't waste a good bottle of wine when you cannot concentrate on anything other than burying your sorrows.

While it is impossible to eliminate (nor would we want to) all surrounding stimuli which may impact our tasting, it is important to identify what may be altering the perception of the taste. Minimally, we need to determine if it is due to the wine being off or something about us or our environment being off. The important thing is to be able to identify if stimulus errors have occurred, so you have a framework to understand and react accordingly.

Matching Wine and Food

Eating, while drinking wine and sharing time with friends, is one of life's great pleasures. A university professor told us 35 years ago: "Your life is broken if you cannot find time each day to break bread and share drink with friends." I never forgot that and have used the approach to monitor if my life is broken or not. Unfortunately, when building a career and chasing the elusive goal of trying to make more money, it was too easy to grab food and drinks on the go, and not to follow my professor's advice. As I started to appreciate and live life more and understand that life is a journey, not an end point, I focused more of my life on breaking bread and sharing drink with others. I challenge and recommend you to follow a similar approach if you are not already.

This book is not about matching food and wine. There are some tremendous resources available which accomplish that. I am not going to provide lists of foods and matching wines. There are plenty of sources which provide excellent advice on that topic. I do want to provide some general observations and suggestions on how to get the most out of food and wine matching. They fall into the following categories:

- Wine drinking almost demands the presence of food
- The taste of wine changes when combined with different foods
- The combination of wine and food is usually better together than alone
- White with fish, red with meat is a start, but only a starting point for achieving a fine gustatory experience

Chapter 9: Wine and Taste covers significant ground on how food and wine matching works. I now provide some practical suggestions for ensuring we are getting the most out of combining wine and food.

Drinking wine on its own is pleasurable. I like to have a glass when I return from work and sit down to blog or work through some administrative activities. I enjoy a glass when reading. A glass of good wine feels like an extension of my body, an integrated part of my presence. It heightens awareness, creativity and helps facilitate thought processes. My mind, heart and soul function better when drinking wine. Wine is as nourishing (in different ways) as food for me.

I do not drink wine on an empty stomach. I only drink a glass of wine on its own if I have eaten within the last several hours. If it has been longer, than I make up a small cheese plate, or possibly eat a biscuit or roll before drinking a glass. While I want my palate fresh and nothing to interfere with the wine drinking experience, by the time the wine enters my stomach, I want it to mingle with some food. The alcohol (and potentially acid) from wine absorbs at a better rate if combined with food. Several glasses of wine without any food in the stomach can cause a sense of unbalance. Therefore, it is a good idea to have some food in your stomach prior to introducing a solitary glass or two.

The perception of wine's taste changes drastically when combined with food. Based on the wine and the food introduced, this change can be positive or negative. In *Chapter 9: Wine and Taste*, we explored the physiological reasons this occurs. Obviously, you will want to match foods that enhance the experience instead of detracting from it. This requires both knowledge and experience.

The same wine will taste one way when you are eating chocolate and differently with mushroom soup. In one case, a wine will match beautifully with one food choice and taste horrible with another. For example, I would enjoy drinking an aged Chardonnay with a hearty, thick creamy mushroom soup, but would never consider putting Chardonnay in my mouth after having a bite of dark chocolate.

But chocolate comes in many different flavors, including dark, milk, white (which is not really chocolate at all as the cocoa has been removed, but it still tastes and feels like chocolate), or altered with chili, caramel, peppermint and other flavored infusions. Additionally, crushed nuts or marshmallows may be added to change the texture of chocolate. Based on the specific secondary characteristics, some chocolates would go best with Pinot Noir, spicy Shiraz, Cabernet Sauvignon, or Port or Muscat. And based on the type of nut used, I may even make a choice of a red wine aged in burnt or toasted oak to pick up on nut flavors. (While chocolate is being used as an example here, this is true of all foods taking on various combinations of taste.)

As discussed earlier in this book, assessing and determining what you like about a particular type of wine is contextual to your individual tastes. The same would be true for food; when combining the two, the variety of responses grows exponentially. Only you can determine what you like. However, based on the physiological principles at play, some standards exist that provide a good starting point in terms of food and wine combinations that should work well together. For example, an aged Chardonnay with buttery or creamy foods; a Sauvignon Blanc with whitefish; and a lighter Pinot Noir with non-beef meats such as pork or duck are good combinations as the dominant characteristics of the food and wine work in balance with regard to taste and mouthfeel.

These combinations usually work well together. There are

simple charts and taste wheels on the Internet which provide grape types matched to food types which can be accessed for free to provide basic ideas. The charts do not explain why, but only 'what' to match. Neither do they discuss how the taste of wine changes based on the primary and secondary ingredients or cooking method involved.

The primary or dominant characteristic of food is usually the main and largest ingredient such as beef, pork, duck, lamb, chicken or fish. The secondary characteristics come from sauces used, seasoning or the manner in which the main ingredient was cooked (boiled versus grilled, for example). Having lobster does not dictate having Sauvignon Blanc just because you are having seafood. Lobster could be boiled and served with butter, grilled (and therefore a bit tougher / dryer in texture), served in tomato-based bisque, or baked in cheese as a lobster mornay. In each case the lobster demands a different wine. This is the huge impact secondary food characteristics play in the choice of what wine best matches the food.

Similarly, a wine's primary and dominant characteristic is the grape itself. However, secondary characteristics are introduced through the different soil types and climatic conditions where the grapes are grown, and the process of how the wine is made and aged. Winemakers talk about fermentation bouquet, processing bouquet and aging bouquet. There are many different ways to achieve growing great grapes and making wine that provides variety in the wines we drink.

A simple example is eating a beef steak and considering which Australian Shiraz to best go with it. Hunter Valley Shiraz is often described as spicy whereas Barossa Valley Shiraz is often described as fruity. Therefore, if I was having the beef steak with a peppercorn sauce, I would choose a Hunter Valley Shiraz, and if I was eating the beef steak with 'au juice' or a mushroom sauce, I would choose the Barossa Valley Shiraz.

But there are many different methods for making both Hunter Valley and Barossa Shiraz. Additionally, there are a lot of different types of beef steaks, ways to prepare them and sauces to serve with them. In many instances, I would choose a Cabernet Sauvignon over a Shiraz, or a blend of both grapes could be suitable in many situations.

The important thing to remember and start to experience is that the reason you consider one food type or wine to be superior to another is because of the secondary characteristics, not just the primary or dominant ones. Even before you have the knowledge or experience to identify or articulate this, you intuitively know that one is superior to the other. With some practice and experience you continue to improve and enhance your food and wine matching abilities.

Food and wine matching may sound complicated, and one could make it complicated. I have some experience, but often guess at what types of wine to bring to dinner, especially if we are going out (and I have not decided what to eat yet), or if someone else is cooking and I do not know what they are cooking. (In these cases and if I have the time, I will review the restaurant menu online or ask my friend what he or she is planning on cooking, so I can do a better job of selecting the right wine.) Fortunately, many different wines will work very well with the same food. And through a little knowledge and a little experience, you can continue to get better and better at matching food and wine more appropriately.

Summary

This has been a long chapter with many pragmatic and easy to follow techniques for improving wine drinking as it relates to your sense of smell and taste. Smell and taste are highly stimulated when drinking wine. There are a number of things you can do to improve and heighten the impact. Over time, they become second nature – you won't have to think about them as you inherently are more comfortable with various aspects of wine drinking.

Notes

100. Robards, *Book of Wine*, 27.
101. Peynaud, *The Taste of Wine*, 239.
102. Robards, *Book of Wine*, 18.
103. Peynaud, *The Taste of Wine*, 100.
104. Ibid., 97-98.
105. Ibid., 93.
106. Robinson, *How To Taste Wine*, 72.
107. Amerine and Roessler, *Wines: Their Sensory Evaluation*, 9.

Chapter 13
Improving Sight Sensations

The previous chapter focused on improving how we smell and taste wine. For most people, these are the two senses used most when wine drinking. But it is our sense of sight that first encounters wine and influences our experience greatly.

Wine is best drunk in glasses that are clear and without decoration, pattern or color; that feature and focus attention on the wine, not the glassware. The glass should be completely clear, without distraction. The glass shape should be tulip-shaped, suitable in size and shape for the wine you are about to drink. This is the most visibly appealing aspect of glassware. Chiseled crystal glassware only serves to hide the beauty of the wine itself. While using leaded etched crystal shows you have expensive tastes, it does not exhibit good taste with wine.

The glass should have a narrower top rim than middle. If you use glasses where the top of the glass is wider than the middle, you immediately projected you know little about how to enjoy smelling and tasting wine. If I am handed a glass widening towards the top rim, I have already assessed the wine which will be poured into it to be of questionable quality. Even if it is of good quality, I am disappointed I will not be able enjoy it fully. This critical judgment has been rendered by just looking at the glass. Make sure your glasses are properly shaped. It is easy and inexpensive to do.

Wine Sense : The Art of Appreciating Wine

Curved in at top to retain smell

Wine is observed by looking down into the top of the glass and by tilting the wine at a 45° angle to provide the longest observation plane without spilling the wine. Wine is best observed when viewed through glass against a white background. Use a white tablecloth for displaying bottles, decanters and glasses. When standing around the table, everyone can then tilt their glasses to a 45° angle and best observe the color and fragility of the wine against the white background. This provides clear visual indications if the wine is suitable for drinking.

You are able to immediately assess the age and fragility of wine by viewing it. If the lighter colored outer rim of the wine touching the glass is nonexistent or narrow, then the wine is young and probably tight. If it is thin to moderate, then the wine is likely ready to drink. If there is a light colored and wide outer rim, the wine is old and fragile. (It still may be a very good wine, but should be drunk immediately.)

There is a lot to learn from viewing wine against a white backdrop. In addition to a white tablecloth, use a white serviette (cloth or paper) when serving. Always have a serviette ready to wipe a loose drop off the decanter or glass to remove the risk of any drops falling to the table or floor. The white serviette also provides a white background for viewing wine away from the tablecloth or if the tablecloth is not white.

The visual display of wine bottles, labels, decanters, glassware and other wine paraphernalia provides a beautiful backdrop to any wine drinking. While it does not change the actual quality of the wine, it can certainly add to the perception of taste and the overall enjoyment of the experience.

After decanting, I keep the bottles around for several reasons. The first is that they may be used if there is leftover wine and I need to re-bottle it. Additionally, bottle shape and label design add to the beauty of the setting. A number of books and research papers have been written on the topic of wine label design and aesthetics. Many people buy wine based on the label design without knowing anything more about the quality of the wine in the bottle. This is why wine manufacturers focus so much time on labels. And if we are willing to pay for wine based on the design, why not use the visible bottle and labels for visual appreciation? Additionally the label provides useful information on the grapes used, where grapes have been sourced, where the wine was made, vintage, and alcohol level. which are important for assessing and comparing our wine drinking experiences. In general, more information on the label (or back label) indicates a better quality wine.

If I have decanted several wines, I keep the wine bottles and decanters together so people can see both the wine as it is displayed in the decanter and the information displayed on the bottles. If it is a wine tasting, then the bottles and decanters are lined up on a counter. If it is a meal, the bottles and decanters are placed on the table and within reach for review.

Bottle size on its own can be an impressive visual sight. A 1.5-liter magnum bottle displays strength and unity (since it presents a lot of wine we are all sharing), and a 3-liter bottle even more so. I occasionally use a magnum if I have a large number of guests sharing wine, but never used a 3-liter or larger bottle: larger bottles are difficult to maneuver and consume too much table and counter space. They look impressive in a winery's cellar, but are too cumbersome and will visually impair most wine drinking experiences.

There is beauty in the occasional magnum and 750-ml bottles of various shapes and smaller 375-ml bottles of dessert wines. Occasionally, dessert wines or fortified wines come in sleek 500-ml bottles which are visually appealing. Having a variety of different bottle shapes and sizes provides a wonderful collage of what you are drinking. Use the bottles and labels to enhance the visual experience.

Another key visual impact is filling the glass only to the level of the widest point in the glass bowl. This means the glass is usually filled to between the one-third and two-fifth level. As explained earlier, this provides optimal exchange of wine and air to continue to soften and mature the wine while in your glass. It also provides safety room in anticipation that you will be swirling your wine. Filling a wine glass higher than maximum width is counter-productive and visually unsightly. When someone does this (often a waiter in a restaurant who has not been trained properly), they are limiting the impact of smelling and tasting the wine. The visual impact of filling a glass too high disgusts me - it shows the servers or hosts know nothing of wine. Like providing a white tablecloth, knowing how high to fill a glass of wine provides important visual effects the people involved know how to make the wine drinking experience an enjoyable one.

I have never spent more than $20 for a decanter. I have about ten decanters in total. The traditional decanter shape and size works well; in fact, far better than many more exotically shaped ones. When I have several wines opened for a comparative tasting, the visual display of the wine in the decanters next to the original bottles the wine came in, is quite visually impactful and will not be improved using more exotic and expensive decanters.

I acknowledge some decanters are both functional and visually attractive, including the Duck decanter and the series of Black Tie decanters by Riedel. I have been given the Black Tie Smile decanter and another Riedel decanter as gifts. They cost several hundred dollars and do not improve the smell or taste of the wine over using a flat pan or milk jug to decant. However, they provide significant visual impact highlighting the wine we will soon be drinking. When having a dinner party and opening three or four bottles of wine, I will use the Riedel Black Tie Smile decanter to feature the best red wine. This draws attention to and builds anticipation for serving that wine, usually later with the meal.

I personally am not willing to spend several hundred dollars on a decanter when any container will do in terms of optimizing the smell and taste of the wine. (I would never use a pan or milk jug as it would be visually detracting from the wine drinking experience.) I like having one or two visually beautiful decanters displaying feature wines on the table. If you consider buying one or several of these beautiful decanters for visual display, make sure they are well balanced, and provide the basic function of rapidly exchanging wine and air which is the main purpose of the decanting process. I have seen exotic looking decanters for $4,000 that make great conversation pieces, but actually do not provide the basic function of a decanter. I always favor function over form, but if I can get function and form together in a decanter, I will do that for one or two. But form without function, especially for a $4,000 decanter, is a waste of money!

If you are serving several bottles of red wine together, make sure you have adequate lighting to exhibit the differences in the color of red wines. This is important in being able to tell them apart visually and also representative of the differences in grape and quality. A candlelight dinner or one with poor quality lighting makes all red wines look alike.

We mentioned in the last chapter how easy it is to be deceived by stimulus errors. This is especially true when our sense of sight is involved. We are so confident in what we perceive through sight that it overrides what we experience through our other senses. Sometimes people selling us wine intentionally create stimulus errors to entice us to purchase more or pay a higher price than we should. (This topic is discussed in detail in *Chapter 17: Buying and Storing Wine*.) Typical visual stimulus errors you should be aware of and consciously avoid include:

- Do not assess wine sealed with cork as better than wine sealed with screw cap.
- Do not assess wine in a box being worse than wine in a bottle.
- Do not view a bottle with a fancy or imported label as containing better wine than those with simple labels.
- Avoid being tricked to believe white wine with red wine dye tastes like red wine.
- Avoid dark, aesthetic tasting room settings, which increases the perception we are drinking a higher quality wine.
- Be careful not to be lenient in judging a wine when in the presence of the winemaker, other winery staff, or so-called 'experts' who are proclaiming the wine excellent when it is not.

Even the very best winemakers (outside of Europe) are switching their iconic brands over to screw caps. This should not in any way influence perception of wine quality. And while wine in a box is usually made from the mass of grapes available which have not been reserved for better quality wines, there are certainly boxed wines that are better than some bottled wines. I have had some decent wines out of a box which were suitable for the occasion and enjoyable to drink. Had I stuck with the attitude that wine in a box is insufferable, I would have had to go without on some evenings.

While conducting research for this book, I was surprised how much I found on designing wine labels. This is an extremely large field of study and there appears to be more courses on wine label design than there are on winemaking and vineyard management. The industry knows how important wine label design is for wine sales and they work hard at getting labels right. Some people cannot bring themselves to drinking a cleanskin wine (bottle of wine without a label affixed) even if they have confidence they know what wine is in the bottle. They have a preconceived notion that cleanskins are made from low quality grapes (otherwise, why would it be a cleanskin?). I know people who have dismissed extremely fine wines out of refusal to drink anything without a label affixed to it.

There are a number of good reasons cleanskins exist and are sold as such. Sometimes there is a difficult vintage when yield of a particular grape type from the vineyard may not be sufficient to put in the overhead of making a production run that year. The winemaker and sales management may determine the setup cost does not justify a small production run. This leaves very good grapes which may be sold cheaply to others to use in a blend or box wine. The other and usually more profitable option is to do a cleanskin production run and sell at a discount, but with higher margin than they would have received from selling the grapes to someone else. Other batches of grapes may be set aside as they may not know quite what to do with the grapes until decisions involving other grapes (often harvested later) and made. They may have too many good grapes of different varietals that have been allocated to produce the targeted amount of wine sales for the year. They do not want to flood the market driving prices lower, so they will sell the remaining grapes in cleanskins.

I recently sold some excess wine from inventory. I had a number of cleanskins of very good wine and vintages and proper provenance to show that the wine inside the label-less bottle was the wine I claimed it to be. My cleanskin stock sold out immediately to people who understood they were getting great wines in great vintages at a significant discount. Don't be mistrustful and dismiss a wine because of no label or a simply-designed label. Knowing what is in the bottle is far more important than what is on the label.

Earlier in the book, we have discussed the stimulus and deception that can be caused when drinking white wine with red dye in it. With practice and experience, you will gain more confidence about what grapes you are drinking regardless of the wine's color. There are other stimulus errors that can occur through a wine's color or color characteristics such as hue and depth. Most of us have a preconception that a good red wine should have a certain color and that the color should be a rich brick red. However, it is important to observe and evaluate the color of wine within each grape category. A high quality Pinot Noir or Zinfandel will be lighter in color than Cabernet Sauvignon or Shiraz. Shiraz that looks like Zinfandel is likely to be tepid, while Zinfandel that looks like Shiraz is likely over-oxidized or has issues of clarity. Therefore, you should not view a wine only on its color without knowing what varietal it is or what the vintage is. Wines darken in color over time and if you have an expectation of what a wine's color should be, you may end up drinking a poor quality wine that has great color. Study and understand wine color charts for various grapes and ages to become comfortable of how a wine's coloring should look.

Even wine experts are fooled by red dye in white wine. Dr. Charles Spence, an expert in cross-modal sense interaction states that the reason red coloring in wine is such a powerful driver of what we experience is that redness typically equates with the ripening of fruits in nature.[108] This is also the reason red dye is added to meat and other food products and liquids. Red is perceived to be an indication of health.

The last two topics on stimulus errors as they relate to over-buying and over-paying for wine will be discussed in *Chapter 17: Buying and Storing Wine*.

Visual impact does not make wine taste better, but it plays an important part in the wine drinking process (which is why it is a component of wine judging). Be aware of the possibility of visual stimulation being introduced that may lead you to making faulty wine purchasing decisions.

Notes

108. Goode, "Wine and the Brain," 92.

Chapter 14
Improving Feel Sensations

When we think about 'feeling' wine, it is usually associated with mouthfeel, or when wine is inside the mouth. However, feeling wine occurs much earlier in the wine drinking experience: we feel wine and its balance when we pick up the bottle; we feel it when decanting and holding the decanter to pour wine into the glass; we feel it holding the glass and swirling the wine; and we feel it again tilting the wine toward our nose and then our mouth. Only then do we experience mouthfeel.

It is important to strive for balance not only with the wine, but with wine bottles, decanters and glassware. You have no influence in the shape and weight of bottles used unless you are making your own. But you can feel balance holding the bottle properly. It is one of the reasons I do not drink wine from 3-liter bottles or larger. It is impossible to achieve a sense of balance when pouring wine. The feel of a 750-ml bottle and the power and weight of a 1.5-liter bottle provides feeling sensations that adds to the experience. Anything heavier more likely detracts and becomes a physical burden.

Every bottle is heavier on the bottom (due to more glassware across the bottom and in many cases an indented bottom) than the top (where the neck is tapered). This allows the bottle to stand firmly with little risk of knocking it over. Given the slightly below-median balance point, you should be holding every bottle slightly below mid-height when pouring. If the bottle is hurting or putting pressure on your wrist, adjust accordingly. As wine is poured out of the bottle, the balance is lowered and your grip should be adjusted to match. This may not seem that big a deal, but balance on its own is worth pursuing and you avoid the possibility of injuring your wrist.

When re-bottling wine after decanting it, you are pouring the wine through a funnel which usually has limited width and if you are not adjusting and holding the wine properly, you might pour wine too quickly causing a spill and losing wine that could be put to better use by drinking it, not wiping it off the counter!

Sometimes wineries use slightly heavier bottles for wine. This is typically done with more expensive wines where another $0.50 - $1 per bottle cost can be more easily absorbed. It is done to reduce the amount of accidental breakage and preserve the wine's value. It also provides a feeling of stronger, higher quality wine. A heavier bottle improves my opinion of how good the wine is going to be (another example of stimulus error intentionally introduced by wine industry). While the actual taste has not changed, my perception of it has. I feel the winemaker has done his or her best to bring me high quality wine.

Decanters are not as well balanced as wine bottles, so pouring from them requires more skill. The best approach is to use two hands with one around the neck of the decanter and the other one under the base. There are a few decanters that have built in handles that work well. I have bought several inexpensive ones with handles and Riedel's famous Duck decanter is a great example of a beautifully formed decanter with perfect balance. Decanters with handles are best suited when continuously filling glasses from the decanter such as during a dinner party. They are the easiest to use and to feel without distraction when serving.

I have an abundance of traditional decanters used for tasting, but have never paid more than $20 for any of those decanters. I have a Riedel Black Tie Smile decanter for visual impact and balance (even though I consider it a two-handed decanter). I also have several $15 - $20 decanters with handles for serving wine during a sit-down dinner party. I am a traditionalist and believe the shape provided by the Riedel Duck decanter or similar is the ideal decanter for both visual impact and feel. More exotic and visually impressive decanters often feel fragile and unbalanced which is another reason I do not use them.

The benefit of proper glassware for improving smell and taste cannot be over-emphasized. Good glassware also provides good balance and sense of feel. I consider the Riedel Vinum line to be the ideal traditional glassware range for a wine drinker in terms of good value for money. The Riedel Sommelier line is more elegant and provides a slighter lighter feel, but it is twice the price. I have several glasses from the Sommelier line for Port and Sauternes which I consider 'special' drinks. I have also purchased some of the Vinum XL glass sets because there have been good offers on them. They feel more celebratory in my hand because they have a higher and distinctive feeling stem. I enjoy drinking from the Vinum and Vinum XL range for the way they feel. They provide the best balance and overall feeling and value for money in my opinion.

Your glass should not be filled to the top. This makes the glass uncomfortable to hold and prone to spilling. The glass should be about one-third full; this makes it easier to hold and balance and swirling is a more easily achieved. A glass too full is uncomfortable to hold and requires concentration which should be focused on smelling and tasting the wine, not on holding the glass.

Later in the book, I provide an evolution of myself as a wine drinker and how I learned to enjoy and appreciate wine more over time. I do this as I believe the journey is educational. I also believe that it takes some of the mystery and fear out of embarking on a similar journey. The first two characteristics of fine wine I learned to notice and appreciate had to do with balance and mouthfeel. While I could tell a wine tasted and smelled good, it was the ability to feel a fine wine (in my mouth) which I could identify and articulate first.

Wine changes in flavor and feeling over a period of time in your mouth. It is recommended that you keep wine in your mouth for up to a minute before swallowing completely or expectorating (spitting). Different parts of the mouth and tongue feel and detect flavors differently. Therefore, while in the mouth, it is important to toss the wine around several times to ensure your entire mouth feels the wine. You then truly feel all a wine has to offer as each part of the mouth provides different sensations. You can also sense how the feeling changes over time. Take several small swallows as swallowing provides feelings in your throat (and rest of head) as it forces wine retronasally into your olfactory region. Aspirate (suck in air between your lips and teeth to continue the air exchange with the wine) to continue to agitate and enjoy the feel of the wine on your palate.

The other key mouthfeel sensation is caused by the amount of tannin in wine and how it adheres to the inside of the cheeks. Heavy tannins (which are also found in teas) can provide a puckering or suction feeling on your cheeks. As described in *Chapter 10: Wine and Feel*, and for good wines, some of this is pleasant, but too much is not. I like to feel well-integrated tannins as I know that this is the sign of a good wine and the tannin has provided structure for the wine to age well over a long period of time. If the tannin is in perfect balance with other wine characteristics, it feels great in your mouth. If not balanced, and especially in a younger or poorer quality wine, it feels like a cat fight is underway!

In a previous chapter, we discussed the benefits of decanting, filtering and aerating wine when it comes to improving smell and taste. Filtering, in particular, removes any free floating tannin so you do not introduce a gritty mouthfeel from the tannin particulars. Decanting and aerating (aerating is just a method to speed the decanting process) softens the wine and provides an improved mouthfeel.

When drinking unbalanced wine, there is little that can be done to make it balanced. It is possible that leaving it sit overnight and tasting it the next day could improve overall feel, but will not improve balance. Aspirating and tossing the wine around in your mouth improves it slightly.

What can be controlled is the ability to ensure your palate is fresh and has the ability to absorb everything a wine has on offer. During wine tasting, it is always important to take time between sips to let the previous wine finish. Usually a time equal to the time you had the wine in your mouth is adequate. Therefore, I tend not to sip more than once every two or three minutes. During the course of an evening, I will also take several 5 - 15 minute breaks without drinking to let my palate rest.

Even with this approach, you may have palate build-up during an evening. This creates a carry-over effect from the previous wine's influence. It limits the ability to enjoy new wines as the palate is conditioned by the previous wine. When people taste wines serially over short duration, they often create sequencing errors, due to false impact noticed in later wines caused by the sensation of the earlier-drunk wines. It is difficult to keep a palate fresh in this situation.

Freshen your palate by eating a spoonful of sorbet, or have a piece of bread or a non-salty biscuit. Drinking water does not help directly, but can be useful in terms of keeping you from drinking more wine and worsening the problem. Water also helps rinse wine which has been absorbed and extracted by eating sorbet or bread.

I once spent ten straight days sampling a lot of wine and

drinking wine with meals during that time. I did not realize it, but by day seven, my palate was destroyed. No wine tasted good during the last three days. Several months later, I tried a number of those wines again with a fresh palate, and realized several were outstanding. The cumulative effect of wine drinking had altered the state of my mouth, numbing it to the point I was not able to taste properly.

Make sure ample time exists between tastings to cleanse and restore your palate. Also make sure to eat some sorbet or bread during a long evening to cleanse the palate. This will provide optimal ability to achieve good mouthfeel. But the most important thing about ensuring good mouthfeel is to make sure you have selected the right bottle of wine in the first place and that it has aged the proper length of time in the cellar. Once opened, there is very little you can do to improve mouthfeel beyond decanting.

One additional topic is how you feel overall while drinking wine. Drinking wine in moderation usually makes one feel better. However, a number of people have varying degrees of sensitivity to sulfite's used in making wine. I unfortunately have a low tolerance level for sulfite. Sulfite is placed in wine for useful reasons during the winemaking process. Check the labels as it is required by law to mention when sulfites have been added. There should be a notification on the label similar to 'Preservative (220) added.' Sulfites usually completely dissipate after several years. I find if I drink a young white wine or Pinot Noir that I may get a terrible headache, even after only one glass, if it contains sulfites. Therefore, I now ensure my wines have been aged for at least several years to let the sulfites dissipate. If you find you have a low level of tolerance for sulfite, then be careful and drink only wines made without sulfite (many organic wines) or wines which have been aged for several years.

Chapter 15
Improving Sound Sensations

Drinking wine is truly a cross-modal sensory experience. The visual aspect creates anticipation and provides clues as to what the wine will taste like. The combination of smell, taste and feel work in an integrated manner to provide us with great drinking experiences. And while sound does not play as major a part, it does have a role and the role can be improved similarly to how other senses can respond when drinking wine.

Like the sense of sight, sound can be used (and heightened) to help us celebrate. Sounds when drinking heighten the interaction of all other senses. And sound plays an important role creating mood when drinking wine.

There are five areas of sound interaction I try to control and improve:

- sounds to acknowledge or create sense of celebration
- sounds which are testament that we are drinking with pleasure and improving the interaction of other senses
- removing distracting sounds which could harm the wine drinking experience

- providing appropriate level of background noise (which should be minimal)
- sounds of social discourse and sharing the wine drinking experience

The most obvious sound of celebration is the opening of a Champagne cork. It is loud and focuses our attention on the Champagne and the cause of celebration. This is usually followed by a toast as to the reason of gathering and honoring the event or one or more participants. The toast may also acknowledge and bring the group together to remember or praise someone not with us, but whose life around which we all revolve. Regardless of reason, listening to a toast while holding a glass of Champagne brings people together to share a common bond. It starts with the pop of the Champagne cork, is enhanced by the speaker providing a toast, and finishes with us in unison raising and possibly clinking glasses, finishing with the sound of swallowing the wine. Four different sounds (popping, speaking, clinking, swallowing) come together to provide a sense of celebration and fellowship.

In some situations such as an Orthodox wedding, or the signing of a great and difficult to achieve treaty, this can be followed by the sound of breaking glasses by throwing them into the fireplace or onto the floor. I have never participated in such an event, but believe it signals the uniqueness and never to be repeated nature of this one-off event. However, if you are doing this regularly, this is one situation where one might use generic wine glasses instead of Riedel!

There are also sounds made when opening a bottle of table wine. These sounds are not as noticeable as the popping of Champagne, but still evident. Cutting away the seal and peeling it attracts attention. The next faint sound, almost felt more than heard, is the separation of cork from bottle. Older bottles (especially sweet white wine) contain residual sugar which affixes the cork to the glass bottle. Removing a fragile older cork works far better when you have first broken the sugar fixture. This is not possible be using a center drill corkscrew, but is when using the Ah So or similar corkscrew which has two prongs and goes down the side of the glass bottle on the outside of the cork instead of being drilled through the center. Then you can slowly twist the corkscrew to break the seal. Hearing this occur provides a further sense of anticipation (as this is usually only necessary with a much older bottle of wine) that you are closer to enjoying a great bottle, and it is a sound of accomplishment as you now are certain you can remove the cork without it breaking into pieces.

You may hear some popping of an older bottle of wine stored with cork when opening it as some evaporation may have caused a small vacuum to occur in the bottle. If the bottle has been stored overnight with a vacuum pump and rubber stopper, you will hear the popping sound as the vacuum breaks, bringing back memories of the wine you enjoyed the day before and will enjoy again today.

The next sounds include filtering and aerating the wine into a decanter. Much has been written about this previously in terms of significantly improving the way a wine smells, tastes, and feels. It also provides 'wine music' from listening while decanting which alerts you are closer to actually drinking the wine.

Sometimes you are not in a position to decant and aerate a bottle in the traditional manner. You may only have time to pour a glass and start drinking. The Vinturi filter and aerator provides sound while super-dispersing the wine in a matter of seconds. This is not as pleasurable as the sounds provided using more traditional processes for decanting, but does provide a sense of certainty and accomplishment that you have done what you can to make the wine as drinkable as possible when rushed to raise a glass to your lips.

Wine is alive, continuing to change in structure from bottle to glass. With Champagne, you can see and hear the bubbles continuing to rise to the surface in your glass. And still table wines continue to make delicate sounds as they oxidize in a decanter. Riedel has several types of decanters that enhance this sound, making it noticeable, so you can hear the oxidizing process and be certain of the quality and liveliness of wine being decanted.

While sound plays a less important role than other senses, you understand how important it can be in creating anticipation when preparing a bottle for drinking. Sounds also play an important part in ensuring you are doing what you can to heighten other senses when drinking. Swirling wine (which again is described elsewhere for its effect on smell, taste and feel) provides sounds which are often more felt than heard.

Once wine is in the mouth, keep it there for up to a minute, moving it around on your tongue and prolonging the finish. Moving the wine around your mouth provides audible signals, as does continued aspiration, ensuring through the audio sense that you are agitating the wine thoroughly.

When people gather for wine tasting or a meal, eliminate

most, if not all background noise. This type of noise can compete with or distract from the positive sounds which enhance wine drinking pleasure.

Keep windows and doors closed to block out background noise from the street. Ensure the television and stereo are turned off or down. If you cannot block out background noises entirely, then it makes sense to put the stereo on and use non-invasive background music (similar to sounds used for meditation or massage) to mute other noise distractions which could not otherwise be eliminated.

Like many other activities and sensual pleasures, there should be periods of silence during wine drinking to enjoy all of its sensual aspects. This should be followed with periods of wine discourse. The greatest sounds come from talking and sharing with others. Sharing wine discussion helps us to learn more about wine. You learn a lot from others when discussing wine.

If the main point of getting together is to watch sport or a movie, it is inappropriate to interrupt these events to discourse on wine. Then wine drinking takes a background role to focusing on the main event. This setting is for group entertainment with little wine dialog where wine may be discoursed only during breaks or after the event is over. In these cases, I keep my thoughts on wine to myself and enjoy and concentrate on the event. In fact, during such events, I may not be drinking wine at all, but having a beer or soft drink instead.

Wine drinking has developed its own language. It is certainly possible to enjoy and appreciate fine wine without being able to articulate what it is you like about the wine. However, to share the experience with others, some ability of being able to describe what you like and don't like about wine is expected in social gatherings. Is a wine being "fleshy' the same or different from the wine being 'big and robust?' What is really meant (if anything) by saying a wine is 'pretentious?' And if you are not attuned to why some people say Sauvignon Blanc tastes "of cat's pee," or a Riesling has a 'diesel' taste, you may never want to ever try those wines.

Tasting wine appears contextual based on an individual's capabilities, experience and knowledge. The experience is heightened if we can share and have a common vocabulary for doing so. A large part of the requirement for becoming a MW is to be able to describe in consistent terms what you are experiencing when you drink. This is a critical capability for wine critiquing, judging and writing on wine. Several people have put their life's work into creating wine vocabulary and semantics. References for learning more about wine language are provided in *Chapter 20: Further Wine Education*.

While not having the impact that sight, smell, taste and feel have in wine drinking, sounds (both positive and negative) play an important role. Sounds builds anticipation, helps us celebrate, and prepares our other senses to get the most from wine drinking.

Chapter 16
Other Ideas for Improving Wine Drinking

Wine drinking is first experienced via our senses, but is also experienced cognitively and affectively.[109] Wine drinking is enhanced by social interaction and social interaction is enhanced by wine drinking – the two go hand-in-hand. I love and make the effort to gather people together who enjoy being together and have a common love of good food and wine. For such gatherings, we have a somewhat set agenda we intuitively follow.

Upon arrival, we usually serve a sparkling wine or a unique and different type of wine. This immediately establishes a cause for celebration of being together and starts the conversation flowing. It also helps the stomach secrete, building hunger and anticipation for the food to come. The first upon arrival will then discourse over what we are eating and drinking tonight and help pitch in if possible with some of the remaining tasks of meal preparation. We discuss what we are and will be drinking and speculate how it might match with the food. We all learn and get new ideas about some potentially different food and wine pairings we may try in the future. Then during the course of the meal, we have various conversations about all sorts of topics, but definitely share with each other our thoughts on the wine. These types of meals provide a highly integrated experience of drinking and learning together which is invaluable for improving our knowledge of drinking wine.

Other Ideas for Imprvoving Wine Drinking

Meals built around good food and good wine usually have a multitude of people. And it helps to get the right mix of people. We tend to socialize with people who share common interests, be it through work, clubs, or passions. We like to be able to share our wine and wine drinking experiences with others, so try to include at least some people who are wine enthusiasts. As described further in *Chapter 18: Wine Drinking Practice and Experience*, we benefit from and learn more quickly when in the presence of others with more expertise when we are drinking and discoursing about wine.

We try to have a reason for celebration when together with others, or even when opening a good bottle just for ourselves. Celebration creates the perception the wine is better because the overall experience is better. Sometimes we are just celebrating being alive and having good friends. We work with many people who travel to where we live for work and are away from family. We often put on a 'singles and strays' meal to bring us together. This is always a fabulous way to commune with people from all corners of the globe. And our 'singles and strays' appreciate being able to enjoy home-cooked meals and fine wines, instead of having to eat out or getting take-out. Find a reason, any reason, to celebrate to make wine drinking more enjoyable. The wine always tastes better!

When sitting down for a meal of multiple courses or a variety of tapas or taste samplers, try to find wines which are versatile and can move from course to course. Pinot Noir and Pinot Gris tend to be examples of versatile wines. If you have six or eight people attending a meal, then you have enough people to share in each bottle and you can more specifically target wines to food. In general, move from white wine to red wine and from lighter wines to more robust wines. This is not always possible and that is why the concept of versatile wines and keeping several bottles opened on the table helps in matching food and wine.

I am surprised how many serving people in restaurants have not been trained properly in the most basic of wine serving techniques. Many have never opened a wine bottle sealed with cork. If I am bringing an older bottle along, I bring my corkscrew and open it myself. The other most basic requirement for serving wine is pouring wine into the glass. Many servers fill the glass to the top. This is a problem for three reasons. The first is the wine should never be higher than the widest part of the glass, allowing for maximum interaction with air to release the wine's smells. Pouring wine to the top (and much more narrow) part of the glass will choke off the smell of the wine, making it less pleasurable.

The second reason is filling wine to the top makes it impossible to swirl. The third is that not everyone may enjoy the wine or want to drink the same amount. The wine is put to much better use when smaller amounts are tasted first, and more is left for a second round by those who want more. Therefore, unless it is a restaurant where I know the staff is properly trained, I make it clear that I will be serving the wine myself.

Regardless if I am out or at home, I make sure to have a white serviette for serving wine. Placing the serviette under bottle or decanter provides better visual effect and also saves you from spilling a few drops that otherwise may end up on someone's shirt sleeve or the tablecloth. If I am serving wine at home, I make sure to have available cleaning supplies such as soda water, sponges and hand towels in the event an accident occurs. Having a wine accident can ruin the mood of an otherwise nice gathering, so be prepared to quickly address and resolve any accidents.

Indulging in gustatory pleasures such as eating and drinking wine can tax the system and possibly overload it. Therefore, it is always a good idea to be fit and well rested when starting the evening. Make sure everyone is drinking in moderation and at a good pace so as not to over-imbibe. Everyone has a responsibility to monitor, and if necessary, kindly remind each other about the perils of over-indulging. Nothing ruins an evening or its after-effects as much as someone getting sick or having an accident on the way home. I have purchased a home breathalyzer for people to use to ensure it is safe for them to drive home. They are inexpensive (about the cost of a decent bottle of wine). There are also adapters and apps you can use with your smart phone to accomplish the same thing.

Notes

109. Charters, "On the Evaluation of Wine," 168-72.

Chapter 17
Buying and Storing Wine

The book has focused on how wine interacts with the senses and how to improve their use to make wine drinking more enjoyable. The remainder helps you optimize wine drinking through a path of practice and learning. We have covered how the senses work and how to get the most out of them. Yet, that is only useful if the bottle of wine you are opening is worth the effort in the first place. There is a lot we can do to improve wine drinking, but it all starts by opening a good bottle. Therefore I am dedicating almost a quarter of this book to buying and storing wine.

Unless you are involved in the production of wine, purchasing it is the first time you influence your wine drinking experience, positively or negatively. There are a number of questions you should ask, including:

- Do I have a budget?
- What wine do I currently own?
- What wine do I like to drink?
- What should the composition of my cellar look like?
- Do I have the ability to properly store wine?
- How fast will it be consumed?
- How long will these bottles be stored before being

consumed and do my consumption patterns allow me to drink the wine prior to it 'going off?'
- How many bottles of a wine should I purchase?
- Is this vintage better or worse than other vintages?
- Is this wine likely to improve significantly over time and if so, how long should it remain in the cellar?
- Will my taste in wine change over time and if so, will it be aligned with the wine I am purchasing today?
- Where should I buy wine?
- Should I depend on wine reviews or personal tastes?
- Am I able to taste the wine prior to buying it?

The more effort put into your purchase, the far better outcome you will have when you finally drink it. It may appear you need a PhD in wine consumption before buying a bottle, but that is not the case, nor is it necessary for your enjoyment when drinking wine. Like a lot of things, it is sometimes better to jump right in and learn from your experiences and mistakes. And with a little research, you can limit your mistakes and better ensure you are buying great wine at a great price. Both experience and experimentation, combined with some knowledge and research easily improves your wine buying and cellaring habits.

If you do not have a budget, establish one with limits on how much you can spend in total and per bottle. Wine buying can be intoxicating and it is easy to spend more than necessary, possibly even more than you can afford. Avoid the position where you cannot consume your wine before it goes bad (because you have too much and cannot drink it in time). If that occurs, you will pour it down the drain or at best, use it as a cooking wine. I had to do that for about 200 bottles so far and it is not a pleasant experience! I simply did not drink enough wine quick enough, mostly because I did not realize it was past end-of-life. You must have control over your inventory to avoid a similar fate.

There is no better research than tasting wine yourself and understanding what you like. You are the best judge of the style and characteristics that appeal to you. There are many ways to do this, often for free or a small fee. For tasting fine wines, there may be a fee, but this is when it is most important to determine if you really like a wine or not. For the majority of wine, you can attend cellar doors, bottle shop tastings, or selected special tasting events. After having done this several times, you start to develop a sense for what you like and what you will pay for good wine.

Another great way to learn is to have dinner parties where each participant brings a bottle or two, and you taste the wine with different foods and discuss wine with your friends.

Tasting and assessing newly released expensive wines before you buy is risky. It requires a mature palate to determine if a new vintage of expensive wine will improve significantly in ten to twenty years. Drinking a Grand Cru Bordeaux or a Penfolds Grange which is only three to five years old will likely disappoint you. It will come off as too tight, potentially harsh or astringent, and heavy on the palate. It will not be balanced. But if you wait until it is ready to drink to sample it, you are unlikely to find any of the wine left for purchase or if you do find it, you won't be able to afford it! While much wine is consumed immediately (far too much in my opinion) and you may learn to readily determine if you like a wine style for immediate consumption, it is worth learning how to judge a wine for how it will taste a decade or two down the road.

For expensive, long maturing wines, there are the reviews from experts to assist. They should be independent and not associated with any particular winery. It is easy to find reviews through a variety of sources. Search online to find reviews and tasting notes. You can also buy annual review books from renowned experts or subscribe to their online service which is often the most cost-effective way to review current and previous vintage wines.

The first thing is to understand what type of wine you like to drink. What grapes or blends do you enjoy most? Do you like a lighter or heavier style? Does this change based on how and where you are consuming the wine? It does not make sense to buy expensive wine not matching your preferences. We all have different tastes and abilities to appreciate wine, so it is important you gain confidence in determining what you like.

When I refer to cellar, I am not necessarily talking about an underground cave with proper temperature or humidity control and capable of storing thousands of bottles. Your cellar could be a bookcase in the closet or a tray of ten to twenty bottles of wine under the bed; I have used both previously until recently. The important thing is that you do what you can to store wine properly (a topic which will be covered soon). First, we need to determine how big the cellar should be and what should be in it. It may seem strange that I am discussing cellaring wine before we discuss how to buy wine, but wine should only be considered for purchase if it can be cellared properly. Good wine deserves good cellaring. It is necessary to protect your investment.

Most people consume wine within 24 hours of purchase. Many of these purchases are spur of the moment for an event (like a dinner party or to be given as a gift), or to go with dinner that evening. I live in a building with a bottle shop on ground level and am surprised how many people in the elevator have just purchased a bottle for dinner. I make three unsubstantiated (but likely true) proclamations about those purchases:

- With very little knowledge, they could have purchased a far more suitable and higher quality bottle for the same price.
- They paid at least 25% too much for their purchase (unless it was a dirt cheap, low quality wine).
- They are drinking the wine too early and it would be better if cellared a few years.

Bottle shops are in the business of providing choice and selling product. There are limited bottle shops I purchase from, as most of my purchasing is direct from the cellar door or at auction. It is the purchaser's responsibility to know what wine they want to purchase before entering the bottle shop premises. Simple research is easy and worthwhile if you have any interest in wine whatsoever. It provides more control and confidence in getting the right bottle at the right price. Obtaining this knowledge is covered later in this chapter.

People ask me to walk through bottle shops with them to provide understanding of what wines would be good buys. This takes only several minutes and has armed my friends with a sense of knowledge and confidence when they need to make their next purchases (while they continue to learn how to do this on their own). They use a smart phone camera to take pictures of the label and write a caption ('great value,' 'goes well with Thai food,' etc.) for each photo. There are also smart phone applications that allow you to scan a wine label, and retrieve tasting notes and purchasing information from different sources. This provides you the information you need to have confidence in buying the bottle at the right price.

Early in my wine drinking days, I spent 25% - 35% more than I should have. The cost per bottle does not improve the taste of wine, but getting better value improves the joy and perception of quality. It also provides more funds to buy better wines in the future. I realize also that I purchased far too much wine, due to not having established a budget and set limit, and also by not understanding my consumption patterns properly. That combined with not having a proper inventory management system meant I overbought and overpaid by a lot!

The key to buying the right amount of wine at the right price is to build a cellar of wine from which you select most of your bottles for consumption. I rarely buy wine for immediate consumption. I do not buy in a bottle shop for the reasons mentioned above. I buy (and highly recommend that you buy) to cellar wine. When you need to consume a bottle, go to your cellar (again your cellar could be anything from closet space to a more professional basement cellar) to retrieve a bottle. This approach provides you with the best choice available, the best guarantee that the wine is imminently drinkable and that you have purchased the bottle at the right price.

How Big Should Your Cellar Be?

This varies by individual, but can be easily calculated. First set a budget and know your consumption patterns; then determine how large your cellar needs to be.

Wine in storage is an asset, and like other asset classes, it can increase or decrease in value. It is not an asset though like equities, bonds, or investment property which can easily be sold and converted near-term to cash. It is an asset that we usually consume. I never buy wine as an investment or with the intent of selling it later. However, I do put some time into understanding which wines are likely to go up or down in value and why. This has been useful to help adjust inventory by selling some excess wine. It is important to realize that the wine you have in storage is an asset that required capital to put it there in the first place and is capital you could have used elsewhere, such as paying down debt, investing in other asset classes, or purchasing other things.

Maintaining a cellar comes at a cost which is the cost of financing the inventory and the cost of the cellaring itself. Based on the type of cellaring used (a book case in the closet or building a professional cellar), the total cost of financing and cellaring will be approximately 5% - 10% of the cost of the wine annually. This may seem exorbitant. That is one of the reasons most people do not cellar wine.

I believe the investment for cellaring is wise as it allows you to drink far better wine at much lower costs. There are also hybrid cellaring approaches to keep the cost of your cellar low.

Buying vintage wine (one that is ten or more years old) to consume immediately usually costs more than what you would have paid for it originally, even including the cellaring and finance costs. (This has been somewhat impacted by the recent Global Financial Crisis, but still generally holds.) There is also greater risk with aged wine that unless you know the provenance of the wine before you bought it, you have the risk that it may have been stored improperly. Cellaring wine also provides far greater choice that is not available to others for vintage wine; exceptional wines usually sell out quickly. It is not worth cellaring cheap wine though or wine that will not last, but having a cellaring strategy makes sense for fine wine.

What size should a cellar be? Should you have a cellaring approach that contains 50 bottles, 500 bottles or 5,000 bottles? There are two main questions to answer to determine cellar size. These are:

How many bottles do you consume per year?

What is the average age of the bottles you consume?

Multiply those factors together and you will have an approximation of how many bottles you should have in the cellar. Think about and estimate a response to these questions. If you drink two bottles per week on average and drink wines that should be cellared for five years, then you should have a cellar to store 500 bottles (100 bottles consumed per year times 5 years.) If you drink on average four bottles per week and drink finer wines that require cellaring for ten years on average, then you would need a cellar to store about 2,000 bottles.

In general, people tend to over estimate how much they need. There are a lot of factors affecting this that should be considered:

- How many people are really consuming wine week in and week out? (Take into account the size of your family, how many larger functions for which you use wine, etc.
- How old and healthy are you? Do you need to reduce

your wine drinking as you get older?
- Much wine is being made to mature earlier and be drunk after only a few years, therefore requires shorter cellaring

Our drinking habits change over time. My wife and I drink less now than previously due to my wife having to watch the amount of alcohol that goes through her liver. I am drinking slightly smaller quantities per meal. Additionally, we tend to have more meals with just the two of us now or smaller gatherings than when we were both working full-time and dined with larger groups of people. I also am better at buying vintage wine at auction which means the bottle lays in my cellar far less time than had I bought it upon release. In general, I am buying finer, but fewer wines which require less storage time.

Given these factors, reduce your cellaring requirements to 75% of the amount calculated above. If the amount of wine consumed per year times the number of years required for cellaring is 1,000 bottles, then having storage arrangements for 750 bottles should be adequate. And if you find you have received a gift of a couple hundred bottles from someone else's estate, you can always temporarily use other external storage capabilities. There are numerous commercial wine cellaring options available from paying by the bottle in a shared and managed space to having your own dedicated cellar with 24/7 access. I have provided links to several of these in *Chapter 21: Other References*.

What Should I Do for Cellaring Wine?

Different wine storage approaches exist and a hybrid approach is likely most suitable. I built two cellars in previous homes. I spent $6,000 to build a cellar in my garage to hold 1,200 bottles. Assuming the cellar was full and the useful life cycle was 15 years, this means in current costs, my storage cost per bottle is approximately 35 cents per bottle per year. This is an inexpensive option. However, I sold the house six months after building the cellar, so the actual storage cost was significantly higher! In my next house, which I thought was going to be my lifetime residence; I spent $15,000 to build a cellar to hold 3,000 bottles. But fate intervened causing us to sell that house also, and never using the wine cellar.

I currently use an external storage provider which costs about

$3 per bottle per year. That is much more expensive than building a home cellar, but I have not had to allocate up-front capital. I have the flexibility to reduce or terminate this option whenever my needs change. They also provide services such as having wine shipped directly to the cellar which ensures the wine spends minimal amount of time outside controlled environments. I do not need to be available to receive a shipment as the facility is staffed. Additionally, they provide events allowing us to meet people with a common interest in wine. I have met several people and we have exchanged wine and experiences to broaden each other's knowledge. Therefore, the $3 per bottle per year covers more than just storage, but is an expensive proposition for storing wine you paid $10 for originally, so other alternatives should be considered for less expensive bottles.

Once wine has been bottled, there is nothing you can do to improve its quality, except store it properly and determine the best time to open it. The winery has done everything possible to ensure your wine has been made from the best grapes, using the best process to let the wine age and mature. And with proper cellaring, the wine should achieve its potential while in your cellar.

Principles for Wine Cellaring

The primary principles in wine storage are to keep the temperature constant and avoid extreme temperatures. Large changes in temperature can cause a cork to expand and contract, causing cork faults which allow air more rapidly into the bottle, prematurely oxidizing and ruining it. Even if sealed with screw cap, large changes in temperature place the wine's structure under duress, possibly rupturing it, and losing any possibility of the wine becoming balanced. Therefore, it is important that wine stays at a constant temperature with changes in temperature no more than a few degrees Celsius (or several degrees Fahrenheit). Anything more can potentially harm the wine beyond repair. One or two short durations with small changes in temperature is not a problem, but if the wine is undergoing frequent large changes due to seasonal swings, then the wine will be at risk.

The specific temperature does not matter as much as consistency of temperature. The warmer the temperature, the quicker the wine matures. If the wine matures too quickly, it can break down and become undrinkable. If wine is stored at colder temperature, it matures more slowly, prolonging its drinking life. It is important to understand and monitor the temperatures at which the wine is stored. Only then will you understand the optimal time to drink each bottle. Each cellar should have a thermometer and humidity recording device, optimally one that records the highs and lows for temperature and humidity achieved. This provides the information required to determine if your cellar has suitable conditions or if your wine is potentially at risk.

Bottle size also plays a significant role in how long to cellar wine. Each doubling of bottle size requires an additional 3 - 5 years of cellaring. Therefore, a good Magnum (1.5-liter bottle) should be cellared for several more years than the same wine in a 750-ml bottle and a 3-liter bottle several years longer than a Magnum. The reason for the longer cellaring of larger bottles is there is proportionally less air than wine in the bottle, slowing the wine's aging.

It is impossible to predict the exact time at which to open and drink a bottle of wine. Fortunately a wine's quality (and value) changes at a very slow rate. For good wines, we may have a period of a decade or more where the wine is in optimal, or close to optimal, drinking condition. If you wait too long, there is little you can do to improve the quality of the wine after opening it. Extreme oxidation cannot be reversed. If you open a bottle of wine too early, as presented in *Chapter 12: Improving Smell and Taste Sensations*, there are several things you can do to improve the quality of an immature wine such as decanting it longer, aerating it, and agitating it through swirling. You may even let it sit another day. You can quickly accelerate (some components of) the aging process of young wine when opened to somewhat improve its quality, but there is nothing you can do once the wine is past its prime to return it to optimal drinking quality. Therefore, it is better to err on the side of drinking wine earlier rather than later.

For single bottles of great wines, read multiple reviews and tasting notes which predict when the wine is most drinkable. Read how the wine is drinking by others who have opened bottles early. Plan to drink the wine around the consensus mid-point in the range. You may have several sources predicting the optimal drinking range which differ by several years at the end points of the range. If one trusted reviewer provides a range of 2016 - 2024 and another 2014 - 2020, consider the best time to drink the wine would be between the years 2016 and 2020. I would drink the single bottle in 2018 or just before or after to determine how good it is. As mentioned previously, the Coravin is another option for extracting a glass to try to help determine if the wine is ready to drink while maintaining the integrity of the rest of the bottle for later if you have found the wine requires more time.

When you have multiple bottles of the same wine, drink a single bottle early in the optimal drinking period (or even earlier if you want to experiment and compare) to rely on your personal experience (and not have to depend totally on others) to determine how the wine is aging and how long it should be cellared. You can then plan your consumption pattern for the remaining bottles. (In the example above, I would drink the first bottle in 2014 or 2015.) If you find a good wine has not developed in structure the way you thought it would, and only has several years left, you can then plan to consume the rest quickly. If you find the wine still a bit tight and has astringent tannins, then you know this wine will last a long time, and can take longer before trying another bottle.

I suggest planning to drink wine according to a bell-shaped curve when you have half a dozen or more of the same wine. Sample a bottle or two early in the recommended drinking range to assess its aging potential. Drink most bottles during a three- to six-year period in the middle of the range. After that, you start to risk some deterioration. However, with some fine to excellent wines, there is a good chance they continue to improve even further. Therefore, I 'take a risk' and leave a bottle or two until later in the optimal drinking period or even slightly beyond to see if I can achieve a truly unique drinking experience; one which is surprising in its pleasure and not to be repeated. However, this comes at a small risk that the bottle will be less than optimal instead of unique and pleasurable. But the thrill of taking this chance and often getting a great bottle is worth it for me.

To manage this, you must understand how wine ages by varietal, style and cellaring conditions and monitor it. Before I got on top of this, I was losing too many bottles which ultimately had to be poured out. I now have an inventory management system which outlines the best range of years over which to drink each wine in cellar and when the optimal drinking year is. Each varietal is different, but in general white wines cellar less than reds. The amount of tannin in a wine is the largest influence as to how long it should remain in the cellar. The other large influence on aging is acid. For both white and red wines, sufficient acid is required to maintain freshness while aging. Some varietals, such as Riesling, are naturally high in acid while others such as Sauvignon Blanc are not and should be drunk much earlier. If you understand the varietal and the vintage conditions of a wine, you will have a much better understanding of for how long to cellar a particular bottle.

Most commercial wine storage cellars keep a constant temperature of 14° Celsius (57° Fahrenheit). Your wine will be fine if it is stored a few degrees warmer or cooler as long as the temperature is constant. Wine ages more quickly in warmer temperatures and more slowly in colder ones. If stored at 18° Celsius instead of 14°, consider opening the bottle a few years earlier. Similarly, if you are storing the wine at colder temperatures, wait a few years longer than recommended. If you store the wine at too cold conditions (like 5° Celsius), the wine may outlast you and you will never get to drink it - aging virtually stops. I have been able to maintain several bottles of very old white wines at optimal drinking beyond their expected life by keeping them in a refrigerator at 2° Celsius (just above freezing). This has allowed me to save the wine over a longer period of time until we were able to have a special reason to celebrate. (I sometimes identify a person tagged to a specific bottle of wine and make a promise to drink that bottle with them, but it may take several years before we can get together under the right circumstances to do that.)

As a matter of course, wine should never be stored in direct sunlight. If it is, the wine will rise quickly in temperature, cooling again overnight on a daily basis. The UV rays affect the organic compounds in wine (creating hydrogen sulphide compounds), causing the wine to develop fault. A wine in direct sunlight will not last long and may even taste terrible upon opening. People make the mistake of placing a wine refrigerator with a glass door in direct sunlight. They feel they are protected because they have the temperature set to 14° Celsius (57° Fahrenheit). However, UV light still finds its way through glass and can damage the wine. Keep wine away from direct sunlight.

There are various views on the importance of humidity and its import on wine storage. If you have bottles sealed with cork, the cork needs to remain moist and therefore, a relative humidity of somewhere between 60% - 80% should be targeted, with a range of 70% - 75% considered ideal.

Regardless of cellaring approach and whether the wine is sealed with cork or screw cap, you should lay bottles down horizontally if you have the room. For bottles sealed with cork, this is necessary to keep the cork moist and the seal intact. If the cork dries out (which can occur after six to eight months), too much air will seep into the bottle and ruin the wine. The only exception to this rule is for sparkling wines which tend to mature better standing up and the carbon dioxide inherent in sparkling wines provides a natural buffer from the wine becoming oxidized.

For wines sealed with screw cap, the seal should be perfectly intact and you do not need to worry about air leakage under normal situations. But to be safe and if room permits, lay bottles horizontally in case there is a problem or imperfection with the seal. Laying bottles horizontally creates a secure seal with the liquid. A surprising number of bottles under screw cap have (not obvious) imperfections caused when transporting or racking the wines. Horizontal storage helps secure the seal in situations where this occurs and is a good insurance policy.

The most important reason to lay a bottle (even if sealed with screw cap) horizontally, is to maximize the air-wine interchange to help mature at the proper rate. The debate and argument (some people have) over using screw cap is that it limits the slow introduction of air into the wine and thus the wine may not mature to the level of greatness it could if sealed with cork. Minimally they argue the process is slowed and takes too long to realize the full potential of the wine. While this is technically true, the difference is so minor that it would not be noticeable by almost anyone who enjoys drinking wine. Additionally, the benefit of not losing bottles to bad corks more than compensates any undetectable difference in quality.

Wines sealed with screw cap continue to mature at a normal rate from the interaction of the air which is captured when the bottle is filled. This has more of an influence on the proper aging of wine than the minute amount of additional air exchanged through cork. Laying bottles horizontally triples the surface area for wine-air interchange. This has been tried and tested for thousands of years, and there is no reason to change it!

Both the temperature at which the wine is cellared and the orientation of the bottle will impact the aging process and time required. While I do not have quantifiable proof (nor do I know of any that exists), I believe that temperature plays more of a role than bottle orientation. That is one of the reasons I am willing to set bottles upright if they are cheaper bottles using screw cap if I am going to drink them within several years. More expensive bottles that require five or more years of cellaring should always lie down horizontally, regardless if cork or screw cap is used.

In general, wine can be handled and transported occasionally, but you should avoid constant vibration to bottles or any rough shaking of bottles while they are being stored or moved. It is not necessary to turn bottles in the cellar as some have claimed. This is a myth created from the need to shake sediment out of Champagne bottles.

Let wine sit undisturbed and you will get the best result in terms of aging and the treatment of residual sediment. Ideally, bottles should only be moved and stood up just prior to opening them.

In every case, remember three main principles for safe wine storage:

1. Keep temperature constant.
2. Keep wine away from sunlight.
3. Lay bottles horizontally.

Options for Cellars

Never store wine above a stove or oven. Extreme heat conditions will 'bake' wine quickly. Wine should not be stored in locations where ambient heat changes significantly over the course of the day or year. Similarly, wine should never be stored in the trunk of a car or left outside when heat or cold will be extreme.

There exists a variety of cellaring options which have different price points and risk involving how well and long your wine will last. Options range from not spending any money on storage to around $3 per bottle per year. Some involve an up-front outlay of capital while others do not.

For ten to twenty bottles of wine, it does not matter where or how you store them since they are likely to be consumed in short order and unlikely to become damaged. However, if you have several bottles you know require a longer period of time to cellar, you should determine a method for doing so. Once you start to accumulate thirty bottles or more, you should find a small place to create your 'cellar.'

Good ideas for spaces include underground (as the temperature is consistent over time), and in buffered spaces such as closets or store rooms. Do not use a cabinet next to hot water pipes or heating conduits. Do not use a space next to an oven or dryer. Otherwise any closet, cabinet, or storage space should work well. The lower in the house, the better off you are avoiding changes in temperature.

You are likely to have less temperature change inside the house than outside unless you burrow into the ground. Ground temperature does not change much throughout the season; it may only vary by a couple of degrees. (If you do store fine wine outside, you also need to consider security.)

Regardless of intended location, place a thermometer there first to ensure the temperature changes significantly on a daily or annual basis. Having a thermometer that records the high and low temperature can be very useful in monitoring this accurately.

Stacking wine bottles on top of each other can get heavy. Once the right storage space is found, use a small bookcase or shelving to provide racking for organizing the wine. Not all wine bottles have the same shape, so it is good to have at least several different shelves for organizing and stacking bottles. To buffer the wine further from changes in temperature, you can cover the bookcase or shelving with a blanket or Styrofoam sheets to create buffered air pockets.

Prior to building my own cellar, I bought some Styrofoam containers which held a dozen bottles each. The containers cost $50, but I expect there are cheaper versions now. This allowed me to further buffer my best bottles from temperature change. This approach is almost cost-free and provides adequate storage and protection. However, if you have acquired several hundred bottles of better quality wines, you should consider a more professional cellaring approach.

As mentioned previously, I built two professional wine cellars at home, but in neither case did I recoup my investment capital. To properly build out a cellar with ideal temperature and humidity control, you need to buy an air conditioner unit which goes down to 8° Celsius (46° Fahrenheit) in case you wanted to use a slower time frame for aging your wine. A wine air conditioner unit like this and for capacity of cellaring about 2,000 bottles would cost $2,500 - $4,000 based on features. The colder temperature setting could also be used for larger cellars and having varying temperatures the further the wine is away from the air conditioner. Many larger commercial cellars and restaurants have multiple chambers at different temperatures with sparkling wine and whites stored at colder temperature than reds.

If you build a professional cellar in your home, you should also make sure to provide a false wall with several inches of air space between the inner and exterior wall. Since the cellar is constantly cooler than outside the cellar, condensation problems on the exterior side of a single wall are common. Creating a false wall reduces this problem.

For smaller spaces using storage location in your house, you can consider going with a normal room air conditioner at much lower cost. A home air conditioner for this purpose would cost about $1,200 and only cool your cellar to 16° - 18° Celsius (61° - 65° Fahrenheit), but this is certainly adequate, as the temperature remains constant and is an excellent temperature for storing finer red wines. I know people who have done this as an alternative to spending more for a wine air conditioner in an attempt to keep their cost down. If you go this route, have a method to adequately address the water drainage for humidity build-up.

Another attractive alternative for storing wine is semi-portable wine refrigerators. Vintec and others make portable wine refrigerators that hold 24 to several hundred bottles. They have variable temperature control, some with dual settings to store both red wines and a cooler temperature to store and immediately serve white wines. Based on the brand, capacity and features, your annual wine storage would be about $1 - $2 per bottle, which is cheaper than an external shared commercial wine cellar, but more expensive than building your own cellar. However, it has lower capital outlay and is portable, so you can bring it along if you move.

When having two residences, we used a hybrid approach for getting the best value and ensuring the protection and quality of our wine. We have about 2,000 bottles of wine stored as follows:

- 1,800 bottles in a commercial storage locker with 7 day access from 7 am – 11 pm (The facility has redundant electrical and air conditioning capabilities and humidity control. The wine is insured against physical damage.)
- 135 bottles in Vintec wine refrigerator in apartment for good selection of wines for dinners and immediate consumption
- 20 bottles in buffered storage in apartment for wines sealed with screw cap that do not require temperature control as they will be drunk in next several months
- 8 – 10 wines in the refrigerator for immediate chilled white wine drinking
- 30 bottles in Vintec in our country home
- 40 bottles in buffered storage in our country home for wines sealed with screw cap that do not require temperature control as they will be drunk in next several months

- 10 bottles in the country home refrigerator for immediate chilled white wine drinking

This approach provides a good selection of wines, even when required spur of the moment. The 1,800-bottle vault is only 15 minutes from our apartment. I am not going to build another in-house cellar until I am absolutely certain of where I will permanently be living. My current approach is more expensive, but provides the flexibility to move and avoid significant capital outlay which may not be recouped. Since writing this, we have moved permanently to our place in the country and have consolidated our cellar areas, but still use the hybrid approach for best overall value until I build a more permanent wine cellar.

I get visual pleasure having wine close to me, being able to study labels and being able to select a wine. I buy with intent of cellaring and take pleasure selecting wines from the cellar to consume. By cellaring wine, I am certain I save far more than I spend on cellaring plus I have certainty of the wine's provenance. I also know I have a good selection to choose from which I am familiar with and am able to make a selection with confidence for any occasion.

Regardless if you determine your cellaring needs to be 50, 500, or 5,000 bottles, there is a cellaring approach that should work effectively for you. Start small with little or no capital outlay and expand over time as required.

What Should be in the Cellar?

This will always be a matter of personal choice. However, there are several guidelines you should follow:

- Have wines that are ready to drink now; others that mature over time.
- Have wines close to serving temperature for immediate consumption.
- Do not accumulate more than you can drink in any given time period.
- Drinking habits change, usually reducing over time, so do not over-collect.
- Maintain good selection across varietals and price points.

- Keep up-to-date inventory of each bottle in your cellar.

The definition of cellar used herein has comprised a primary location and several secondary locations. The secondary locations are smaller in size, usually consisting of a refrigerator, wine refrigerator, or closet which contains wines for near-term drinking. The secondary locations (unless temperature controlled wine refrigerator) generally have greater temperature variations which would place the wine at risk if stored for a prolonged period of time. Never store fine wines in locations where temperature varies.

It is all right to keep wine in a refrigerator for many years (if you can afford the space). These wines mature slowly as the temperature is just above freezing. If you have an exceptional white wine at end of life, but want to save for an exceptional event (like a wedding anniversary or a 50th birthday party) that is several years away, you can store the bottle in the refrigerator to significantly retard further maturation.

If there is limited refrigerator space, consider buying a small secondary refrigerator to maintain bottles that are ready to drink or require very slow aging. Many people have a second refrigerator for chilling wine and beer. A second refrigerator can be small, inexpensive and stored in any open space in the garage, basement, or storage room.

I keep eight to ten bottles of white wine refrigerated and available for any occasion. The stock comprises good and an excellent Chardonnay, Riesling, Semillon, Sauvignon Blanc or Sauvignon Blanc blend, a good and an excellent Sparkling wine or Sparkling Shiraz, Moscato, and a decent dessert wine. We have a larger primary refrigerator to accommodate this many bottles. We also usually buy fresh food almost daily or remove it from the freezer when needed, so we do not need to reserve all the space for food. If I am planning a larger meal at home or wine to bring along to a BYO function, then I will move bottles from my primary cellar to the refrigerator in preparation for the upcoming meal in the next day or two. But on a daily basis, I always have a bottle of most white varietals ready to drink when needed.

Any wines stored at room temperature (in closet, under bed or on pantry shelf) should be drunk within several months. These wines are at risk if left for prolonged periods outside of controlled temperature storage. The risk is reduced somewhat if sealed with screw cap instead of cork as you do not need to worry about cork damage caused by temperature change. Limit the number of bottles outside of temperature controlled facilities to no more than ten to fifteen bottles and make sure to consume them in a reasonable time frame.

For reds, store several different varietals such as several brands of Cabernet Sauvignon, Shiraz, Pinot Noir, Sangiovese, and possibly one or two secondary grapes such as a Tempranillo or Malbec. However, most secondary grape varietals could be considered fine wines and therefore stored in the primary temperature-controlled cellar and only removed several days before drinking them.

Wine in the refrigerator and in room temperature storage is intended to be consumed immediately or near-term, whereas almost all wine stored in the primary cellar should be purposed to age for future consumption. If you are looking at a primary cellar of 500 or more bottles, plan to buy and consume the wine across various age groupings and varietals. While your tastes may vary, I believe my approach provides good general guidelines for what should be in your cellar, so I will share that with you.

I drink wine regularly and get great pleasure from drinking wine. I like to have access to a wine to match every likely occasion that I expect to experience. Therefore, I require having a cellar that contains 150 – 200 bottles which are drinkable immediately. This covers most major and secondary grape varietals, five or more major producers for each primary varietal (Shiraz, Cabernet Sauvignon, etc.) and several producers for each secondary varietal. I have coverage of different regions and styles in each varietal. Most of this group of 150 – 200 bottles will have some age on it, being in the range of 5 – 8 years for the whites and 10 — 20 years for the reds. One-quarter will have cost under $25 per bottle, half the stock between $25 and $40 per bottle, 15% between $40 and $60 per bottle with the remaining 10% costing over $60 per bottle. (Only several bottles are over $200 per bottle.)

150 – 200 'ready-to-drink' bottles provides enough coverage across varietals, style, geography and terroir, domestic and import, and value. The rest of the cellar is aging wines to back-fill the 'ready-to-drink' group on an annual rolling basis. The last section helped you calculate how many bottles in total should be in your cellar based on likely consumption patterns. Now we will discuss the composition of those bottles.

You are cellaring not just for your personal taste, but also to share with others. The composition of your cellar should cater to preferences of others you dine and share wine with. The following guidelines should work for most readers with some small amount of exceptions to cater for specific requirements. A good set of general rules are:

- Have more red wine than white wine as it takes longer to age red wine. (While I drink 70% red to 30% white wine, my cellar is 80% red due to the requirements for longer aging.)

- The spread across vintages should be roughly equal (within a couple of years). Reds should be spread over a 15 year planning horizon (with about 5% or so of very fine red wines being older than that), and white wines being split over a two to eight year planning horizon with very few bottles older than that.

- Primary grape varietals should make up roughly two-thirds of your cellar, with secondary grapes making up the remainder. If you embrace diversity and comparative tasting, then allocate a higher percentage to secondary grapes.

- To provide choice within a particular varietal, 70% of your holdings should be of known, well-respected brands, and 30% for more exotic styles, and lesser known brands.

- At least 75% of your cellar should be in the typical alcohol range of 12% - 14.5% alcohol content. The remaining should be lower alcohol with very little higher than 14.5% for table wines.

- Each wine bought and cellared should represent good value (more on achieving this in next section). My general rule for cellaring is the same for immediate consumption (this should make sense as I am back-filling my immediate consumption pool continuously). One-quarter of cellar under $25 per bottle; one-half between $25 and $40, and about one-quarter costing over $40 per bottle.

- 90% - 95% of bottle sizes should be 750 ml. The other 5% - 10% should be half bottles (375 ml) or magnums

(1.5-liter bottles). 750-ml bottles provide the best ability to select the right number of bottles and variety of wines for most situations. Using a magnum for a larger party occasionally makes sense and most of the half bottles should be dessert wines.

When it comes to the mix of red and white wine, you buy white wine more frequently and turn it over in the cellar more frequently than with red wine. Storing too much white wine runs the risk that you will not be able to drink it in time before it deteriorates.

In general for red wines, segment cellar holdings by vintage as follows:

- 20% younger than 3 years old
- 20% between 3 and 5 years old
- 20% between 5 and 7 years old
- 20% between 7 and 10 years old
- 15% between 10 and 15 years old
- 5% more than 15 years old

White wine should have a similar, but accelerated, pattern:

- 35% younger than 3 years old (many of these would be drinkable immediately, especially Sauvignon Blanc or Chardonnay)
- 35% between 3 and 5 years old
- 20% between 5 and 8 years old
- 10% more than 8 years old

For finer white wines that were built to last, you should adjust percentages and ranges accordingly, as they should be cellared a few years longer.

Regarding alcohol content, I prefer staying in the lower to middle of the acceptable range. This is an example where my tastes have changed over the last decade. I used to only appreciate and drink big, robust, high alcohol red wines. The bigger the punch, the more I liked it. However, I have switched significantly to lower alcohol (12% - 13%) old-world style red wines. Occasionally, I still pull out a higher-alcohol wine to go with a hearty red meat or to juice up a cold winter day by serving it with a roast. I am also enjoying the very light alcohol wines (8% - 8.5%) on their own or with afternoon cheese and meat plates.

Over time, my cellar is becoming smaller and the average bottle price is getting higher. This is because as I age (unfortunately more quickly than the wine in my cellar!), I drink less, my tastes and expectations have improved, and I am purchasing already aged, vintage wines for immediate consumption (at auction). At a certain point, it just does not make sense to purchase current releases and let them cellar as I run the risk of my palate not working anymore, or being too old, too sick, or dead to be able to drink at all!

Organize your cellar to place just purchased wines requiring aging of at least five years cellaring to be stored in the least convenient locations. Place them on higher shelves or behind other wines of more immediate consumption. You do not need to access or move these boxes for some time. If you want to taste a bottle or two prior to its optimal drinking period to see how they are maturing, then remove a bottle (or two) and place them in a more immediately accessible part of the cellar. This could be a unit for single bottle storage or stacked with other bottles in a bin.

The key to maintaining a proper cellar comprising the right mix of wine is to constantly be monitoring your inventory and adjusting it from time-to-time. I recently had to accelerate the disposal (through selling off) of my older Cabernet Sauvignon as I had too much to consume in the period it was optimally drinkable. I was also running low of high quality Chardonnays that needed replenishment. You need to understand where your stock is long (too much) or short and react accordingly. Fortunately, if you find you have too many aged wines, there is a good market of wine enthusiasts who are glad to pay a premium for already aged wines they can consume immediately. (Ideas on selling excess wine are covered at the end of this chapter.)

It is easy to lose control of your cellar, especially as it grows and as you accumulate more wine which requires longer aging. I finally built a simple database (there are also tools and systems you can buy or subscribe to inexpensively) to fully understand my total inventory. I was shocked! I had almost 4,000 bottles of wine and realized that about 60 bottles were definitely well past optimal drinking and needed to be disposed of. I also had another 150 bottles at risk and would need to be consumed immediately if they were still drinkable. I also had too large an amount for certain varietals and needed to sell some off.

I sold a lot of wine, consumed more and finally after two years, have gotten my cellar down to under 2,000 bottles. It is only now that I need to think about replenishing certain varietals and styles.

Keep on top of your inventory to minimize wine loss. It is relatively easy to build and manage a wine database, including being able to enter and refer to tasting notes, and to assess the value and provenance of your inventory. I present some ideas in *Chapter 19: Tools and Systems for Managing Your Wine Inventory* on how to do this.

What Should I Look for When Buying Wine?

I have bought far more wine than I required; secondly, I paid far too much for it. Up until several years ago, I was being sold more wine than I was in the control of buying. The cellar door sales manager and staff or bottle shop owner would have more knowledge and desire to push certain wine on me and I did not have the knowledge or desire to avoid it. They always made me feel special and that I was getting a unique wine at a great price that I could pull out later to share and impress others. Through those interactions and not being able to articulate what I liked about wine, I estimated I paid about 25% over what I needed to pay on average. And since I have purchased about $200,000 worth of wine throughout my life, this means I wasted about $50,000 which could have been saved or spent better elsewhere.

Additionally, I wanted to please the Cellar door or shop owner (after all, he made me feel special!) and because I was convinced the wine was special, I wanted to get as much as I could. Over the years, I estimate that I probably bought twice as much wine as I needed. This has been verified since by having sold off about half of my wine to get my cellar to manageable levels.

Had I known better how to buy wine – instead of being sold wine – I would have spent only about $150,000. And had I only bought half of what I did, that means I would have spent only $75,000 in total instead of $200,000. I don't care who you are, that is a lot of money! That is why I am dedicating a full chapter to storing and buying wine. By learning how to taste and appreciate wine through this book, you are in a position earlier than I was to figure this out.

We all make mistakes and spend money on wine we do not like. By knowing more and by having a little more experience, you can have the confidence to buy what you want, not what is being sold to you.

The other thing working in your favor now is wine apps on mobile devices for wine shopping and price comparisons. You now have immediate access to a plethora of different options of where and how to buy wine. Some individual bottle prices will differ by 300% based on where you buy it. You have many arbitrage options available today.

I greatly value relationships I have developed with people in the wine industry. There are a number of cellar door managers, winemakers and bottle shop owners with whom I have become friends. We share a common passion. I now know enough to know who has treated me with integrity and who has not. I buy from those who have served me honestly. I do not look for the lowest price on a given bottle. I value the seller's knowledge and the service they provide on my behalf. But I expect to be treated fairly and now know when that has been the case.

There are a variety of different channels for buying wine, and you should explore all of them. I buy most of my wine direct from cellar doors and online. I also review and occasionally pick up some great wines at auction.

The important thing is I now have enough knowledge, experience and confidence to know what to buy and what to bypass and why. It does not require a lot of experience. From a little more drinking and experience as guided by this book and the increased knowledge you will have after reading it, you should be in a good position to buy smartly, according to your needs, not the needs of others.

The other day, one of my work colleagues purchased a bottle of wine as a going away gift for one of her team members. She got the recommendation from the bottle shop owner, but decided to ask me afterward if it was a good bottle or not. I told her it was a good bottle and would likely be appreciated by the person receiving it. I then asked her how much she paid for it. She paid $42 for the 2010 vintage. I told her she got an acceptable price for it. I did not want to disappoint her by telling her I knew how to buy a far better vintage of the same wine (the 2008) which was more drinkable immediately for $26. That is a significant difference. By exploring multiple channels you become comfortable with the best way to buy all of your wine.

Even when not buying wine over the last two years (while adjusting my cellar down to more reasonable levels), I constantly have been reviewing wine auctions, wine exchanges, monthly reviews, wine sales prices and cellar door prices. To make sure you can buy the wine you want at close to the best price possible, you need to keep monitoring and analyzing the market. This does not take much time and is a passion for me, so it is both enjoyable and a worthwhile investment of my time. I also record in my database what I paid for each bottle and comments such as if I got a volume discount or any other reason I was able to purchase the wine at other than the normal retail price. If you buy at the right time, the seller's desire to move the wine and yours to buy it are much better aligned. They may have some overstock, or just need to free the warehouse for the next vintage. This is the best time to buy. Another good buying situation is when a major order has been canceled. Sometimes, orders are bottled and labeled for export and the order canceled. The winery cannot sell the wine through normal channels without relabeling which would add costs to the wine and is difficult to do. Since the earlier prospective buyer who canceled their order has already subsidized the order (they may have had to forfeit a 25% cancellation fee, for example), this wine can be bought at an attractive price point. I have been able to buy some nice Chardonnay which were $30 per bottle that I was able to pick up for $16. I was able to receive far better pricing by accepting a label not compliant for Australian retail sales.

I also subscribe to several global and local research databases which provide all known selling prices of a specific wine and where you can buy it. I don't always go for the lowest price. I make sure I know the reputation of the vendor, and the provenance of the wine before buying. It is usually worth paying a little more to reduce the risk of getting a fake or poorly cared for bottle. Provenance for wine is like provenance and certification of original artwork. You know and value an original painting by a famous artist far more than a fake, and finding you got a 'great' price for a fake is a situation you want to avoid. Similarly, I do not want to pay $300 for a 25-year-old Penfolds Grange only to find out it was a bottle given to someone who kept it in the closet standing upwards for the last 25 years because they don't drink and then gave it to someone who knew something about Grange who sold it at auction. With proper provenance, $300 for 25-year-old Grange would be an outstanding buy, even for the worst vintages. But it is an expensive mistake buying Grange that tastes like vinegar!

I was following a bottle of 1982 Château Haut Brion at auction which had an opening bid of $410. I expected I could get this bottle for under $500. It also had the highest level of provenance achievable. There was authenticated proof the bottle was purchased directly from a French distributor and has been properly stored for the bottle's life. This bottle would usually cost $1,600 - $1,800 per bottle, but if no one else has a similar interest level, then I could get this bottle at a great price. And I was interested as I have never had a bottle of Château Haut Brion (even though it is on my 'wine bucket list'). Had it not had a high provenance rating, I would not have considered it.

For any purchase this expensive though, I wanted to make sure the wine was going to be good. I read community and professional tasting notes to learn that for this 30-year-old wine, some bottles had been spectacular and some not so great, even from two bottles purchased and stored under exactly the same conditions. This concerned me as the tasting notes had more unfavorable reviews and the consistency between great and poor reviews widened over the last 5 - 8 years. This led me to believe there could be cork problems and I had increased risk of buying a bad bottle, even though the brand and provenance were exceptional. If this was a bottle of wine under $100, I would likely take the risk, but at $410 or higher for the bottle, I decided to pass. For that money, I can buy a dozen or two dozen very good to excellent wines.

Pay attention to bottle color when buying aged, expensive wine. In *Chapter 7: Wine and Sight*, we discussed the importance of opaque bottles for storing wine properly. This is common practice today, but less so 20 - 50 years ago. Many great wines produced in the 1960s and 1970s were bottled in clear glass. If they have been stored properly and out of light, these wines should be as good as if they were stored in an opaque bottle. If you know an expensive aged wine was bottled in clear glass, it is doubly important to check the provenance to ensure it has been stored and handled with utmost care. Otherwise, you run a larger risk the wine is undrinkable.

We have discussed the mistakes of buying too much and paying too much. Another common mistake is to purchase too much of a specific vintage. There are reasons this is tempting. Unlike art and music which can be appreciated again and again, once a particular wine of specific vintage is gone, it is gone forever. When we find a truly great wine to our liking, we want to have a supply for ongoing consumption. However, wine will not last forever, no matter how well you care for it. Wine matures, improves and then deteriorates over time. At some point, the wine is no longer drinkable.

When I have found wine I really liked at a good price point, I would have bought between four and eight dozen bottles of that wine. This is a lot of the same wine to drink over the period it is drinkable. Having to consume the same bottle again and again cuts into your ability to explore and discover other great wines. And the reality is that each of these vintages have been superseded by better, more recent vintages. There will always be a better wine and better vintage. Vineyard management and winemaking techniques have improved considerably in the last fifty years, and on average, all wine continues to improve in quality and value. You do not need to worry about running out of great wine.

Next year there will be better wines to drink than the wines you have in your cellar today, due to many factors:

- Each year, winemakers learn more and improve.
- Each great vintage is followed by another within the next several years.
- You find other wine brands, styles and winemakers as good or better than ones previously thought 'the best.'
- Vineyard management and winemaking technology and process are constantly improving.
- Your wine knowledge and appreciation constantly changes, possibly causing misalignment with large previous purchases now in cellar.
- New hybrid varietals and styles provide choices not available previously.

Having too much of a particular type and vintage of wine inhibits your opportunity to buy newly found, and likely better wines. I had to pass on some great wines in the last several years as I have been selling off excess wine to get my cellar under control. I was drinking what I previously thought was a great wine, only to have to forego what I now know was a better wine. (Yes, another first world problem with which we must deal!) I no longer fear running out of a specific wine. I know there always will be better choices available tomorrow.

I also have turned the ritual of sharing and drinking my last few bottles of a particularly great wine into a matter for celebration. I think about whom I want to share that bottle with and on what occasion it should be drunk. Unlike viewing art work or listening to music, the experience of drinking a last bottle cannot be repeated. This is a special occasion and I celebrate it for its own purpose, even if not used for celebrating anything else. Instead of fearing running out of a particular great wine, I now embrace the passing of the final bottle as a special occasion to celebrate. And by purchasing fewer dozens, I experience my 'last bottle passing' more often!

I no longer buy more than one or in very limited situations two dozen of any wine, no matter how great or good a value it is. Unless you are buying wine for an investment or to on-sell later, you should never buy more than a dozen or two of any given wine. There is always a better and better-valued wine around the corner. And if you are on a smaller budget and drink less, then limit any given wine and vintage to six bottles.

In summary, general principles for buying wine include:

- Don't buy too much in total
- Don't pay too much per bottle
- Don't buy too much of a particular wine and vintage
- Know your current cellar's inventory
- Gain a little experience and knowledge (this book supplemented by ongoing drinking should be sufficient, but learning more as outlined in *Part Four: Where to Next?* helps)
- Use the technology available via mobile to supplement knowledge
- Check out multiple sales channels and compare prices

I listen to and use the opinions of others. I supplement that with my experience and building confidence in what I like and why. I now focus on quality, not brand. Too many people buy on brand and pay too much. Brand can represent a historical reflection of the quality of winemaking, but winemakers change brands and ultimately the best ones create their own brand. There have been some great brands that have had off years due to the vintage and the particular winemaker at the time, and some innocuous brands that have had some great wines due to the reverse effects. Scruton reminds us: "The most important thing to remember when exploring

Burgundy is that the world is full of people who are both very rich and very stupid, who can be relied upon to spend virtually unlimited sums of money on products which they know nothing about except that other people as rich and stupid as themselves are spending unlimited sums of money on them."[110] Scruton bluntly points out the cost of doing so, and the benefit of gaining a little knowledge to be able to avoid spending too much solely on brand. I personally paid too much early on not having the confidence myself to discriminate good wine from good brands.

Fine wines have a higher cost structure than average wines. This is usually due to higher capital and maintenance costs, land values for the best vineyards producing the best grapes, and higher labor costs associated with more selective harvesting techniques. The grapes used in Château d'Yquem have a very high labor cost associated with them as there are multiple (as many as ten or eleven) pickings over the average harvest season of 21 days. They identify and pick grapes when the botrytis effect is exactly right. Most wineries which produce Botrytis Semillon only have one picking when they think the 'average' is best and then pick all the grapes at once. While this certainly saves on labor, it also diminishes the quality of grapes that go into most dessert wines. Some iconic brands such as Penfolds Grange, use grapes that cost twenty times as much as the cost of the grapes going into medium quality Shiraz. From a cost perspective there is some justification why certain better quality wines are higher priced.

But there is not a uniform correlation between mark-up percentages and wine quality. Brand tends to skew the price upwards more than the quality justifies. Some winemakers, after winning a few medals in one good year, think their wine deserves to be priced at a premium, and they continue to push that premium as long as consumers pay for brand and not quality. I no longer buy from these wineries. If the brand is justified on quality, I am glad to purchase and have some top-notch bottles in my cellar of the iconic brands. But all too often, the brand is not justified by quality. One indication I use to judge the integrity of producer is if they skip a vintage every now and then for their iconic brands because the grape quality that year did not justified a premium label. I also look for wineries that have refused to raise their prices after being awarded medals. These are wineries more concerned about quality than brand.

Do not be deceived by brand. Brands are a useful indicator of quality, but no guarantee. A recent study of social media reviews estimates one-quarter of reviews are fake. Technology can be used to create a more positive brand than a product deserves. In general, you overpay significantly if you buy on brand alone. We have friends who are wine judges and serious wine drinkers, and they love finding a new winery where they have been able to get a great bottle for $15. They were so delighted to gift us a bottle of a Canberra region Sangiovese that tasted like a $200 Reserve Chianti and only pay $15 for the bottle. They had confidence in buying what they tasted in the bottle, not the label on the bottle.

It is also important to understand some of the basics of wine so as not to be deceived by people trying to convince you a wine is of a higher quality than it really is. For example, a wine with tears looks good in the glass, but tears are not a sign of quality (as some in the industry will tell you); tears are a sign of high alcohol content, as alcohol is more volatile than water causing the tears to form.

Another aspect of successful wine buying is to understand where the grapes were sourced. A winery located in a particular region does not mean the grapes came from that region. You can usually find where grapes are sourced by looking at the label. It is important to understand how well the grapes grow in a particular region and in selected small land parcels in those regions. Based on where the grapes are grown, the components in the same varietal of grapes can be triple or quadruple that of the grape from another region. Terroir matters, and having an understanding what terroir is best for what grapes gives you a real leg up buying better quality wines for less money.

Successfully buying wine at the right price involves knowing three things:

1. Who was the winemaker?
2. Where were the grapes sourced?
3. What vintage is the wine?

These three aspects of wine provide the best indication of how good the wine is. The winemaker imparts his or her style on the wine, reducing faults and bringing the best out of the grapes; the native soil and climatic conditions in any given year impact how good the grapes are to start with. In the next chapter we present how to obtain this type of knowledge. Price is more a factor of brand than winemaker, grape location and vintage. If you focus on these three aspects, you will buy better quality wines at better prices than by paying for brand.

From Where Should You Buy Wine?

There are a variety of channels from which to purchase or otherwise acquire wine. They include:

- direct from wineries
- bottle shops
- auctions
- exchanges
- personal collections
- promoted tastings within the wine industry
- trading wine with others or in lieu of other services

In general, you should consider all channels when purchasing wine. There are different reasons for using specific channels. The benefits one channel may provide over another is price, knowledge, service, timeliness, convenience or general ambient experience. I use all channels to buy and to continue to learn.

Do not take advantage of the service and knowledge provided by one channel and then get online to purchase the cheapest bottle you can find. In addition to being risky, it undermines the relationships you can build in the industry and eliminates channel options you may want to use in the future. Knowingly wasting someone's time if you are going to purchase elsewhere is not the way to build long-term and valued relationships.

Therefore, after a little research, I know which channel I want to explore and why. In one case, such as buying from a winery, I do so because I want to provide myself and others with a broader tasting experience and good afternoon out. I may purchase from a bottle shop because I know the owner or staff has significant knowledge of the wine they serve and they may be able to steer me to an better bottle than the one I was considering buying. I may go to a wine industry tasting to try some samples before I buy if it is a new wine I am trying. As a general rule, I always like to taste before buying, and expect to do so when purchasing larger quantities or better wines.

Therefore, know what you value when using a channel and what you expect to achieve through that channel.

Purchasing Wine Directly from Winery

I buy most of my wine at cellar door. Having lived in Sydney previously, means most of my wines come from The Hunter Valley. Fortunately, The Hunter Valley has some great wines and I am privileged to have purchased a lot of my wine there. But it can also be limiting in terms of finding out what other wines are on offer around Australia and globally. I use other channels to expand my vision and to sample and learn to appreciate other wines. Fortunately, several of the wineries in The Hunter Valley are part of larger conglomerates and represent a variety of wineries across Australia and internationally. I have been able to go to the cellar door, sample other wines from Victoria and South Australia and build a more diversified cellar. In a sense, these conglomerates are bringing their cellar door to me in The Hunter Valley instead of me having to visit their wineries elsewhere.

You are limited by geography if the cellar door is your only channel. But there are ways to expand reaching more cellar doors. The best method is to plan a vacation visiting cellar doors in various regions. I know many people who vacation in Barossa Valley, Margaret River, Napa Valley, Italy or France. The vacations may revolve around wine or have other purposes, but time is found to visit wineries to taste and purchase wine to ship home. There are several professional travel agents who can organize wine tours to exotic places with great reputations for wine, combining the best of a wine tour with other highlights and visitor attractions.

And more and more, the cellar door is coming to you. Many wine industry groups and restaurants offer tastings or meals combined with tastings where the winery visits where you live to promote their wines. Usually the owner, winemaker or sales manager conducts the tasting. These tastings and meals may have current releases, but often also present older vintages which are still for sale. I have taken in several restaurant meals like this with matching wines and accompanied by an education of the winery and their wines. Sydney would have 20 - 30 events like this annually to introduce you to 'cellar doors' that have come to you.

But as much as possible, visit the cellar doors as there are many benefits, including:

- ability to taste before buying;
- comparatively taste different but similar wines;

- accessing and interacting with staff, often including the winemaker;
- ambient setting for great meal and day out;
- arranging private tasting functions, often free or at low cost; and
- ability to tour facilities.

I usually only buy wine I have tasted prior to purchase. Being at the cellar door, you can sample before buying. Comparing various wines is a great way to build experience and increase your knowledge on what wine you like.

Many wineries in Australia provide free tastings for most of their range; some wineries in Australia and globally charge you. While I enjoy participating in free tastings, I have become more comfortable paying for them. First off, it frees you from any guilt you may have about needing to make a 'mercy' purchase. Some wineries provide lavish tastings with free cheese plates, free wine and free access to their facilities and people. However, while their wine may be drinkable, they may not meet your purchasing needs. Yet, you feel obligated to show the winery thanks and invoke a mercy purchase!

Charging for a tasting helps defray the winery's cost, allowing them to serve more people. Wineries often charge a nominal fee such as $5 to taste five wines and then waive it if you buy a bottle or more. I think this is very reasonable as it cuts down on the number of freeloaders passing through and allows the staff to concentrate on serving those with an interest in learning more and possibly purchasing more.

Since most people who visit wineries drink decent (but not fine) quality wines and many of them are out to visit a winery for a good time, the cellar door usually excludes their most expensive and iconic wines from tasting. While I spend some time at the standard cellar door, especially if it is my first time to the winery, I will always ask for the sales manager and discuss options with them for tasting some of their iconic wines. This usually results in a private tasting with better quality wines sampled and the knowledge gained. Most wineries are staffed with at least one or two senior staff members to identify and look after more serious wine fans. They know that the per-visit purchase from someone who fits this description is far higher than for your average cellar door customer.

- To help establish relationships and receive greater access for tasting higher-end vintage wines, do the following:
- If not already connected with Sales Manager or a senior staff member, ask for them.
- Explain that you sought their winery out for specific reasons, such as reading a great review of their wine, or that a friend recommended them.
- Establish your enthusiasm about wine and provide a proof point such as mentioning you want to explore adding to your inventory.
- Explain what you like and are looking for, including higher-end vintage wines.
- Offer to pay for tasting these wines and willingness to buy a bottle if not available for tasting.

You will then likely be ushered to a private tasting room or area at cellar door which is away from the general crowds. You will have a more intimate and mutually beneficial understanding and relationship. In this setting, you do not need to fight for the divided attention of a person serving multiple people. Additionally, you will be provided more wines across their range to compare and establish what you believe is the right value point. Usually better glassware more appropriate for tasting particular varietals is used, and often a cheese platter or some tapas are provided.

This is a far better situation to quickly learn what wines you like and why. You may think this type of attention requires you to buy something, but it does not. Your obligation is to explain what you like or don't like about the wine and why the wine may or may not meet your purchasing needs. Compare the wine to similar wines from a different winery you thought provided better or worse value; or explain the wine does not meet the style you were expecting; the winery benefits from this type of feedback.

One of the great benefits, regardless if in the general tasting area or a private tasting room, of being at the cellar door is to be able to compare a variety of similar wines at different price points. A winery may have three or four different Shiraz for you to taste. The difference in taste and price usually is due to the quality of grapes used. Even though they are all Shiraz grapes, highly selective, better grapes are separated and reserved for the top end of the range. The grapes may have come from several vineyards and have been blended together for the lower end of the range. Some may have been set aside and represent a single vineyard grape selection.

The wines will have some, if not many, similar characteristics, but also some differences, and given your personal tastes and preferences, you may find you like the $16 bottle better than the $30 bottle. I love finding situations like this. You may identify more with and appreciate the balance and multiple nuances from a blend of grapes than the sharper focus of grapes from a single vineyard. By tasting these wines side-by-side, you quickly know and become confident in which wine is most suitable for you. Comparative tastings at cellar door provide an acute set of experiences to develop how your senses are attuned to different wines and understand why. This is one of the major reasons I visit cellar doors to taste; I can drink a number of similar, but different wines to compare and learn quickly.

Comparative tasting is so important that many wineries exchange bottles of their wines with other wineries so their staff can taste and compare between wineries. This helps each winery's staff members learn quickly; then better explain how their wine rates and what the differences are to its competitors. This is common to do with each new vintage release. I happened to be at one winery when the staff was comparing a dozen different Shiraz from around the region and was asked if I would like to participate. It was a great experience and we were able to compare notes and hear what the winemaker and the sales manager thought of the different wines compared to their own.

I know many wineries also train new staff members by sending them for half a day to another winery to have their staff taste and compare other winery's wines. For a new staff member, within a month, they may have been to four or five other wineries and have had a solid education by comparative tasting. If it is used by the wineries to train their staff, there is no reason you should not do it yourself!

Most people in the food and wine industry are among the nicest and most generous people in any industry. They have common passions and are always looking for ways to share when with others. They experience genuine joy seeing others learn and appreciate food and wine more. And they love to talk about their own product – how it was made, why it is special, what techniques were used to create specific characteristics and so on. Many chefs and winemakers have shared with me their recipes and secrets and will with you if you just ask. It is quite easy and pleasant to interact with people in the wine industry. Most of them have a real love for their work and desire sharing it with others. Most are willing to spend an extraordinary amount of time with you if you have similar interests and passions. I have learned most of what I know about wine from talking to people in the industry; most of it from interacting with people through the cellar door.

Do not be afraid to ask questions or forward requests. I have asked some very prominent people in the wine industry for help in researching and writing this book and have been surprised by the outpouring of help. I have received private research, links to topics to help me learn more, and reviews, comments and willingness to associate their name with this book. It could be said that much of this book was researched at the cellar door!

Wineries provide some of the nicest locations to take a day away. They are usually set in beautiful locations with rolling hills, nice architecture and great views. Many wineries have restaurants or minimally a kitchen to prepare food. Wineries are great places to relax, meet and socialize with friends.

But be careful not to let the great location and ambiance create a stimulus error. I have been in some cellar rooms that have been dark and ambient, sharing in a cheese plate provided by the winery. I have been caught up in the experience, leading to over-judging the wine's quality. Similarly, being in the presence of the winemaker makes us less critical of the wine's quality. This has led to paying too much for wine and finding out several months later in a different location that the wine was not that good! Do not be seduced by location and ambiance and give the wine greater credit than it deserves.

Wineries make great venues for weddings, birthday parties and other events. They are excellent for corporate events and client functions. I can personally attest to the strengthening of business relationships once we have established a common bond of wine appreciation. But for the most part, I enjoy visiting wineries for the ambiance and the exploration. More wineries are becoming child and family-friendly. Many wineries provide guided tours of the facilities and show you how the wine is made. These tours are fun and educational and worth doing at least once per winery.

Almost all wineries tend to be at least several hours away from major cities. And while they are worth it if the trip is several hours or less, some wineries are further away. Therefore, look for opportunities (as described previously) on how to bring a winery or several wineries to you. More and more of them see the value in touring different major cities and partnering with restaurants to do a meal with matching wines.

We have invited a winery to do a tasting at our place several times. The winery showed up with wine (and in some cases a chef and food), glasses, etc. They are used to and have the ability to be portable as they participate in multiple food and wine shows annually. In return, I provided fifty guests, several who were wine judges, sommeliers, or others in the wine industry and corporate friends ready to try and buy.

For these events, the winery sells a lot of wine on the evening and is also pleased to have introduced more people to the winery who later come to the cellar door or order online. They also receive independent endorsement and reviews from others in the wine industry and the guests in general. The guests and myself receive a real education and ability to taste a lot of different wines. My guests have a great time and think I threw a great party, but all I have done is to provide a venue and broker a meeting between potential buyers and a seller. This is a great way to get the winery to come to you if you cannot get to the winery.

I buy from wineries because of the overall ambiance and experience and because I can taste before I buy. I do not buy from wineries for the price. You may think wineries would have lower prices because they cut out the distributer and the retailer, but that is not the case. While their prices are competitive, especially if you can get a volume discount or become a cellar door member (which can provide good discounts, but does come with obligations), the wineries must maintain margins. They are also prohibited from selling at a lower price than the bottle shops. I once paid $64 per bottle for great wine at the cellar door and was pleased to be able to secure it several days before the official release. I then saw that same bottle in a very large chain of bottle shops for $49 per bottle! I was shocked and disappointed. In discussing it with the winery, I realized the buying power of this large chain and understood the contracts in place. Since this wine did sell out quickly I was glad to have secured it even though I paid a premium for it. You may not get the lowest price at the cellar door, but you will get great value and service along with the ability to buy some wines not available through bottle shops. I also have occasionally been able to buy older wines and odd lots for significantly lower prices when the winery has needed to clear inventory for the current vintage.

To get significantly discounted prices, I joined several winery loyalty programs. You can usually get about 20% off the price per bottle. You also usually have an obligation to buy one or two dozen each year, year-in and year-out. I do not like this obligation as some vintages are significantly better or worse than others. I usually only buy every several years and when I know it has been a great vintage. But if you are a regular and known buyer, the winery will likely keep you as a loyalty member while not encumbering you with the mandatory purchase obligations on an annual basis. Again just ask!

Winery visits are a great way to have fun while learning a lot. You can usually combine a few wineries together in day trip. If you are going to be drinking a lot among several different wineries, make sure to have a designated driver or hire a coach and a driver for a group of you.

Purchasing Wine from Bottle Shops

Bottle shops provide many of the benefits of visiting a winery. Bottle shops have wineries visit them to conduct tastings, providing another channel for bringing the winery to you. Some schedule regular monthly or even weekly tasting events. They provide the ability to interact with knowledgeable people in the wine industry. While most bottle shops lack the ambiance of a winery, just seeing all those different bottles displayed and available for purchase is ambiance enough for me!

I have built up experience knowing what wines I like and what to pay for them over time. I keep notes of how much I paid for wine and how it tasted. Yet, this does not prepare me entirely for what I will find in any given bottle shop. I engage with the store owner and quickly assess if they have any knowledge that may be of use for my purchasing decision. There is a big difference in service when the shop owner is in the store or the clerk is a wine fan who loves their work, as compared to a cashier who only knows how to total your purchases.

I have found several stores that provide convenient access where I can trust and get help to select the right bottle. I appreciate and am willing to pay slightly more for this when buying a single bottle. The bottle shop in the building I used to live in, however, does not have this level of service and has lost my trust. The shop owner has proven he is more interested in dumping his past due stock than he is on selling good quality wine that has been stored properly. And when he is not there, the hired help has not been helpful. They have not been trained nor have the knowledge required to serve customers with even the most basic set of information regarding the product line.

Upon our escaping an ordeal we had living overseas, and upon our return to Australia, we moved into our building. I wanted a really nice bottle of wine to celebrate. We did not have a car at the time and my wine was stored in a commercial cellar fifteen miles away. Therefore, I went to the first bottle shop I could find and purchased a nice bottle of wine. I knew I could buy this bottle elsewhere for about $85, but I paid $150 for the bottle in the shop in my building as I wanted to celebrate that evening. When I opened it, I could tell immediately it had not been stored properly. The bottle was not bad enough to consider returning it nor did I have any confidence another bottle would be better. We wanted to celebrate our return to Australia and I did not want my quality standard to get in the way of that.

But I never went back. Fortunately within a week of living in the area, I found another bottle shop five blocks away which had much better service, far better prices, and held tastings which were useful in helping me become re-accustomed to Australian Rieslings after some time overseas. Within four weeks of our return, I had a car and was able to get to my cellar to start to stock a small cellar in my apartment.

Six months later, we held a dinner party and one of my friends brought a bottle of wine as a token of his appreciation. Since we had already selected the wines for dinner, I set aside the bottle gifted me for later drinking. Within a few days, I had the opportunity to consider opening this bottle. When I reviewed the vintage, the grapes used and where they were from, I had a concern that this bottle could be well past due for drinking. I felt it needed to be drunk right away (if at all), so I opened it and tested it. Unfortunately, this bottle was, as expected, well past its drinking age.

I did not really want to embarrass my friend, but I also knew he was growing in his appreciation of fine wine and I wanted to understand why he purchased this bottle. He told me that he purchased it from the bottle shop in my building (as he was running late and had no other choice), and that the owner told him he had the same bottle a few weeks ago and it was outstanding. This was a $65 bottle of wine and I am certain that the owner was lying as this wine was well past due. My friend did not buy a bad bottle (the cork was perfect) - all bottles from this vintage would be bad by then.

I took the full bottle down to the shop and talked to the owner, and asked him how he could have recommended this bottle to a customer. I recommended all of his remaining bottles should be removed from the shelf as they were well past drinking age. He immediately wanted to put the blame on me by questioning my palate, then questioning if I had left the bottle in the window and 'baked' the wine. I assured him that neither was the issue.

I then asked if he would consider providing a replacement bottle at his recommendation, even a decent $30 bottle would do, but he refused. He then told me that the bottle was probably good when I opened it, but it clearly did not taste good now because a day had passed and I probably did not stopper the bottle up properly. He said that had he tested the bottle immediately upon opening it that he probably could do something about, but not now. I explained that I did come down to his store immediately after opening it the previous evening, but he had already shut for business.

I explained to him that he may be lucky enough to get away with his unethical antics with many people, but certainly not with all. I have never shopped there again and I recommend to my friends never to shop there either. And if I need a bottle that is beyond what I have in my apartment cellar, I now go to the bottle shop five blocks away. And if anyone is asking for a bottle shop in the area, I recommend the one five blocks away.

It is highly useful to have a local bottle shop you can trust where the wine is being well cared for and the owners and clerks know what they are doing. If you are in a different location from where you normally shop, you need to ensure you are buying a bottle that will not disappoint. You should do five things:

1. Make a quick tour of the bottle shop and understand choices available.
2. Engage the owner or clerk to see if they have any recommendations, promotions, or bottles not shown that might be of interest (of course, you should have some idea of what you want to buy and be able to explain that to them). Also ask how his wines are stored and transferred to the shop.
3. Read the label describing the wine, and ask the help if they know anything about this wine or similar wines. I always ask if they have vintage or tasting notes.
4. Then use your smart phone to see if you can find any ratings or tasting notes on the wine.
5. When purchasing the wine, only select a bottle lying horizontally if sealed with cork. Also ensure the seal is intact and not leaking.

Some people refuse to engage with shop help (or sommeliers in restaurants) because they do not trust the help is motivated to serve rather than just moving product. I do not agree with this. I tend to trust people until they give me a reason not to (like the shop owner who owns the bottle shop in my apartment building). Then I vote with my feet and leave. There are shops where the help is knowledgeable and passionate about wine. Many have personal experience with the wines they sell. The shops usually have access to information provided by wineries or distributors. Ask for and take advantage of this information. If they don't have much information, then use your mobile device (almost everyone has one now, right?) to research the wines you are considering. (This is quite easy to do and will be explained in more detail later in the book.) There are some great free or low-cost applications and a wealth of information on over a million different wines on the Internet to supplement whatever personal knowledge you may be able to get in the shop.

It is almost impossible to tell if wine in a bottle shop has been stored and transported properly. Bottle shops will typically turn over the wine quick enough that, for the most part, it should not be an issue. However, if picking up a bottle sealed with cork, only select a bottle lying horizontally. Most bottle shops lay most of the bottles down (as it keeps the corks moist and it saves space), but usually have several bottles standing up more prominently displayed and accessible. Most staff would have been trained to rotate the bottles and replace those that were standing and sold with the ones lying horizontally, but you can never be sure; some help just don't know or care. To be certain, grab a bottle lying horizontally. Regardless if cork or screw cap, check the seal to ensure the cork is intact and not bleeding, or that the screw cap is perfectly sealed with no faults or leakage points. For fine wine over $100 per bottle, only select wine stored properly in temperature-controlled storage. Fine wines turn over at a much slower rate and you do not want to buy fine wine that has matured too quickly without realizing it. Had I followed my own advice when returning from overseas, I would not have purchased a bad bottle for $150!

The main advantages of dealing with a bottle shop are convenience and choice. I buy most of my wine online from a bottle shop in Melbourne (even though I live in Sydney). I have only been in their store twice, but have purchased a lot of wine from them over the last fifteen years. The very first time I entered their store when visiting Melbourne, I was impressed with the quality and value of the wine they recommended. I then called and ordered some more wine from them. I came to trust their staff and have developed a long-term relationship. They are familiar with my tastes, source a lot of French and other European wines and often recommend wines I know to be of very good quality and value.

It is good to have several different bottle shops you can trust. I tend to buy by the case, but there are times when I need a bottle or two for a function that may have just arisen. Using a trusted shop that knows your preferences and value points helps you to make good selections.

Purchasing Wine at Auction

The single most important benefit of buying at auction is you can achieve substantially better prices than you can at a winery cellar door or bottle shop. Most auctions are done online, over a defined period of time, similar to buying through eBay. And there may be multiple auctions open at a time.

The other benefit of auctions is being able to search for and find specific bottles that cannot be sourced otherwise. We were able to pick up a 1971 Château d'Yquem and a 1971 Penfolds Grange on auction to have for my wife's 40th birthday. Both of these are truly great bottles and the only way to find them was by searching through auction sites. Fortunately, there are free or very inexpensive online tools to help, so it only takes seconds.

Unlike at a winery or bottle shop where you can receive expertise from ownership and staff, you need to bring your own knowledge to an auction. I use auctions to find a special bottle every now and then, but then I know exactly what I am looking for and have a price in mind in terms of how much it is worth and how much I am willing to pay. I quickly review newly listed auctions to see if there are any great values. By knowing the inventory in my cellar, I can decide if I want to replenish a specific varietal or style of wine and if I should consider buying some via auction. I always set the highest price I will pay in advance so I know when to pass and look at other options in the future.

Every now and then, you can get some great values. Based on availability and if there is a general wine glut or stock is scarce, prices will vary significantly. Therefore, it is important to monitor auction sites regularly to be able to understand what the prices are. Professional horse handicappers will watch a thousand races but only bet on ten to twenty. They will only bet when they know there is a very high chance of winning and when the odds are long enough to far exceed the risk. Most races are uncallable or too risky. A similar approach should be taken to monitoring wine prices via auctions. You should be constantly checking and updating your views on pricing, but seldom be buying. Every now and then a great value will appear, and by being prepared, you can then pick up great wine at great value.

Wine auctioneers will usually take a 25% or 30% margin on what they sell. This is divided between buyer and seller. The auction final price is not what you pay. The price you pay with commission will be 10% - 15% higher.

Not all auction houses are created equal. Some take provenance very seriously and others do not. I only buy form the ones that take provenance seriously. The importance of provenance is discussed earlier in this chapter. Even if a particular bottle cannot achieve any level of provenance, you know the auction houses that treat it seriously will value the wine accordingly. The higher the provenance level, the higher the asking price for the wine.

When provenance cannot be verified, there is a higher risk that the bottle may not have been stored properly. It is still likely to be a good bottle (especially if you know the bottle is sealed with screw cap) and could be worth the price. Just make sure that you are not paying top dollar for a bottle without provenance as you are assuming the risk. Both the 1971 Château d'Yquem and 1971 Penfolds Grange were purchased without provenance and both wines were absolutely perfect. But I wanted the bottles to give to my wife, knowing the act of caring enough and putting in the effort to get the wine would be appreciated, and I was lucky. I did not pay top dollar for these wines, and felt the price was worth the risk. (There was also a bottle of back-up wine for each, even though it was not the exact same bottle.) To improve my chances, I asked for and received a photo of the bottle to view the wine's color. While this does not guarantee it is a good bottle, I could possibly tell by the color if it was likely to have a fault.

In addition to provenance, I check community and professional tasting notes to better understand how the wine has held up over the years. There are a number of free resources you can review, but for about $300 in total annually, I use three well-respected reviewers that provide global coverage and have a massive amount of wine reviews and other useful resources. The three I use are:

- Jancis Robinson: Europe focused
- Robert Parker: US and Americas focused
- James Halliday: Australia focused

My best buys on great wines come through auction. You need to bring your own knowledge, but that should be less of a worry after finishing this book. You need to accept you are taking some risk that you will buy an occasional bad bottle. But the savings you make on the other bottles should more than make up for the occasional bad one.

Purchasing Wine via an Exchange

Buying from an exchange is similar to buying at auction, except the prices are fixed. It is similar to the *'Buy It Now'* option on eBay. The benefits and risks are almost identical to buying at auction. You may not get the occasional steal that you could get at a lower price at auction, but in return and if you see great value, you can purchase immediately without running the risk you will be outbid later.

Like buying at auction, you should ensure provenance of the wine before you buy. And similar to an auction, an exchange will take a 25% - 30% margin split between buyer and seller.

Buying from a Personal Collection

Buying from someone's personal cellar can provide even better value – but potentially at higher risk – than buying at auction or from an exchange. Private sellers would not add commission (unless they are selling on someone else's behalf, but then the seller would pay the commission). Therefore, it is possible you can get the same wine up to 30% cheaper than buying from auction or an exchange, assuming the private seller has a good idea of wine market pricing.

When buying from a private seller, you have the ability to negotiate more, especially if you want to buy volume or the total collection. Be warned though that many sellers have an emotional attachment to their wine and may be more challenging to deal with than a third-party auction or exchange broker. The owner has made an emotional and financial investment in storing the wine. However, the owner may be desperate or in a position where they must sell and sell quickly. Therefore, you may have some ability to negotiate even further.

The prices that a 'common sense' wine owner would list should be similar or 10% - 20% or so lower than what you would find at auction or on an exchange. However, with further negotiations, you should expect to be able to buy at 15% - 30% lower prices than through auction or exchange. And if you sense some desperation on behalf of the owner, and you are willing to close the sale then and there, you may be able to achieve prices 25% - 50% lower than what you would pay at auction or exchange.

Substantial savings can be achieved and unique bottles acquired when buying from a private collection. You should explore the wine's provenance carefully and not just accept the owner's verbal version of how they acquired and stored their wine (unless you know and trust them). A reputable auction house or exchange would be checking their provenance and so should you. It might even be the case that the private collection was offered to several auction houses or exchanges and rejected because the provenance was questionable. Ask for receipts when the wine was purchased so you know how long the wine had been in the owner's hands. Ask for pictures or even visit their cellar or view their receipts if the owner has been storing their wine in a commercial wine cellar. Ask how often the wine has been transferred and how it was transferred. You should be able to quickly assess if the owner of the wine is ethical and has cared about the wine's storage.

It may be possible that you may want to sell some of your wine in the future, either privately or through an auction house or exchange. I never thought I would ever sell off any of mine, but I have sold quite a bit and will continue to do so in the future to continually adjust cellar levels. There are a number of reasons why you may elect to sell, including:

- Your tastes have changed and the wine you like has changed with it.
- Your ability to sense has been altered.
- You have made the decision to drink less for health or other physical reasons.
- Your partner or wine drinking friends are drinking less.
- You realize you have too much of a particular type of wine that may go past due before you can get to it.
- Some of your holdings have increased significantly and are now worth more to you by selling them instead of drinking them.
- You may just need to turn physical assets into liquid assets (no pun intended).

I do not purchase wine as an investment. I purchase wine to drink and am assuming you do also. By buying wine and storing it, circumstances and market conditions may cause significant increases in the value of some of your wines. Therefore, while I originally purchased wine for consumption, I may now elect to sell all or part of it. I also recognize that many of the just-mentioned factors for selling wine apply to me. My wife has to watch her alcohol intake to ensure she does not damage her liver. More and more of my friends are regularly detoxing. And I have certainly had a change in the mixture of varietals, style and types of wine that I find appealing.

I now constantly monitor and adjust my wine cellar and in general continue to reduce inventory levels. It is impossible to predict exactly what you find appealing in the future. Much wine has been built to last into the future. A wine you were excited to buy a decade ago, may not be the wine you want to drink today. This does not mean it is a bad wine or was a bad choice initially. It is likely still a very good wine and of appeal to others whose tastes are similar to the taste you liked a decade ago. Therefore, I now assume that any wine I buy may be a wine for future sale. While I hope I will consume most of the wine I buy, I am not sure exactly which ones I will consume in the future and which ones I should consider selling, so I treat the purchase of every bottle as a bottle I may sell later.

Wine is far easier to sell and you will achieve higher prices if you can provide an accurate history of the wine in terms of where it was purchased and how it has been stored and transported over its life. There are several things you should be conscious of in terms of record keeping to make it easier to sell wine in the future. I was not conscious of this previously, but now do as a matter of course, including:

- Keep all purchase receipts and scan and index them (also provide a link to the file name or URL stored in that record in your wine database if you keep one)
- Keep a storage log of where the wine has been stored (my wine database has several fields on provenance)
- Keep records of any supporting information and receipts for cellaring regardless if it is your own or you rent a commercial cellar
- Take pictures of your wine and date-stamp when they entered your cellar. This combined with your purchase receipt provides the highest level of provenance you can achieve

This may seem like a lot of work, but it is not. First of all, your wine purchases should be infrequent, so it is not that often that you need to update records. Secondly, with some simple systems that you can build, download for free or subscribe to, you have access to the tools you need to be able to do this (described in *Chapter 19: Tools and Systems for Managing Your Wine Inventory*). By putting in a small amount of effort now, you will be able to achieve higher prices selling your wine than you would without proper provenance.

Promoted Tastings within the Wine Industry

I attend a number of wine industry tastings, but rarely buy at them. They provide the benefits of bringing people together to taste and discuss wines from several wineries. These events can provide further experience, but are not often a good time to purchase wine. These events are primarily sales events, and the prices are standard retail prices. You may have an offer to get 10% off if you buy that evening. I have found people get caught up in the evening and buy on the spur of the moment. In my opinion, this is not the right time or incentive for purchasing wine. The experience should be valued as it provides additional insight in wine drinking in general and these wineries and wines in particular. However, it is likely that you will find these same wines in major bottle shops for similar or less price than you would be paying that evening.

The only time to consider buying at these events is if it is a pre-release tasting for a highly sought-after wine with limited supply, or a re-release of a museum wine which is not on the market currently. Both would be highly sought-after wines and having access to purchasing some, even while paying top dollar, would be a benefit of which you may want to take advantage.

Trading Wine or in lieu of Other Services

Regardless if you are purchasing or selling wine, using a bartering exchange may be a way to acquire or dispose of wine without any money being involved. Barter exchanges or private agreements for the exchange of goods and services can work extremely well when the other party values what you have on offer more than you do.

There are wine bartering sites that allow you to list the wines you would like to barter and view other people's inventory and propose trades with others in the network. Additionally, there are broader bartering sites that allow you to do the same, but offer non-wine goods or services in exchange for wine (or wine in exchange for other non-wine goods and services being offered).

Or you may just enter into individual agreements with other people. I have bartered wine in exchange for restaurant meals. As you may know, we love to cook at home. We do so for three reasons:
- It is far cheaper to eat at home living in Australia than it is eating at restaurants.

- It is healthy and connects us with the simple activity of living.
- Cooking has greatly improved my ability of smell and taste and has enhanced my wine drinking experiences.

We still eat meals out and greatly enjoy the experience. And we know several of the best chefs and restaurant owners around town. When eating out, about 20% of the cost of the meal is for the food. The other 80% is for the real estate, the labor and other incidentals. Therefore, if a restaurant owner has an empty table and can fill it and charge 50% of what they normally would, it would improve their profit margin for the evening. Restaurants also typically sell wine at two to three times what they paid for it to cover their profit, cleaning and service.

I provide wine to two restaurants in exchange for three-course meals. The restaurant is only spending 20% on our food and this is more than covered by the bottle of wine I have provided them in return. They do not need to buy that bottle from a distributor and can sell it now for profit to someone else. And while I have parted with a bottle of wine I could have consumed or sold elsewhere, I do not have to go through the trouble of trying to find another buyer; I have exchanged it for something of far greater value to me which is an excellent meal out!

You may have professional skills or other assets you can barter in exchange for wine. It may be as simple as doing gardening or landscaping for someone with a good collection of wine or a winery itself. Or you could possibly be providing some weekend accounting to a business that sells wine. The possibilities are endless even though they may be difficult to source. Earlier in my career, I wrote a simple computer program for someone and was paid with a bottle of 1961 Château Lafite!

Transporting Wine

Wine ages best when at rest over long periods of time. However, every now and then, we need to transport wine between locations. What ruins wine the quickest is extreme temperatures. Wine is also heavy and if you are purchasing a couple of dozen bottles, space and effort is required to transport it. We ship wine from the cellar door to our commercial cellar. Both the winery and the commercial cellar are staffed and trained to handle the wine properly. Wineries have strong relationships with transport companies and know which ones to use for the best care. They only use transport companies that have good records and serve them well.

There are regular times the transport companies come by the wineries and the wineries have daily processes to package and ship the wine. The trucks then deliver the wine to the commercial cellar knowing someone is there who can immediately receive and put it into controlled storage. There is virtually no time involved where the wine is out of controlled temperatures. I buy enough wine that the wineries almost always ship the wine for free for me. If I am buying from a new winery for the first time, I may have to pay a shipping charge of $10 or $12 per dozen. However, I think this is well worth it as I know the wine is being looked after properly and I avoid needing to transport and care for it myself.

Most of you will not be using a staffed commercial cellar to receive your wine. I know a number of people who have their wine shipped to their work location as work locations have the ability to sign for and receive goods during the business day. Do check that this is in accordance with your company policies of using corporate facilities for personal use. Or have it delivered to a Post Office address or through a courier service where you can either have it on-delivered when you are at home to receive your wine, or can go to the courier company offices to pick it up. Do not have wine delivered to your home and sit at the door step. If you are not around to bring it inside and there are extreme weather conditions, you are putting the wine at risk; worse, it may be stolen.

If I am only buying a few bottles, I carry them in a bag or small box, place them in the car, immediately drive home and place them in appropriate storage conditions. If you are driving a long distance and running the air conditioner or heater to stabilize temperatures in the car or the trunk, the wine should be fine. However, if you are stopping overnight or stopping for a prolonged period of time on a day with extreme temperatures, you should remove the wine from the car and place it in normal temperature conditions. Avoid having wine in a car when the car reaches extreme temperatures, either hot or cold. Extreme temperatures easily damage the wine's structure, ruining it. If I have wine in a car which will be outside in extreme temperature conditions for longer than 90 minutes, I will remove the wine from the car. You would not leave a dog in a car in these conditions, and you should not leave wine in these conditions either!

A friend of mine moved from the US to Jakarta, Indonesia about a decade ago. He shipped 300 bottles of fine wine with him to enjoy. Due to problems with the shipping company and a dock workers strike, his wine sat out on the docks in Jakarta for three weeks in extremely hot temperature. I remember spending an evening having dinner at his house and drinking a number of bottles of wine. I brought three 'good' bottles along from Australia with me, but we had to open eight of his bottles to get two that were drinkable. Most of his 300 bottles were ruined and the remainder far from their potential.

If you are going to relocate a large number of bottles of fine wine, make sure you put in the effort and cost to transport them in refrigerated containers. Refrigerated storage is more expensive, but worth it if you are shipping $20,000 of wine. To keep costs down, you can share or top up the refrigerated storage container with goods of someone else. This might mean your wine arrives a few weeks after the rest of your goods, but the cost of shipping will be a lot less and your wine protected during transport.

Transporting wine should not be a problem if you avoid extreme conditions as suggested above. If it is a few bottles, move it yourself. If it is several dozen and transporting them domestically, have the wineries transport them for you. If it is a lot of wine to ship internationally, then consider using refrigerated storage. Chances are that your container will be stored somewhere near the middle of the boat and away from the most extreme conditions, but you cannot guarantee this, so it is best to consider paying for refrigeration.

Selling Wine

Every now and then, you may find yourself in a position where you may want to sell wine. There are a number of reputable dealers who sell wine via the same methods from which you may buy wine mentioned above such as auction sites, exchanges, and private sellers. I list a number of the ones I know to be reputable in the Australian market in *Chapter 21: Other References*. Each of these sites has slightly different commission schedules and approaches, but they split the commission between the buyer and seller so if you are selling, you should expect to have 10% – 15% deducted as commission.

The first step after contacting an auction house or exchange is to provide a list of wines (brand, vintage, varietal, etc.) for them to prepare a valuation for you. Also be prepared to provide provenance (as discussed above) as it will increase your selling price point and improve clearance rate. Provenance has several different levels of authority, and is treated differently by different auction houses, but needless to say, the better the provenance, the higher the price when the hammer strikes!

I have sold about 1,200 bottles privately (using emails to friends and posters in the building around where I lived), and about 600 bottles through auctions and exchanges. This has allowed me to adjust my cellar stock and better align what is in my cellar to what I am drinking now, not what I thought I would be drinking ten years ago. If you buy carefully and in accordance with the advice in this chapter, you should not be in a position where you need to sell off wine, but again, you may find you have a medical issue or your tastes have changed, so it is always a possibility. And if you are going to sell, you want to be in a position where you can get the best price.

Notes

110. Scruton, *I Drink Therefore I am*, 37.

Chapter 18
Wine Drinking Practice & Experience

Todd states, "we are, in general, simply much less good at smelling and tasting than we are at seeing, hearing and touching."[111] While difficult, Korsmeyer explains, "taste is an educable faculty,"[112] pointing out that developing a trained palate is more difficult than developing a trained ear. Yet, it is certainly possible for many. Todd claims the ability of gradually accumulating knowledge and experience to affect what one perceives, and how one evaluates this, is quite remarkable.[113] This chapter provides ideas and a path for improving wine drinking abilities through continued training to develop the senses further.

You may have attended trade school, university or even a graduate program. You may have felt pressure to compete and complete these programs. They may have seemed like drudgery while going through them. The motivation was to acquire skills, a degree or certification for work. Fortunately gaining wine drinking knowledge and experience is not like that. You can do it according to your own desires, and with little budget.

There exists formal training and certifications to achieve becoming a noted wine judge or sommelier. But neither is required to appreciate fine wine. I first acquired taste for beer and hard alcohol. I did not enjoy either much, but they did provide alcoholic consumption, enabling me to fit in during my university days and party with others. But the focus was on alcohol, not taste.

I could not articulate what I liked about one wine over another. I just knew that I enjoyed some wines more than others. I was fortunate in being able to appreciate a few good wines and being able to determine in many cases which wines were better than others. I was accumulating experience, but not translating it into knowledge. It was only after sharing meals with others who possessed more knowledge that I started to understand why I was enjoying specific wines. I started to know in general, that I liked Cabernet Sauvignon or Shiraz better than Merlot. I occasionally had a fine red which appeared more elegant and became attracted to Red Zinfandel and Pinot Noir, but also found some of them tepid and nondescript.

I enjoyed red wines better than whites. I was introduced to and generally liked some decent Chardonnay, Riesling and a variety of New Zealand Sauvignon Blanc. But I could not determine flavors or pick out characteristics in wine. I then learned to identify mouthfeel and balance. My first abilities to describe wine were along the lines of the following statements:

- I like the way it sits in my mouth.
- I can still taste it after swallowing.
- I am enjoying the flavors.
- I feel the wine on my cheeks (tannins).

Mouthfeel and balance are the first things most people learn and start to understand about fine wines and why they like one wine over another. You do not need a lot of experience to determine if a wine is balanced or not. If I had a good wine I really enjoyed, I would remember the winery and grape (but not likely take notice of the vintage) so I could buy it again. Mouthfeel played a more dominant part of the experience at that phase in my wine tasting life than the differences from vintage to vintage.

Based on the large amount of travel for work, I had the opportunity to try wines from around the world. I also had enough cumulative airline loyalty points, and was designated as a 'road warrior,' so was flying business class most of the time and occasionally first class. This provided access to excellent wine choices from the countries where the airline was headquartered and where the airline was flying. I also had time to sip and think about the wines and read the tasting notes provided by the airline sommeliers that choose the wine for the flights.

I remember having received an upgrade and being able to fly Singapore Airlines First Class for the first time around 1990 and drinking the Château Brane-Cantenac from the Margaux region in France. I knew I had to get this wine again. It stood out as one of the finer wines I ever had. Fortunately, several weeks later, while flying through Frankfurt, I was able to pick up two bottles in duty free. I savored this wine while drinking those two bottles. I started to truly appreciate fine wine, reflect on it and wanted to figure out why I enjoyed some wines so much. This was the wine that was a turning point for me. I currently have four bottles of the 2005 (a brilliant Bordeaux vintage) Château Brane-Cantenac in my cellar to drink over the next decade. The idea of drinking this great wine from a great vintage fills me with excitement!

Eating better and drinking better provided greater appreciation of wine and what was possible. The other thing was that as I sampled more and different wines, that there were so many different types of wines that tasted great, or tasted great in the right circumstances. Wine appreciation became seductive. Winemaking is a simple manufacturing process using high quality ingredients and quality control to influence major differences among wines. But it is more than just a manufacturing process. It is an art form, it requires individual craftsmanship, it is a thrilling risk-taking adventure, and it is almost religious. Jesus turns water into wine, as he tells His disciples during The Last Supper "This is my blood of the covenant, which is poured out for many for the forgiveness of sins. I tell you, I will not drink from this fruit of the vine from now on until that day when I drink it anew with you in my Father's kingdom." (Mt, 26:28-29, NIV). And we depend on our winemakers to provide similar religious experiences for us!

Becoming a wine expert can be daunting and appear counter-productive to your ability to enjoy wine if you put too much pressure on yourself. But some knowledge and experience can help to:

- learn why and how to appreciate wine;
- make your drinking and eating experiences much more enjoyable;
- provide insights in buying fine wine at the best prices; and

- provide confidence you know enough about what you like to share that with others.

I had a slow and accidental path to learning how to appreciate and value wine in my life. Looking back, I wish I would have had people around me to start and promote the process earlier in life and to guide me to learn much more quickly with focused attention. My 'accidental' approach finally evolved, but cost me many thousands of dollars during the journey; I also missed many great wine drinking experiences along the way.

This book provides you guidance and a framework to taking a similar journey much more quickly and less expensively. There are a number of components to wine appreciation which can be easily and enjoyably followed to gain knowledge and experience:

- smelling and tasting practice sessions
- food / wine comparative tasting
- tasting through the variety of channels mentioned in the previous chapter (cellar doors, bottle shop tastings, wine industry promoted tastings, etc.)
- hosting your own tastings
- degustation meals or meals with wine competitions
- reading books on various aspects of wine
- wine research
- note taking
- vintage charts
- wine courses / classes
- building an expert network
- cooking

Smith reminds us: "The experience of tasting provides the only route to such knowledge. We need to start by tasting and do what we can to gain the most out of our tasting experiences. And through more tasting and concentration and reflection when we taste, our brain becomes rewired and trained to more easily and naturally identify and appreciate the qualities that make up a fine wine."[114] Experiments and research of brain scans of novice and experienced tasters have proven this.[115] This research underlies the importance of the learning component in wine appreciation. The research also indicates how we may become experts in wine appreciation in one culture and geography, but when we move into different styles of winemaking and other cultures that we may need to start again as novices and be retrained. I have personally found that to be the case with my initial dislike of certain foreign wines until I opened my mind to them and tried a few more. I have now grown to like a variety of different styles from different geographies and the diversity of many different types of wine adds greatly to the overall pleasure derived from wine drinking.

There is no optimal way to build knowledge and experience. Yet, there exists a few standard practices to ensure you are learning and gaining experience more quickly than if you do not follow those practices. One of them is to continue to work on and improve your sense of concentration and to remove distractions so you can concentrate more. Another is to make sure you are physically fit and that your senses are working properly. Most importantly, continue to drink and sample wine!

I define knowledge as learning and experience as doing. It would be a mistake to focus too much on learning and not doing or the other way around. I believe that you should weave the two together in turn as each area provides useful input to the other and builds upon the other. Knowledge is gained more quickly when fueled by experience and experience is more meaningful and insightful with relevant and pre-existing knowledge. As a matter of guidance, with regards to learning wine appreciation or almost any other topic, I believe that about one-third of time should be spent on knowledge (learning) and two-thirds on experience (doing). That seems to work for me and I believe it is a good guideline for most people.

Smelling and Tasting Practice Sessions

One of the first and most useful books I read on wine tasting was Jancis Robinson's *How to Taste Wine*. This book is approachable and provides exercises to help you smell and taste better; it helps you discriminate between various wine flavors. She outlines a number of exercises on wine tasting you can do alone or in small groups of like-minded friends. Doing the exercises in this book is a great way to start to improve your wine tasting.

Another good set of exercises you can perform, either with normal eating experiences or as a planned exercise with different targeted foods, is to try different combinations of wines and foods at the same time. It helps to take notes during this as there will be many different combinations of wine and food possible and you will be doing this ongoing. Identify what combinations work well and why. For example, I found out that Riesling goes well with apple, but not peach and that a Semillon goes well with peach, but not apple. I did this by trying the different combinations when I had access to the fruits and the wines side-by-side. This has led me to select Iced Riesling dessert wine with apple pie or apple tart for dessert, or a Botrytis Semillon with peach cobbler.

Whenever you have minimally two different food types and two different wines, try each of the four or more combinations to determine which ones work best and take note as to why you like some combinations better than others. You will start to better identify features such as acidity, sweetness, and the texture of various wines. There are a number of specific simple events which are easy to host, providing the opportunity to match food and wine without anyone knowing that research is a by-product of enjoying such an event! You can provide several different wines combined with cheese platters, different types of chocolates, or a plate of charcuterie (various meat slices). All of these make for a pleasant food and wine experience and can be used as a prelude or après-dining experience to expand your wine knowledge. I am recommending these exercises not only to help you identify food and wine pairings, but as a set of exercises to identify and understand what it is about the wine and its characteristics that you are experiencing. Various different food types provide different contextual situations which highlight increased sensitivity to sweetness, acidity, astringency, etc.

Another more academic, but useful exercise is to use the sets of wine smells provided by Le Nez Du Vin. These come in smaller sets focused on white wines, red wines, wine faults, and so forth or you can buy the complete set of all wine smells. These exercises help you to more easily determine wine smells by presenting you with a typical set of smells for various wines. By practicing these exercises, you will more easily be able to identify what smells are associated with what grapes.

When participating in these exercises initially, you will focus on how a single sense is reacting to the experience. Wine, however, is a cross-modal sensory set of experiences using your eyes, nose and mouth all working in harmony to provide a holistic experience.

When swallowing, take note of what is happening in your olfactory passage. While tasting, concentrate on both the flavors and the tactile sensations you are experiencing. Over time, you will more readily pick up on the beautiful nuances provided by complex and fine wines across all the senses.

These are all exercises that you can do alone or in a group and are a good way to provide a foundation for improving your ability to smell and taste wine. There are a number of other experiences you can participate in to continue to gain experience and therefore, more knowledge. And as we see, wine education can be combined with, and an easy by-product of, enjoyable events and gatherings!

Food / Wine Comparative Tasting

Any time you have the opportunity to do comparative tastings (multiple bottles of wines and different food types), take advantage of it. When dining at home, I may have two or three bottles of wine open at a time that I am trying with food that evening. If I have leftovers that will be served the next evening, then I may open a different bottle of wine to try with it. Once we made a large tray of lasagna which we had three times over six days. I tried a different wine each time to be able to compare which characteristics of the wine I liked most with lasagna. I tried Shiraz, Grenache and Tannat, and was able to conclude I would not use Tannat with the type of lasagna we make. I preferred the Grenache, but would also use a spicy Hunter Valley Shiraz when we decide to put more seasoning (pepper and chili) in the lasagna.

I occasionally eat out at a steak house with a group of friends who each bring a different wine to compare. One of us might have a Wagyu steak; another, the slow roast; and the third, the Scotch Fillet. We usually have two or three bottles of red wine open at the time the steaks are served, and we will share a bite of our steaks with each other and be able to try with each wine. This gives each of us the opportunity to try multiple (three different steaks and three different wines provides nine pairings!) combinations in one sitting and discuss what combinations we enjoyed the most and why. This is a great way to learn what food and wine go well together. I have done similar at seafood restaurants using white wines and Pinot Noir with fish and crustaceans.

Another good opportunity to do comparative tastings is

when you are out at an Indian, Chinese, or Korean restaurant and are eating 'community' style. This is where everyone orders a dish (or someone orders on everyone's behalf) and the dishes are shared. You self-serve a small portion of many different dishes. This provides the ability to compare wines with different primary ingredients (chicken, pork, beef, fish) and also different secondary ingredients (mild or hot curries, oyster sauce, different spices, etc.) with different wines.

When starting out, only compare two wines and foods. With more experience, increase the numbers as you will be able to discern and remember the differences of more wines more easily. And if the wines are of different varietals, styles and matched with food over the course of a long evening, you may be able to compare eight to a dozen wines once you have gained experience and the ability to discern finer nuances of difference between them.

Comparing wines side-by-side is the best way I know to learn, and to have a great time while learning!

Tastings Through a Variety of Channels

In the previous chapter, we described the benefits of buying wine through various channels. One of the major benefits of several channels such as the cellar door, bottles shops, and wine industry promoted tastings is the ability to try before you buy. Another benefit is to be able to learn about and sample the wines provided and compare. A day of cellar door tastings around a given region may allow you to taste 20 – 50 different wines in a day, based on how close the wineries are together and if you are swallowing or spitting!

Bottle shops regularly schedule tastings as do many wine industry forums. Most are free, but some may cost a little to subsidize the cost of putting on the event. When visiting wineries, you do not need to call ahead or make a commitment unless the winery is not usually open to the general public. The need to call ahead is rare in the US and Australia, but many wineries in Europe require that you call ahead. And if you want to do a tasting with more than four people, call ahead to ensure you can get served. The wineries appreciate the heads up and will often provide a dedicated person and area to serve you and answer questions.

Some bottle shops also offer regular tastings. They host regular weekly or monthly tastings. Unless it is a pre-release party for an iconic brand, almost all bottle shop tastings are free. Wine industry promoted tastings will vary in price based on who is wearing the cost of the venue, wine and any guest speakers or wine industry stalwarts who are attending.

All these types of tastings provide you the ability to try before you buy; the main point attending them is to learn more about wine and to gain experience discerning good from bad, and what varietals, styles or characteristics you find enjoyable. Like exercise or practicing a musical instrument, the more you train and practice, the better you become at it!

You should participate in tastings on a regular basis. I try to do at least two or three wine region trips annually, visiting twenty or thirty different wineries in total. I also try to take in about ten bottle shop or wine industry tastings per year. I target bottle shop or wine industry tastings that are presenting three or four different wineries at a time if possible. This is further supplemented by hosting or attending friend's wine or dinner parties where we are sampling a variety of wine.

And at least several times per week, I will try a new bottle or a bottle that has aged for some time since the last time I drank it. Therefore, through the participation of tastings at wineries and other venues, sharing meals and drinking at home, I am able to try about 100 different wines per year. (Note that this does not mean I have drunk 100 full bottles of wine as many of the tastings are only a sip followed by expectorating the wine.)

Doing this year after year quickly provides experience where you have tried 500 – 1,000 different wines or the same wine over its aging period. Considering the limited investment in time, you will have gained real experience and hopefully expertise during that time. You will be able to much more easily determine what you like about wine, and have more confidence when purchasing wine. And having read several books on wine tasting and wine appreciation during that time will further enhance and improve your capabilities.

Hosting Your Own Tastings

Holding your own tastings provides similar ability to gain experience as those mentioned in the previous section. I discuss it separately as there are dimensions to hosting a tasting that provide the ability to learn more, more quickly. By being the one to prepare the tasting, you need to focus on what the theme will be if it is a comparative tasting. Will you be sampling the same wine over different vintages; the same grape, but from different regions; the same grape and vintage within a region; different styles of white or red wines; or some other theme? Just thinking about theme forces you to review what you find interesting in wine, and why and how you are going to describe that to others.

You also need to think through if you are going to serve a meal, tapas, cheese and crackers or something else with wine. This makes you think about what foods will go well with the wines or if some wines should be changed to match the food served. You also need to think about the use of decanters and if you should decant each wine and for how long prior to tasting. And you are likely to have some wine left over, so you need to think about how you will store that wine and use it in the near future.

The mental gymnastics to host a tasting exercises your brain and reinforces and strengthens what you already know about wine. It may seem difficult at first, but becomes easier each time you do it. Events like this can turn into special evenings, but they do take a little effort. It is effort I believe is well worth the investment, but it does take several hours of preparation beforehand and a while to clean up afterward.

If you are concerned about funding all the wine and food, you can charge people a token amount to cover wine and food costs, and I have found people more than willing to do this to participate. Or you can ask each to bring some type of food and a bottle of wine. However, make sure to provide guidance to each individual so you do not end of with the same wines, or food and wines which do not match well. And by having to think through what each person should bring, you are again reinforcing what you know and value about wine.

By hosting several wine tastings or meals for friends which consist of several courses and matching wines, you become much more knowledgeable about wine. You will also become known as a great host!

Degustation Meals or Meals with Wine Competitions

Experience is gained the quickest and most effectively, in my opinion, when you are doing comparative tastings across a number of different wines and also when matched to suitable foods. Degustation meals tend to have five to seven courses, and cost about $100

- $200 per head. I know of several with six or seven courses and matching wines that cost $150. The meal portions are smaller than if you ordered a full serve as you are indulging in many more courses than the standard two or three you would have as a normal meal.

The wines are selected by the restaurant sommelier to suit the food. Sometimes they will select two different wines you can choose from for some of the courses to compare which wine you may like better with that particular type of food. These wines can come from the wine list for the restaurant or they may have a special bottle or two for you to try.

More and more, wineries are coming to you by working out dedicated evenings in local restaurants and providing four- or five-course meals matching their wines. Since the winery is doing this as a promotion, they are usually subsidizing part of the cost, making the overall cost of these meals still around $100 - $150 per head. I have been able to eat some excellent meals at my favorite restaurants and sample some great wines this way.

Another great way to enjoy a meal and learn about wine is when two wineries go head-to-head and have you compare their wines side-by-side with each meal course. Two wineries with similar wine listings will compete throughout a four- or five-course meal with the winemakers or owners providing insights on their particular wine. You are then asked to judge the wines and score which one you like best. This provides good feedback to the wineries and makes you think about what you like in a wine. Since you are comparing two wines which are often quite similar, you start to pick up on the nuances of each wine and the slight differences to better train your palate.

In this case, the wineries usually select the wines they want to have you judge and then they have the restaurant match the meal to those wines. I was recently at one where two great Hunter Valley wineries compared Semillon, Chardonnay, a very good Shiraz, their top-end Shiraz, and a dessert wine.

By doing degustation meals, and meals which have one or more attending wineries, you can learn a great deal about wine in a short period of time. And you usually also get a great meal and fine wine at a very reasonable price!

Reading Books

Reading and learning about wine would seem less enjoyable than drinking it! Hopefully you understand and agree that drinking wine is a sensory, if not aesthetic, experience and has unique characteristics not present when drinking other liquids. Hopefully, you agree life is better with wine!

The experience to enjoy and appreciate wine is greatly enhanced through reading and other forms of wine education. There are a variety of different approaches to wine education and a plethora of sources. I enjoy reading about wine and usually have a glass in hand when reading or blogging on wine.

I had read about ten books on wine in their entirety and parts of many others when I wanted to learn more about a specific wine topic. Additionally, I have twenty more reference books and a number of very inexpensive books I bought in used bookstores that I thought could possibly be useful at some point in the future even though I did not have a specific interest or need when I bought them. These usually cost under $5 and sit in a separate shelf in the bookcase.

The main books I have on wine fit into the following categories:

- History of wine
- Wine appreciation
- How to taste wine
- Philosophy of wine
- Food and wine matching
- Wine lifestyle
- Making wine
- Wine regions
- Wine references such as description of grapes and varietals, dictionaries, encyclopedias

For the immediate benefit and enhancement of heightening your drinking pleasure, you should read books on how to taste wine and wine appreciation. This book falls into those categories as do a number of books referenced in *Chapter 20: Further Wine Education*.

This should be followed by a book on food and wine matching to provide insights as to what foods and wines go well together and why. This will have an immediate and positive impact on enjoying both food and wine. And as you grow in wine appreciation and if wine is the center of the meal instead of the compliment to the meal, you should also get a book on matching food to the wine, not the other way around! Several exist.

Books in the categories described in the last paragraph are useful for improving your sensory experience with wine. They educate you on what is happening to you physically and sensually when drinking wine and how to improve sensory experiences. Reading on the topics of making wine, wine regions and the philosophy of wine improve your cognitive appreciation of wine, while reading on wine lifestyle and the history of wine improve your affective appreciation of wine. As described in *Part One: Wine and the Senses*, the sensory, cognitive and affective dimensions come together to provide the wonderment that wine drinking has to offer.

Reading about wine can never replace the experience or joy of drinking wine, but it certainly can enhance both – in fact, reading about and researching wine is necessary to improve the wine drinking experience. I recommend reading books as outlined below:

Sensory:

- How to taste wine
- Wine appreciation
- Food and wine matching

Cognitive:

- Making wine
- Wine regions
- Philosophy of wine
- Grape varietals

Affective:

- Wine lifestyle
- History of wine

As a general reading and study plan, I would read two or three Sensory books, followed by two or three Cognitive books, then one more Sensory book and one more Cognitive book. Affective books may be read and enjoyed throughout.

It is less exciting to read books sequentially and in their entirety. I find that when I have a topic of particular interest or am curious about some aspect of wine, it is best to just research that topic through books or online sources. By interspersing reading and wine drinking, you will develop quickly and effectively in terms of greatly improving your wine drinking experiences.

While I still enjoy sitting down and reading physical books, I am accessing my books much more through electronic media devices. This means a lot less heft to carry around. It also saves time and money as follows:

- Electronic books are usually significantly less expensive than physical books
- They can be delivered immediately and put to good use providing knowledge which reduces near-term spend on food and wine
- They save time by reducing the number of return trips needed to go to the store or wine cellar since the information is immediately available
- They provide price checks on wine to make sure one is getting a good deal if you need to pick up a bottle or two in a bottle shop. They also may provide a proof point which can be used to get a matching price from the shop owner

Many of the books referenced in *Chapter 20: Further Wine Education* are available in both electronic and printed format, so check and determine which format you desire. For me, if it is available (and formatted well) in electronic format, I will purchase it that way.

There are also a number of good wine magazines available. These provide reviews of wine currently available, reviews of certain winemakers and wineries, notice of upcoming events, and other articles of insight. I subscribed to two of them and occasionally buy an issue off the rack if there is a feature of particular interest. However, some magazines are stilted towards their advertisers and therefore, less credible sources as independent reviewers. Additionally, many of the articles (or similar articles) contained in magazines, can now be found online for free. I enjoy being able to occasionally sit, relax and read up on current events in wine, but do not use wine magazines as a major source for gaining experience or knowledge.

Wine Research

General wine learning comes from reading several books on wine along with practical drinking experience. To further enhance the drinking experience, it is important to have more targeted access to knowledge about specific wines and topics which are easy to find and digest in the spur of the moment. Doing this frequently provides a treasure cove of information that adds to your overall knowledge and appreciation of wine. It can also save you a great deal of money when you have that 'need to buy it now' feeling about a particular bottle, by checking the Internet quickly to see if the price is acceptable and the tasting notes support your desire to buy it.

I once was caught up in the moment celebrating our 10th wedding anniversary and was sitting next to the restaurant's glass-encased wine cellar staring at a bottle of 1989 Château Margaux. They wanted $1,850 in the restaurant for the bottle. Using my smartphone app, and within a minute, I found I could purchase that bottle for about $250 in the US and for less than $500 in Australia. That certainly relieved me of the 'need to buy it now' moment!

Throughout my wine drinking history, I have learned the value of research to answer questions, understand more, and to help satisfy my curiosity about certain aspects of wine. The research has become more frequent and necessary when writing my blog. But my research skills have improved significantly since I started writing this book. There is a tremendous amount of useful information to be found on the Internet with regard to wine. It varies from the silly to serious, summary to detail, and covers almost any aspect of wine you feel you need to know more about. The intent of this book is not to provide you an overview on how to research. The intent is to enhance your knowledge and appreciation of wine drinking, so this section will be focused on 'where to look' instead of 'how to look.' However, several easy to understand tips on how to improve your research capabilities will increase your productivity and allow you more time to drink than to read about drinking.

Here are a few suggestions to keep in mind while conducting research:

- The Internet is the beginning and end of research capabilities and should be the primary source for quickly finding something (make sure to assess the credibility or provenance of information you find though as it will vary greatly in quality and truthfulness)
- Do not forget to supplement the Internet with other channels such as visiting bottle shops, reviewing and subscribing to wine magazines, and sharing time discussing wine with others of similar interests and more knowledge than you (i.e., building an expert network)
- Visit wine research facilities such as universities which offer viticulture or oenology programs
- Know precisely, or minimally, directionally what you are looking for to determine what keywords to use (Entering 'wine' returned 528 million hits the last time I tried it!)
- If a particular search string does not work, try a few slightly different, but similar, variations to narrow in more precisely what you are seeking
- Always have a version of a search engine with you, via phone or tablet
- Tag specific master indexes for wine-related content
- Supplement 'free content' with some inexpensive access to wine-specific knowledge sources
- Collect URLs to bodies of wine-specific research as published by viticulture or oenology programs (I use Evernote to tag and store my wine resources)
- Have access and ask for help when required from expert researchers (my wife can find things in minutes that I could not in an hour!)
- Take a little time up front to organize your research material into folders or directories (and possibly tag with keywords) to be able to find them in the future when needed

- Take every caution to respect and not violate copyright protection

As with a lot of things, continued practice significantly improves researching capabilities.

A lot of great research can be found at no cost. And some targeted material can be secured for a couple of dollars. Significant and comprehensive bodies of research can be acquired for under $100 per source. If you require more expensive materials, it is probably best to review or borrow it from a wine academic facility.

The real cost of wine research is not doing any and being ignorant! And the next significant cost is in the time it takes you to find and review materials. I pay (but not too much) for accessing research when I need it. With all the material available, it is impossible to find the time to read it end-to-end. It is also of less interest when you are reviewing materials sequentially instead of targeting and focusing on the specific topic of interest, regardless of if it is finding the market value of a particular bottle, a description of grape varietal, tasting notes, etc.

Some research stands the test of time and is useful perpetually, once you have secured it. Other research changes year-to-year and should be subscribed to for a small annual fee. A good example of this would be annual wine reviews for new releases and tasting notes.

What I do for research access and materials may or may not be suitable for you. Just as our taste in wine may differ, our taste in research may differ.

I have about 40 books on wine comprising the topic areas as described in the just-previous section. 25 of them are specifically for research. The others have been read mostly sequentially in their own right and covering a multitude of useful wine topics to help build general knowledge.

I also subscribed to three comprehensive wine review sources. They are:

- Jancis Robinson: especially for Europe
- Robert Parker: especially for the US and Americas
- James Halliday: especially for Australia

This provides comprehensive global coverage including professional reviews and tasting notes, access to blogs and other useful articles. I review a number of free community and amateur tastings notes which are useful, but trust (and am willing to pay for that trust) in the three sources mentioned here. I have subscribed to several other review and tasting databases in the past which I have not renewed because they were poorly constructed and difficult to navigate and they also had major gaps in their coverage. In total, I spend about $250 for these research options. However, based on how you package them, you are often provided with a print or electronic version of their associated magazines and/or annual review books. I used to buy annual review books on wine which were useful, but are no longer necessary by having subscriptions to the databases and other online sources.

I supplement my research books and online database subscriptions by subscribing to one monthly printed wine magazine. (I also receive a second one through Halliday's service based on my subscription package.) This provides good ongoing learning and also provides lists of upcoming events and paid advertisement which keeps me current and reminds me to check out wine product company websites. I do this every couple of months to see how the technology has changed or what new products may be available. While I rarely buy anything, it keeps me current and aware of some things that I may make a decision to buy in the future.

The other key annual subscription I have is for *Wine Searcher Pro*. There is a free version of this application and other similar applications you can obtain. I pay $39 per year for the professional version, as it provides access to all global sources and price information it can find when trawling the Internet to provide you with great competitive information on the value of and what you should pay for wine. It also provides integrated tasting notes, including the professional sources I mentioned that I subscribe to (but only allows you into them if you have the subscription).

The three wine review database subscriptions mentioned above and *Wine Searcher Pro* make up the bulk of my annual spend on research materials and cost me about $300 per year in total. Most everything else is either free or available for a couple of dollars.

One key area of online research material is books that can be bought outright through Amazon or retail bookstores. However, many of these books are very expensive (over $100) and sometimes I only want access to read several pages or a chapter of particular interest. Many of these books can be accessed online through Google Books or other subscription sources for academic books.

You can access Google Books for free and are allowed to read online. You cannot download the books, but you can access and read them for free. This works great if it is only several pages of content you are looking for.

There are several other academic subscription sites you can subscribe to for an annual or monthly fee. These sites cover many different types of books, including wine books. The books can be downloaded in PDF format and read on your laptop, phone or tablet. PDFs can be opened in the Amazon Kindle application or a PDF reader like Adobe Acrobat. I tend not to use these services, even though they could provide great value if you wanted to subscribe for a month and download a great number of relevant books. If you really want a text as reference that you cannot get elsewhere, yet do not want to buy the physical book, then you can subscribe to these sites for several dollars for a 24-hour period to download it.

As mentioned, make sure to respect and follow copyright. For the most part, the sites mentioned are legitimate sites and you can usually tell if a downloaded PDF has been formatted and looks as you would expect the physical copy to look. However, some PDF files, which are easy to identify, are illegitimate copies that have been scanned. These can be easily identified because the pages are off-90° perfect centering, or have handwritten notes in the margin! You should reject obtaining these copies as you are most likely violating copyright.

There are also a number of great research papers specifically on wine that are published on the Internet. Many of these have been associated with different viticulture or oenology schools or wine industry associations.

Another source is YouTube. More and more channels are dedicated to wine-related videos. I had heard great things about the Ah So cork removal device and had received one as a gift. When I finally encountered a bottle with a twenty-year-old soggy and fragile cork, I knew the Ah So was the only cork removal device that had a chance of removing the cork without pushing small cork pieces into the wine. But I did not know how to use the Ah So in practice yet. Three minutes watching a YouTube video took care of that.

I have been surprised by how much is on offer for free on the Internet. Use it and keep using it whenever you need to find out something new.

Note Taking

It is difficult to remember how a wine tasted from several years ago. With practice and more experience, your wine tasting ability will improve and be easier to recall. But most of us do not possess eidetic (photographic) memory.

Taking notes can help increase your memory and databank of wine tasting recollections. Just by writing something down, you remember it better and more permanently. You also have a record to compare how you thought the wine tasted and compare that to other friends and professional tasting notes. You can evaluate if you are picking up on key complexities and nuances of the wine, even years after you have tasted it.

Robinson, in her book *How to Taste Wine*, stresses the importance and one of the easiest ways to learn how to taste wine is by taking notes.[116] This provides a recording of what you like about a wine and helps you balance and gain confidence in what is important in the wine. You are no longer relying on the experts. You want to make sure to take notes so as not to 'waste' the educational value of your wine drinking experience. While you will continue to learn more about wine tasting and appreciation the more you drink, this process is greatly accelerated by note taking. It is easy to do, will only take seconds and pays huge dividends later.

While you may value and trust the judgment of others when it comes to wine tasting, ultimately a wine is only as enjoyable as you perceive it to be. Keeping a record of your own tasting notes provides a basis for requesting certain types of wines in the future. Not only do you know what you like, you will be able to describe that to others who then can recommend and source wines that suit your tastes at an agreeable price point. When tasting at a cellar door, or in a bottle shop, always ask for the winery's tasting notes. I then use them to record my thoughts on the wines I am trying at that point in time. I used to keep a small notebook on hand and in the car so as to be able to record tasting notes about the experience. I now use a smart phone and a note taking app such as Evernote or Notepad to record my thoughts. Additionally, I take a picture of the bottle to ensure I am recording all the information I can. With smartphone technology today, note taking has become far easier.

One challenge is organizing notes so they are useful later. Just writing notes helps cement the content into long-term memory, but the real value comes from being able to access and review them when you need to later. Therefore, I now try to write all notes electronically and if I write them to physical paper, I transfer them when I get the chance into electronic form. I can then easily reorganize them under appropriate headings and with appropriate keywords. For a review of suitable keywords to categorize notes on wine, review *SAZ in the Cellar* website to see what Categories and Tags I have used.

What should you record? For most every tasting, record how you perceived the wine, what tastes you experienced, the vintage, the grapes (sometimes iconic labels change the grapes or blends from vintage to vintage), the winemaker that year, any other pertinent information about that vintage, the cork, etc. I do not follow or restrict myself to a template as a wine judge in a competition would. However, if you have that type of discipline and template, it is a great way to ensure you are rating and recording your notes consistently. I also record what we paid for the wine and if we got any discounts and for what reason.

Many wine inventory and review systems now have the ability for you to integrate your notes and comments with those of others, both the general public and professional rating services such as the three I use. These are relatively easy to set up and use and will be discussed further in *Chapter 19: Tools and Systems for Managing Your Wine Inventory*.

Besides individual wine tasting notes, it is useful to record other things. After most meals, I usually write a few notes on how the wine worked with food and vice versa, especially if I was able to try a couple of different wines with the food. I also record my feelings about drinking wine and what aspects of the experience made it pleasurable or not. This is usually just done sequentially in a journal. At first, I forgot to date stamp these entries, but do so now as it is important sometimes to go back and correlate what other things were happening then and to be able to recognize how tastes change over time.

In terms of the effort expended on note taking and organization, you need to understand why you are doing this. I started note taking for the purpose of being able to understand and remember what I liked about certain types of wine. This meant the approach was a 'write and tuck away' approach. Since I have been blogging and writing more on wine drinking experiences, I have taken a more systematic approach as I find I often need to go back and review previous thoughts on a topic.

In general, I have found that writing things down, even a note or two is useful in improving my wine memory and recall. Having a trove of notes and, especially if linked to other research, can provide an extremely useful base for understanding and enhancing the wine drinking experience.

I sometimes get critical of people who spend most of their time taking photographs to show others that they are living, instead of actually enjoying the experience they are partaking in. I try to avoid that with note taking. I spend most of my time enjoying and appreciating the wine and wine drinking experience. I may send a text to myself to record a thought and then shortly afterward, take time to record more fully what I want to organize for later recall. But taking some notes can be useful in building memory and enhancing wine drinking.

In summary, note taking should be a disciplined exercise for the following reasons:

- It helps you better remember and build a history of what you like and don't like in wine
- It provides information you can use later (such as what vintage for an outstanding wine) to ensure you are making the right purchasing decisions now and in the future
- It provides an understanding and history how your tastes may have changed over time

Vintage Charts

One of the largest variances in wine quality comes from differences in the quality of grapes used. The largest variance in grapes is between seasons due to differences in climatic conditions. Some vintages are completely written off or sold cheaply for use in boxed wine. In other seasons, the vintage is so good, that selected lots are used for special releases as a 'Reserved' wine.

The value and characteristics of a vintage should not be applied globally; in fact, they can vary greatly from region to region and even micro-climate to micro-climate. The 2005 or 2009 Bordeaux vintages are rated as two of the great vintages over the last several decades in Bordeaux, but that does not imply that the 2005 vintage of a wine region in Australia is great. It may be quite the opposite. I saw a photo and email from a friend who exclaimed how great the bottle of 1997 Napa Valley Cabernet Sauvignon was and my first reaction was to shudder, thinking how poorly the Coonawarra (one of the best regions for Cabernet Sauvignon in Australia) Cabernet Sauvignon fared in 1997. But then I remembered the grapes had been grown half-way around the world and it was quite a different set of climatic conditions between the two regions that year.

As mentioned earlier in the book, it is not a good idea to purchase the same wine every year. Its quality can vary greatly year-to-year. By understanding what vintages for what grapes did the best in what years, you can significantly improve the quality of the wine you drink. If you have a choice among several different vintages for a particular wine brand, the simplest thing you can do to improve wine drinking is to determine which vintage is the best and then buy that vintage. Vintage variations in quality differ far more than vintage variations in price upon release. Therefore, it pays handsomely to only buy the best vintages and skip the years in between.

Many good wines sell out first-round retail stock just after they are released. Therefore, you need to get an early understanding of vintage conditions and if it will be a great year or not. In doing so, you should be getting regular weather feeds from various geographies from which you expect you might be buying wine. Follow blogs of the viticulturists and winemakers, and the home page of the wineries from which you are currently thinking of buying. Also, make sure you understand and either participate in the release tasting or pre-release tastings or can get access to reports as this is the first time the vintage's potential is manifested as bottled wine. This is when the ratings and prices are established and the highly valued wines go quickly. You do not need to put much effort into this to form a good idea about what geographies are likely to produce the best grapes that year.

For example, I buy the best examples of Australian Chardonnay either from Margaret River or Hunter Valley; Australian Shiraz from Hunter Valley, several different micro-climates in Victoria, or from Barossa Valley in South Australia. If one of the regions has superior grapes one year, I will only consider buying from that region and skip buying from the others. Or if none of the regions had a great year, I will not buy anything that year and deplete my cellar until another great vintage occurs.

When buying aged wines at auction or on other secondary markets, you have the ability to actually know what a particular vintage tastes like by reviewing tasting notes from a variety of sources. More and more winery websites and industry associations are providing vintage charts to compare all or at least recent vintages year-to-year. These are a great help in understanding and buying the best vintages. The also provide a good guide as to how long you should be cellaring the wine before drinking it.

I cannot over-emphasize the value, especially given the ease and simplicity, of understanding what vintages are better than other vintages. You will buy and drink much better wine once you do.

Wine Courses / Classes

One of the great things about wine drinking is it can be greatly enjoyed by just drinking more wine and gaining a little experience. You can become quite an expert without formal training or certification. There are a number of very short-term (half-day or full-day) training sessions you can take which can quickly accelerate your exposure to and understanding of different wines. They often cost less than $100 for the session, and provide a good way to spend some time among friends and meet others with similar interests. Some segments cover a quick history of wine and how wine is made. But the main focus is on tasting different wines and learning how to evaluate and assess them. This provides a great way to learn about various wine characteristics, which ones are important to you and what you may like or not like in a wine. I have attended two different beginner's courses and enjoyed and learn a lot from both.

There are also self-study programs you can take. One of the best is Kevin Zraly's *Complete Wine Course*. This course has evolved over more than 25 years and provides a great overview of world wines. It also uses QR Codes you can scan with a smart phone application to bring up videos which are used for course segment overviews.

Beginning courses provide a good structure and framework for better understanding wine and getting more from wine. There are some selected and targeted 'master class' sessions you can take which focus on a particular genre or type of wine, be it red, secondary grapes, sparkling or stickies. These usually take several hours and are conducted by someone who has knowledge in that particular field. I find the ones most useful are the ones conducted by a winemaker or sommelier. General sales or marketing staff are usually more prescriptive in delivering the course, whereas winemakers and sommeliers have far deeper knowledge and are more likely to entertain and answer questions.

At this point, the best way to supplement what you learn from reading and attending selected master classes is just to participate in or to host tastings. With several of you participating and learning from each other, and by drinking and sharing your experiences, you will develop an art for wine appreciation very quickly.

Once you have a more cultivated palate and understanding of wine (several years or longer may be necessary to achieve this based on how passionate and diligent you are), you may elect to take an advanced course. However, these are usually targeted for people who plan to work in the wine industry. These courses are more expensive and take a commitment of a week or more to requiring part- or full-time commitment over several months or years.

Beyond an introductory course or two, and possible self-study course, you have the option of taking more courses, but will probably benefit from drinking more, participating in more tastings and reading selective books and other research.

Building an Expert Network

Every industry has its compliment of nice guys and bad apples. But I find more genuinely caring and helpful people in the wine and food industries than any other. It may be the alcohol, but I doubt that is the only factor! I believe there is a natural affinity and alignment in sharing good food and wine with others that extends to people in the industry finding it easy building new friendships. Wine and food people are very approachable.

It is relatively easy to make friends with people in the industry you buy from regularly, especially if you admire and appreciate their product. And sharing a similar passion provides a common point of discourse and companionship. In my case, many of these people have gone from being vendors and service providers to being friends. We continue to meet up and share good meals and wines.

Make it a point to meet and if possible, become friends or at least friendly with those in the industry you do business with. I have found the help of bottle shop owners, cellar door managers, winery event managers, winemakers and viticulturists to be extremely beneficial. They have supplemental knowledge far beyond what we know and can answer questions and provide insights that would otherwise be hidden from us. I am glad and feel fortunate when they take the time during their work to meet with us individually. And it is more treasured when we have the opportunity to spend a meal together. A side benefit of all this is that people in the industry tend to have some of the rarest bottles in their cellars and are glad to bring them out and share over a meal or an evening of conversation when they are with someone they know appreciates good wine!

It is invaluable to befriend winemakers, cellar door managers, sommeliers and others in the industry. They love to discuss their views and can explain why they blended Viognier into Shiraz (to soften it), and provide you inside or backroom experiences not available to others. We have learned much from our wine and food contacts. We also have them attend our dinner parties or wine tastings as they both enjoy it, and we benefit from their insights. There is no better way to learn more than by socializing with people who know more than you do.

Just remember that people in the industry representing a winery or some segment of a wine-related product line will have their own biases. The relationships I covet the most are those in the industry who are completely independent or represent cross-industry concerns. These include wine reviewers, bloggers, and judges.

It is useful to get to know bloggers and other writers in the industry. While there is not any guarantee a blogger is a 'wine expert,' if they are writing on the subject, they probably have some level of wine intellect and enthusiasm. Wine writers in magazines and authors of wine books are more likely to have a level of credible wine knowledge.

After I read a good blog post or good book, I reach out and send an email thanking the author for their contribution. Everyone has always written back. In many cases, they have provided further knowledge or links they thought I might find useful. I have since used many of those contacts to review and provide commentary on how to enhance the integrity, truthfulness and validation of points in this book. I am not certain that I could have written this book, or at least nearly not as well, had I not established and called upon those contacts.

I found the most elite in the industry, such as MWs, and the founders of iconic wine glassware and cellaring devices to be willing to engage in discussion and provide their insights on topics related to wine and improving the wine drinking experience. While I will be providing a substantial amount of links in *Part Four: Where to Next?*, I will not be providing you with the names of the elite contacts that I have made. First it would be a violation of their privacy, and secondly, while I want to help accelerate your attainment of wine knowledge and experience, you cannot short-cut making contacts, let alone friends in the industry. Therefore, it is up to you to reach out to them on your own.

Some suggestions though are in order for how to meet and engage with others in the wine industry. I discussed previously about contacting writers whose work you respect and starting to dialog with them directly. Many can be reached by email just by querying them on the Internet and finding their email, their agents or publishers email, or contacting them directly through their website, blog, Twitter or Facebook page.

Secondly, go to wine events such as Food and Wine shows, industry sponsored events, and regional events which highlight the wines in the area. This allows you to meet a large number of people concurrently and establish good contacts in limited time, as they are gathered together for the events. While visiting wineries, ask to talk to the winemaker. While they may not be on site at that point in time, many are almost always there and are more than willing to talk. To make sure you successfully engage, it is usually good to have tried their wines already and be in a position to compliment or provide constructive feedback; be prepared to ask a question or two to show interest in their product. Ask for their contact information in case you may have any follow-up questions.

The great thing about the Internet and Web 2.0 is how easy it is to connect with others with common interests. I have made about two dozen really good online wine friends based around the world who share a common passion for wine, and am connected with hundreds more. We have used our relationships to exchange some good bottles that were not accessible to the other locally and to share insights into our respective wine geographies, brands and vintages. We have even followed up in some cases with fulfilling specific requests or gaining knowledge that would have been difficult to obtain had our online friendship not existed.

I appreciate the extended network of wine experts I can call on when needed. But ultimately, the easiest group of experts to surround yourself with will likely come from your group of friends or work colleagues. These groups are the most accessible and willing to get together. You have a group of intimates who can mutually support each other, and share with each other. I am constantly asking wine friends for insights and knowledge of wine. It is so easy for wine friends to get together and share common bottles as a point of connection and share ideas while tasting together. Your current friends and colleagues are the quickest and easiest group of 'wine experts' to accumulate, so take advantage of it!

It is useful to have several groups of wine friends who are at different levels of expertise. In some groups, you may be the student; in others, the teacher. Both positions allow you to learn more about wine.

And if you have a group of six to ten of you who all appreciate wine and appreciate each other's company, you should consider the concept of regularly scheduling (quarterly, semi-annually or annually) a 'Last Bottle Dinner." This is where you regularly bring the same, or almost the same, group of people together for a meal and wine. It is meant to be a true gustatory event with four to six courses. I have used three different venues for this and all have been spectacular:

- At-home meal, cooked by us
- At-home meal, cooked by visiting chef
- In restaurant meal with agreed BYO

While the least expensive option is to cook the meal yourself and serve the meal at home, this can be the most difficult and distracting from being able to sit and enjoy the wine and conversation, especially during course-to-course transition. Even with much of the preparation done before-hand, it can still be onerous to serve each course, and clean utensils and dishes throughout the evening.

The other option is to do it in a restaurant and for something like this, your favorite restaurant should be willing to allow you to BYO, even if they are fully licensed. (However, expect to pay a corkage fee.) Then find out who the chef is that evening and either present him with the wine you are bringing and allow him or her to create a meal plan to match the wines, or else agree on a meal plan the chef will make and then determine who will be bringing that great bottle for a particular course. This can be a great evening out for everyone involved without the hassle of having to burden one person or a small team of you to prepare dinner.

The venue I like the best though is to get a chef to come by and cook the meal for us at home. They can usually do this much less expensively than you can in a restaurant as the only thing the chef needs to pay for is their labor and the ingredients. There is no cost for the floor space or corkage either. It is all going into the meal, and the cost per head is usually significantly less than eating out. I also try to do this on an evening when there is no opportunity cost for the chef. For example, if the chef owns a restaurant, I schedule it on the day the restaurant is closed or on one of their slow days when the chief chef is taking a day off.

I also try to find chefs who are 'up-and-coming' with great potential and likely to be the next famous chef. This has allowed me to build strong ongoing relationships by supporting them when they needed and appreciated it. And these chefs have become part of my expert network and group of friends. It has also given me the opportunity to do some consulting for them with regards to building their wine list, what wines to bring along if they are catering a meal for someone else, and to do so in lieu of a couple of free meals!

The wines we bring along are certainly fine and very above average wines. They could be the last or near-to-last bottles of a special wine you want people to share, knowing that this group will savor and enjoy the wine immensely. Even if it is not your last bottle and you still have a decent amount of supply left, it could be a difficult-to-obtain wine that others cannot source. The intent is that each bottle is a unique wine and a treasure to imbibe. The focus is mainly on the wine, but complimented by a great meal and close wine friends. That is why the concept is known as the 'Last Bottle Dinner.'

I have read some real over-the-top stories about last bottle dinners where each participant had to bring a single bottle worth over $2,000, or two bottles worth more than $2,000 in total. Plus each participant had to pay $1,000 for the meal. This type of event is a once in a lifetime type of event, and I hope to be able to participate in one or two at some point in the future. Most people just cannot afford such an extravagance, certainly not on a regular basis. I would rather establish a program of maybe two dinners a year, where we target about $100 per bottle. And if you average about $100 per head for the food, you can have about ten 'Last Bottle Dinners' for the price of the very expensive one I described above!

The 'Last Bottle Dinner' provides a reason for the best of your wine friends to get together regularly and support and learn from each other while having a great time. I have learned as much from these people as I have more iconic figures in the wine industry. Both are important and great to have as contacts.

It is easy to make friends or at least contacts in the wine industry, so be a little extroverted, have something to offer them in return (feedback on product or a compliment and acknowledgment of their work) and you can quickly build a circle of wine friends who can help you enhance your wine drinking experiences.

If possible, find a regular wine group to join or form one yourself. Each month I meet with a group of 25 - 30 other wine enthusiasts, including winemakers, sommeliers, cellar door staff, chefs and others to taste and learn about wine. Each meeting has about a dozen wines to taste, some food to match, and a leader or expert who facilitates the conversation. I learn a lot at each meeting, plus have immediately expanded my network of friends and experts.

Cooking

Great cooks are thought to have a chef's palate. They also tend to have a wine palate, regardless if they know so or not. I have seen several good cooks new to wine be able to discern the grape and region from which the wine came. They were better at it than I was even after a lot of experience. I attributed that to them being "super tasters,' those who have on average about 25% more taste buds and the ability to sense taste characteristics such as sweetness, bitterness, etc., more easily than normal tasters.

But I now realize that this was not likely the case. While they may or may not have a chef's palate, what they did have was a lot of experience and knowledge cooking. The experience they gained cooking is what gave them the ability to appreciate and discern much more about wine flavors and mouthfeel.

I avoided cooking most of my life except for the simplest things such as a grilled cheese sandwich or bacon and eggs for breakfast. I liked the convenience of being served by others. I felt I had more intellectual activities and other pleasures to pursue. I certainly enjoyed eating and the pleasure that great food provided and was willing to pay for it being prepared for me.

My wife decided to take a course of six cooking lessons about four years ago. It changed our lives in many ways. For starters, we were more comfortable preparing dinners and having people come over. This provided us with more social occasions and also saved us a great deal of money when compared to eating in restaurants. We still enjoy the occasional meal out, but cook much, much more at home these days. And I noticed that my wife's ability to taste and discern wine characteristics had improved with the process. But I attributed that to her being another super taster, and was jealous because I was not.

My wife's cooking provided me the ability to focus and learn more about matching wines to the food she was making. This provided a focus and reason for thinking the wine and food matching through in more detail. When going out to eat, I would bring along a white and a red wine and guessing that more people would eat beef or pork or lamb, and based on what my wine mood was that evening, I would select one red over another. However, based on food selections, the wine may have worked well, or not so well. And if it was a non-BYO restaurant, I would often ask the sommelier to recommend a wine. Therefore, when dining out, I did not have reason to think through matching food and wine. But when my wife started cooking and I knew what the menu was going to be for the evening, I could plan and select a wine I knew would work well.

I would think about if a certain style of wine provided better mouthfeel for the food we would be having. I thought more about if I wanted a fruity or spicy Shiraz based on the seasonings being used. And knowing there would be significant mushrooms being used in a cream sauce, I would consider using an aged white wine instead of a red wine to go with beef. My skills in matching food and wine improved because I was thinking more and putting more effort into my wine selections. She became the food gal and me the wine guy!

Then about a year after my wife took cooking lessons, my father had a massive stroke and was in critical care for a month, then transitional care and finally and fortunately made it home again after about four months. My father had to be retaught life's simplest activities. He had to relearn putting on a shirt, brushing his teeth and hair, and getting a fork or spoon of food to his mouth. By watching my father go through therapy, I gained a real appreciation for the very simple pleasures in life, those activities that make up most of our existence.

I started to appreciate and relish doing basic chores and embracing life by cleaning, shopping, and doing all sorts of daily errands. The activities were no longer viewed as being in the way of doing other things – they became the activities and pleasure of life itself. I then decided to take cooking lessons also, while my wife continued to take more advanced lessons. In the last four years, she has taken around twenty lessons and I have taken ten over the last three years.

My initial time in the kitchen was spent mainly helping my wife with my increased knife skills, by peeling, slicing and dicing vegetables. Once she realized I was capable of helping without making things worse, I started to mince garlic and measure and add seasonings and prepare stock. This was extremely useful for me as I was now starting to identify and be able to pick out many different smells. I knew what basil, mint, saffron, and lemon really smelled like and how much was required to provide mild or more intense smells and tastes. I even became familiar and could tell the difference and why and when you would use mild paprika versus smoked paprika.

As I gained confidence, I took over the cooking of full meals. I made soups with a lot of different ingredients, pastas and then some fish and meat dishes. There was joy in cooking for oneself and cooking and sharing with others. Very few things are more fundamental to life and life's enjoyment. Cooking was an eye opening experience for me.

As I cooked more and more meals, I learned when it was acceptable to use a little more or less of a seasoning, and when it was ok to skip or substitute one ingredient for another. I could foretell what the difference would be to the smell and taste. I also was able to discern why a slightly different style or regional variety of wine would work better with the meal I was preparing. My ability to smell and taste had improved greatly and my wine choices with meals reflected that.

Through cooking, I became much better at tasting wine and matching wine to food. My initial ten lessons helped remove the intimidation when shopping for ingredients and when preparing a meal. The lessons showed me that anyone could learn to cook. But it was my growing experience actually shopping, and preparing meals that really improved my cooking. What I soon found out was how much it improved my overall ability to smell and taste and how that would greatly help me with being able to appreciate and drink wine.

It was not that some limited number of blessed people had a super tasting ability or chef's palate. Mostly, chefs developed and improved their natural and normal capabilities through the cooking experience. This should be good news to everyone as it shows that almost all of us (unless we have some severe smelling or tasting impediment or sensitivity) can significantly improve our wine appreciation and discernment through practice and experience. And by taking up and doing some basic cooking, you can increase your abilities even further.

I am certain you will much more greatly enjoy wine drinking if you learn how to cook and do some basic cooking. My abilities to smell and taste have increased more significantly in the last several years than in the previous fifteen because of cooking. The same will happen with you, I expect.

There is a negative side of this though. My nose is more trained and sensitive to all smells, good or bad. Therefore, I am also picking up street smells that I have never noticed before, including dog droppings, decomposing garbage, etc. It is forcing me to pay more attention to the streets I walk and to avoid some that I had not thought were too bad before!

Notes

111. Todd, *Philosophy of Wine*, 12.
112. Korsmeyer, "The Meaning of Taste and the Taste of Meaning," chap. 3.
113. Todd, *Philosophy of Wine*, 34.
114. Smith, "The Objectivity of Tastes and Tasting," 44.
115. Goode, "Wine and the Brain," 87-89.
116. Robinson, *How To Taste Wine*, 77.

Part Four
Where to Next?

Hopefully you now have a better idea of how to improve your wine drinking experiences and have put some of that knowledge and experience to good use.

However, if you want to continue to deepen your knowledge and appreciation of wine (and I hope many of you do because it validates my own wine journey!), this part of the book provides direction on how to pursue that.

The ideas can be applied immediately or you can come back to them in the future after a concentrated effort on gaining wine drinking experience as outlined previously in the book.

Chapter 19
Tools & Systems for Managing Wine Inventory

Wine is an asset that is likely to increase over time, for a period of time. But sooner or later, it will decrease in value, ultimately becoming worthless. If you have less than 100 bottles in your cellar, this is not a big deal. You can easily review and stay on top of inventory, and understand what wines should be drunk immediately and which ones can lie down longer.

I lost control of this (or never really had control of it while building the cellar) with negative effect:

- Too many wines fell past due in terms of optimum drinking, and I had to throw about 60 bottles ($2,000 worth) out and have another 50 - 100 bottles at risk of being at or past end of life
- I had accumulated too much of a particular wine type which I am no longer as interested in drinking
- I feel pressured to drink wines that may be past due or close to past due, even though I am desiring a different bottle

In general having a large cellar became a burden instead of a pleasure. I should have taken action much sooner and updated inventory every time I bought or drank a bottle. I soon had too many boxes of wine and it was burdensome to move them around every time I wanted to get to a particular bottle. Therefore, I increased the size of my cellar and then added a second cellar. My cellaring costs on their own become unmanageable!

I finally organized my cellar and built a database (in Microsoft Excel) to inventory everything I owned. I was shocked and dismayed to realize that I had almost 4,000 bottles. Also, I had a lot of bottles of wine which were unlikely to be worthy of drink. Fortunately, since I was buying fine wine and wine that was built to last, things were not as bad as they could have been. Still, I have disposed of about 60 bad bottles and have another 50 – 100 bottles that may be in doubt. By inventorying and realizing that now, I have been able to work through many of those bottles, some very drinkable and others not. I also have been able to sell down my cellar and now have a total inventory of 1,600 bottles instead of 4,000. You can find out more on selling off your wine in *Chapter 17: Buying and Storing Wine*.

My Microsoft Excel spreadsheet is moderately sophisticated and has a definition for everything required for understanding and managing when to consume wine. I have included some guidelines for building your own database and a copy of the Sheet and Field listings in *Appendix B: Wine Database Format and Field Listing*.

Your system may be as simple as keeping a log of when you bought the wine, what price you paid for it, and any tasting notes associated with the wine if you have tried it. Or it could be a simplified version of the one I use. But one way or another, you should have some idea of how many bottles are in your cellar and in what time period they should be drunk. Then you can determine if you have too many or not enough and adjust your cellar accordingly.

I like an organized system for tasting notes, so keeping detailed information about my wine and my reaction to it is an important part of my system. Yet, having to enter 'standard' information in terms of brands, vintage, grape varietal, etc. is a necessary component of building your own database. There are now available smartphone and tablet applications which allow you to take a picture of a wine label and through wine label recognition, provide you details and other information, including rankings and where to buy wine. However, most of these applications are not tightly integrated into other systems, so I required a lot of data entry into my systems which I wish I could have avoided.

Wine research databases like the three I subscribe to require a good database structure for their basic intent and operation. The Halliday Wine Companion subscription provides the ability to create a cellar inventory, and if they have reviewed the wine, then they will add the information in terms of the type of grape, region, tasting notes and by when it should be drunk. I can then add my own tasting notes to that. This approach saves on having to enter information already obtained from the winery and rating service.

The negative aspects of this are two-fold: It only provides one rating service opinion unless you enter your own tasting notes. And if you no longer wish to use the service, you lose your database, or would need to figure out a way to work with the rating service to extract and reformat the database you have built which has been under their control to get it back under your control. Additionally, no one service will cover all the wines you are likely to have in you cellar.

I believe the best wine inventory and rating system is an open-ended one called Cellar Tracker. Cellar Tracker is a true community system and provides multiple community tasting notes from all over the world. It also provides links and will activate access to the paid wine research and rating systems I subscribe to in addition to many others. Therefore, you are able to combine an expansive set of tasting notes, including your own (which then become part of the broader community and for others to see). It is the best social media site for wine lovers who want to communicate and learn what others have to say.

Started only several years ago by Eric Levine, an ex-Microsoft program manager, and as a system to track his own wine, by early 2013, Cellar Tracker had 250,000 users, nearly 40 million individual bottle entries, and nearly 3.6 million wine reviews from across the globe. It is used by many restaurants to track their wine in support of high-end restaurant operations that take their wine seriously. Another measure of success is that for the last several years, Levine has been ascending the various lists of most influential people in the wine industry globally.

Cellar Tracker charges a reasonable annual subscription based on the number of bottles you have or are planning to have in inventory. And by subscribing to other services into which Cellar Tracker integrates, you can build a very comprehensive and easy to manage wine inventory and management system.

If you are buying wine as an investment, for a restaurant or to possibly on-sell later, having a system like the one I developed or using Cellar Tracker makes a great deal of sense and is worth the investment of time. But if your cellar is only a couple of hundred bottles and you are content with having access to wine tasting notes as you need them, then you do not require a formal wine inventory and management system. Just make sure to keep a handle on what wine should be drunk first and put them in front of the other ones in your cellar.

Chapter 20
Further Wine Education

Much information progressing wine education has already been covered in *Chapter 18: Wine Drinking Practice and Experience*. A plan which comprises two-thirds to three-quarters drinking experience supplemented by one-quarter to one-third cognitive learning through reading, research and other training is, in my opinion, a good approach to most quickly and effectively improve your ability to better appreciate wine.

This chapter identifies specific opportunities to continue your wine education beyond this book and into the future. It identifies opportunities in the following areas:

- Wine books
- Research Subscriptions
- Wine Magazines
- Wine Movies
- Guided Gustatory Tours
- More Advanced Wine Training
- Court of Master Sommeliers (MS)
- Master of Wine (MW)

- Winemaking
- Working in the Wine Industry

The ideas and direct sources for books, coursework and research presented in this chapter are not comprehensive. They represent ideas that have worked for me or ideas validated by other wine enthusiasts. They help you explore and focus your investment of time more effectively. However, it is up to you to continue to tailor what resources you use to enhance your wine drinking experience.

We have already discussed an overview of the categories of wine books you may elect to read and why. We have also presented ideas around half-day or full-day courses in which to participate, such as a wine / chocolate master class, a glassware master class, and an introduction to tasting course. These types of events are fun social events in addition to adding to your wine knowledge and drinking experiences. Since this book is intended for a global audience, I will not be recommending or describing specific wine courses or events as they vary by geography. An overview of such events and how to find them has been presented in *Chapter 18: Wine Drinking Practice and Experience.*

I will offer and describe a list of wine books (since books can be ordered and delivered anywhere in the world) I recommend from which I believe you can learn and benefit most quickly. These books are suitable no matter where you live or the type of wine you drink. Some are more specific or flavored by the geography where the author resides. In those cases, I make note and recommend you may want to look for a similar book, but one more suited to the part of the world in which you reside.

Beyond experiencing and learning from actual wine drinking, I find reading or taking courses to be the best methods for learning more about any topic, including wine. Reading or taking a self-study wine course provides great foundation for wine appreciation. However, it is through interacting with other people, especially experts in the field that you learn the most of relevance for you. Therefore, after the following section on books, I present other fun and more expansive ideas for furthering your wine education and enjoyment.

Wine Books

I am making the assumption that almost everyone who is reading this book has access to the Internet on a regular basis, and can continue to educate themselves without having to build a library of wine books. While I have purchased approximately forty wine books which populate a couple of shelves in my library, I also have a number of electronic books on wine and many free articles which populate my electronic reading devices in Kindle MOBI or PDF format and sit in my Kindle applications or Dropbox.

As required for writing this book and satisfying my thirst for wine drinking, I have over 200 wine books or other articles at my disposal, and there are many more I know I can pull instantly from the Internet as required when I need to dive deeply into a specific topic. I have curated links for future reference, and my recommendation is to drink more and read less, but to read enough to supplement and enhance your knowledge. Using technology today to identify and organize books and other research, you can do this effectively while spending minimal time doing so. To help you, I am sharing my experiences to provide an initial filter on what to read, and in what order so you can get the most out of your reading efforts. You are also provided with a broader set of materials for later use, as needed.

A complete list of books reviewed and referenced in this book is presented in the Bibliography. One technique I used to help me navigate and effectively find more related books on a specific topic of interest is to review the bibliographies of the books I had read and really enjoyed. This helped identify other great books written earlier or supplementary research materials to provide deeper learnings.

As with all learning, it is important to start right and provide a solid foundation. Hopefully, the following recommendations will help you quickly build that foundation. Here are the books I recommend:

Books on wine tasting / wine drinking:

<u>How to Taste Wine</u> (Jancis Robinson): This book, written by one of the wine industry's 'best' is a great first read on learning how to taste and appreciate different wine types. The book provides exercises to help you learn quickly. A recommended must read for beginners enthusiastic to learn more about tasting.

The Taste of Wine: The Art and Science of Wine Appreciation (Emile Peynaud): Peynaud was one of the world's best winemakers and wine instructors. He is known as the "wine expert's expert" and was awarded Winemaker of the Century. This is a great follow-on book to my book if you are 'thirsting' for more on how to taste. Peynaud's book explores deeply and scientifically how wine interacts with the senses, how to taste wine and how to teach wine tasting and wine judging. An absolute 'must-read' if you are willing to put in the effort to gain this level of knowledge. This text was written and translated to English in the mid-1980s, but still relevant today and a true foundational text on wine tasting. If you are only going to read one more book on wine tasting, this would be it.

Wines: Their Sensory Evaluation (Maynard Amerine and Edward Roessler): Written in the mid-1970s, by two prolific wine experts, this text is considered a classic. It focuses on the scientifically-based contents of wine and is supported by numerous detailed, quantifiable studies and statistical tables. The book provides a scientific and dispassionate approach to tasting and judging wine. Part 1 provides an overview of the sensory evaluation of wine, while Part 2 becomes quite scientific. I suggest this book if you want to become a wine judge or be able to scientifically support your wine assessments. It fills some holes, but is redundant to Peynaud's book in terms of the wine sensory criticism and appreciation. While slightly dated in terms of research and selected view points, it is still an excellent textbook on wine tasting, especially from a judge's viewpoint. This book was far ahead of its time when published, and still plays a critical role in the history of wine education.

Kevin Zraly's Complete Wine Course (Kevin Zraly): This book / self-study course has evolved over thirty years. In addition to advice on improving wine tasting, it also provides a good global overview of wine regions and the characteristics of the region's classic wines. Good self-study course on wine and wine tasting.

Jancis Robinson's Wine Course (Jancis Robinson): Another great overview on wine tasting, how to improve your wine tasting experience, and covering wines from various regions around the world. Robinson also has a 2-DVD version of the course if you would rather watch than read on the subject of wine appreciation.

[Note: There are multiple editions of both Zraly's and Robinson's courses, so be careful to either get the current version, or you can get an older version for much less money which may be almost as good. Both of these courses have evolved substantially over time, so I would recommend going with the current edition.]

<u>Essential Winetasting: the complete practical winetasting course</u> (Michael Schuster): This book / course is similar, but simpler and less comprehensive than Zraly's or Robinson's. If you have limited time and require quick uptake, this is a good first self-study course to take; then later you can take one by Zraly or Robinson.

Varietals / types of grapes used in wine making:

I place this category of wine books high on the learning curve for wine appreciation. To learn how to taste wine and distinguish a wine's characteristics, you need to start by understanding the type of grape (or blend of grapes) used in wine. The grape and its quality and unique characteristics have more impact on overall wine quality than any other factor. When wine starts from great grapes, the winemaker only needs to guide the self-creation of the wine with no or little interference. This is one of the main factors that distinguish a great wine from a good wine. Therefore, early on in your wine drinking days, you should have a good overview of wine varietals and the different names they go by in each country.

Jancis Robinson's book, *How to Taste Wine*, provides a useful overview of the major white and red grapes, and is a good place to start, but there are many other great varietals used in winemaking and you should understand these varietals and their characteristics.

<u>Wine Grapes: A Complete Guide to 1,368 Vine Varieties, Including Their Origins and Flavours</u> (Jancis Robinson): This is an extremely comprehensive book on varietals, including cross-references by regions, countries of origin, and temperature range charts for grape growing. This book provides information on far more grape types than any other book in this category. The book is expensive, but worth it for someone who loves to experiment and drink a wide variety of wines. While the

content is magnificent, there have been some complaints about the physical size of the book and the quality of production for such an expensive book. Unless you want the ultimate encyclopedia of wine grapes, you might be better off with one of the smaller, less expensive guides listed in the remainder of this book category.

Grapes & Wines: A Comprehensive Guide to Varieties and Flavours (Oz Clarke & Margaret Rand): This is a comprehensive book on major and minor grape varietals, covering all regions of the world. It presents a difficult and detailed subject in a well-organized manner that is easy to read or to lookup when required to find the answer to a specific question. It discusses regions and their terroir, vine health and other factors that influence grape quality. This book is a must-read, or minimally, a must-have when you need to research specific varietals.

Varietal Wine (James Halliday): This is another good book on wine varietals, covering 80 major grape types and sub-varieties. It is very well organized and presents a cross-reference of grape names as they are used around the world. The book is of most use for those living in and drinking Australian and New Zealand wines, as it covers the grapes' geographic origins and then presents its history and growing regions in Australia and New Zealand. However, the book is certainly of use to wine lovers across the globe.

I would minimally buy one of the three above-mentioned books on grape varietals. However, if you would rather spend the money on a bottle of wine instead of a book describing the different types of grapes and their characteristics, this is a subject area where the Internet provides significant information. There are some useful, if not comprehensive, overviews of grape varieties you can get for free from the Internet. And whenever you need to know more about a grape type, you can search online. However, this approach is more reactive and will take longer to learn about the various varieties of grapes. Therefore, I think it is worthwhile to have at least one book on grape varieties in your library.

Books on philosophy of wine, wine appreciation and wine aesthetics:

Questions of Taste: The Philosophy of Wine (Barry Smith): This group of ten essays brought together and edited by Smith were originally prepared and presented at the first ever conference on philosophy and wine presented in December, 2004. Covering a variety of inter-related wine topics, the book provides a great first overview on the role of wine in life and why we enjoy it so much. Additionally, most chapters provide a list of further references which are highly useful. If you are limited in time to read one book on the topic of wine and philosophy, this should be it.

The Philosophy of Wine: A Case of Truth, Beauty and Intoxication (Cain Todd): A very good text on understanding the role of wine in our life and why it should be appreciated. While heavy on philosophy, it presents a clear view on objectivity versus subjectivity when it comes to wine criticism and provides a framework for being able to evaluate wine and describe it in a systematic manner, explaining why a wine is evaluated the way it is. It also provides a synopsis of wine aesthetics versus wine as a sensory pleasure. This book is a great overall read and highly recommended if you enjoy philosophy in addition to enjoying wine.

I Drink, Therefore I am: A Philosopher's Guide to Wine (Roger Scruton): Scruton is a great philosopher and writer who is also an experienced wine enthusiast. This book is an easy, enjoyable read using Scruton's journey and evolvement as a wine drinker to explain interesting concepts in wine appreciation. In the second part of the book, he becomes more philosophical and provides a framework on evaluating wine and discusses if wine criticism is realistic or perceived. Finally, in the Appendix, he presents ideas on what wine to drink when reading well-known philosophers! Many other books match wine with cheese, chocolate and other foods, but only Scruton would dare to match wines to philosophers!

Wine Style: Using Your Senses to Explore and Enjoy Wine (Mary Ewing-Mulligan and Ed McCarthy): Ewing-Mulligan and McCarthy are the writers of a series of *Wine for Dummies* books. Their book, *Wine Style*, focuses on the various wine styles that exist and the intention winemakers have in making particular wines. It covers different styles of red, white, sparkling and other wines to help explain why we may or may not enjoy light versus full-bodied wine, soft or firm texture mouthfeel, light or heavy tannins, and so on. While you will naturally be able to distinguish what style of wine you enjoy drinking, this book can help you to better understand why and be able to articulate that with others.

Wine and Philosophy: A symposium on Thinking and Drinking (Fritz Allhoff): There are several good contributors to this edited volume. However, I would recommend each of the above four books before this one (in the order presented). This book provides several useful insights, but they become redundant to the context provided in the books above and this book on its own does not justify reading if you have read several of the others first. I was not thinking of providing mention to this book, but felt required to do so, as this is the first book I bought and read on wine and philosophy as I was attracted to the title and table of contents which looked relevant to my interests. While I did not feel misled, I was disappointed after investing the time in this book and then having read each of the four listed above. I do not recommend this book when compared to the ones described above in this reading category.

Approach to Aesthetics: Collected Papers on Philosophical Aesthetics (Frank Sibley): In this great collection of philosophical essays, Sibley covers art and aesthetic appreciation and extends his thinking on how food and wine and other gustatory pursuits are viewed as art forms and aesthetically. Sibley was one of the first to really pursue and treat this field in modern times.

Making Sense of Taste: Food and Philosophy (Carolyn Korsmeyer): A brilliant treatise on the human senses and how they have been valued throughout history. If you want to expand on the material presented in *Chapter 3: Philosophy of Wine and Primary and Secondary Senses* and *Chapter 4: Wine as an Aesthetic Experience*, then you will enjoy reading this book. This book provides an in-depth query of food and wine as an aesthetic experience.

Arguing About Art: Contemporary Philosophical Debates (Edited by Alex

Neil and Aaron Ridley): A collection of essays about art as an aesthetic experience and gustatory pursuits as art and an aesthetic experience. Great essays from Korsmeyer and Telfer on food as art and an aesthetic experience are included.

There are several other books on the subjects and also related research papers. But I would start with *Questions of Taste: The Philosophy of Wine* and go from there if you desire further reading on the subject.

Comprehensive wine overviews and atlas:

<u>Wine</u> (Andre Domine): This text provides 150 pages on a variety of wine topics followed by the rest of the book being an atlas of various wine regions and winery descriptions. It makes a magnificent coffee table book in addition to being a reference book. It is a physically large book, but beautifully presented and relatively inexpensive for what this book has to offer. This is one of the few atlases that cover a reasonable amount of overview about wine in addition to being an atlas.

<u>The World Atlas of Wine</u> (Hugh Johnson & Jancis Robinson): This may be the most popular wine atlas of all time, now reaching its 7th edition. Initially a work by Johnson, it became a voluminous effort and Robinson pitched in to help, and now Robinson has taken over the updating on her own with Johnson stepping back. Similar to *Wine* by Domine, this is primarily an atlas, but has about 50 pages of information covering an overview of wine. It is less voluminous than *Wine*, but still a large book. It also is beautifully presented and can be used as a coffee table book in addition to being a good reference book.

Either or both of these books are highly recommended. While they become slightly out of date over time, they provide a great overview of the world's wine region and major wineries. There are also a number of regional wine atlases covering important wine growing regions such as Bordeaux, Burgundy, Napa Valley, Australia and New Zealand. Many of these exist and comprise different sized geographies, often overlapping each other. These books become dated much more quickly (as a higher percentage of the wineries come and go more quickly than the major world renown wineries), and often cost as much or more than the two global atlases by Domine and Johnson / Robinson.

I have previously spent several hundred dollars on about five of these regional atlases, but now consider that to have been a waste of money. While being comprehensive for the region and beautiful books on their own, I found limited need to review them. However, if you plan on visiting a wine region to taste and study the wines of that region, it may make sense to buy a book on the region beforehand to help you prepare and get the most out of your trip.

I have also found it increasingly easy to find the information I need through my research subscriptions (which are currently updated for my annual subscription cost) and by querying the Internet more broadly. Therefore, I do not recommend buying regional wine atlases unless you really feel the need to have a comprehensive wine library or definite plans to visit those regions.

Wine encyclopedias / dictionaries:

The Oxford Companion to Wine (Jancis Robinson): As one of the wine industry's most noted experts and a prolific and highly competent writer, nobody is more qualified to provide a wine encyclopedia than Robinson. This book is stunningly comprehensive and beautifully presented. I suggest most people should have a wine encyclopedia in their wine library and this is one to consider.

The Australian Wine Encyclopedia (James Halliday): An excellent localized encyclopedia for wine lovers in Australia and New Zealand. This is a great supplement and possible replacement for Robinson's encyclopedia, but only if you live in Australia. I only recommend this text for those living in Australia or who have a strong interest in Australian wine.

In one sense, there is no need to have a wine encyclopedia at all. With Wikipedia being free and having the Internet available for accessing online dictionaries, you can find descriptions for anything you want. However, Wikipedia and other dictionaries were not written by wine experts. Additionally, I like having a dictionary at my side, not just to reference when required, but as a book to read serendipitously to learn more about general wine topics. At the end of the day and while enjoying a glass of good wine, I sometimes pick up Robinson's or Halliday's encyclopedias and browse them to learn more. I have been introduced to some interesting wine topics doing that.

There are several other global wine encyclopedias and a number of regionalized encyclopedias. There are also a number of small, more concise wine dictionaries; some specialized to wine tasting language. While useful, there is much overlap between them. Unless there is a specific focused topic you wish to explore in depth, I would pass on the rest of these encyclopedias (other than Robinson's and possibly Halliday's as analyzed above).

Wine making / science:

<u>Wine Science: Principles and Applications</u> (Ronald Jackson): It is a disservice to this book to put it into any individual category, as this could be the most comprehensive guide to vineyard management, winemaking and wine tasting ever produced. It could be the largest wine book ever at 750 pages that does not include wine atlas information and listings! The book provides significant and detailed background and research on every aspect of wine production that impacts a wine's quality. This background provides a stronger cognitive understanding of what makes fine wine and will help you identify and assess wine characteristics and quality. There is also an excellent chapter on Sensory Perception and Wine Assessment which goes into much more scientific detail than I have presented in this book. I reference these materials to provide what I believe is an adequate overview, but if you want more detailed information, then you should read *Chapter 11* in *Wine Science*. This book is expensive, but provides a tremendous amount of information and is considered a classic.

<u>Making Good Wine: A Manual of Winemaking Practice for Australia and New Zealand</u> (Bryce Rankine): This book is a true classic and prerequisite for anyone who is considering taking up winemaking. The book is a Do-It-Yourself manual on winemaking. While detailed and scientific, it is articulately written and easy to understand. However, some previous knowledge of wine and winemaking would help the reader along the way.

You do not need to understand how wine is made to enjoy

Further Wine Education

tasting it. However, it does provide a significant increase in cognitive knowledge to help you improve your tasting and appreciation for fine wines. While you do not need to understand every aspect unless you plan on becoming a grape grower or winemaker yourself, some understanding is useful. Therefore, I would recommend both of these books, or that you query and find some summary articles on the Internet to provide a cursory overview of winemaking.

Wine history:

Good overviews of wine history are presented in the comprehensive wine overviews mentioned above. If you own one of these books, you are provided with a good summary view. However, if you are interested in more specific and deeper views of wine history and culture, there exist several great books on the topic.

Wine history books will not necessary teach you anything on wine tasting and appreciation directly, but they do provide a cultural and lifestyle context, which can enthuse and excite, making wine drinking more pleasurable. And if you feel uncomfortable describing and sharing your thoughts on wine tasting, these books provide some interesting stories about wine drinking that you can share instead!

<u>Gods Men and Wine</u> (William Younger): If there is a better book on wine history and culture, I am not aware of it. This is an exceptional read – a real treasure! It was published in 1966, but then ancient wine history has not changed much in the last 50 years! As far as I am aware, this book is out of print, but you can find a used copy (and a few new copies at considerably higher prices) through used books on Amazon and other online book sites. That is the way I secured my copy and at a reasonable price. This book describes in some depth how wine was such an important part of various cultures. If you love history and love wine, you will love this book!

<u>Wine: A Cultural History</u> (John Variano): This is another popular book on wine history and culture. It provides a different perspective and view on the importance of various regions and their role and influence in the global wine world. It also provides beautiful photo plates that make the concepts in the book visual.

Divine Vintage: Following the Wine Trail from Genesis to the Modern Age (Randall Heskett & Joel Butler): This is a fascinating and unique text which follows the history of wine through the Christian Bible, and the influence wine had of Biblical proportions. It is deeply researched and if you like Christian History or theology and wine, you should find this an interesting read. The second part of the book provides an atlas of current wineries which are on Biblical lands which existed at the very beginning of the ancient wine history. This book is not for everyone, but for those interested in both religion and wine, you will be reading a truly unique book!

Wine lifestyle:

Making Sense of Wine (Matt Kramer): This book is an enjoyable read and covers many aspects of wine drinking and how to achieve pleasure through drinking wine. Good overall, 'feel good' book on wine appreciation and lifestyle.

The Red Wine Diet (Roger Corder): *The Red Wine Diet* credibly explains the health benefits of red wine. It shows how to use appropriate amounts of red wine to provide an increase in antioxidants and lower hypertension to improve overall health. It goes further and provides healthy food recipes into an overall lifestyle plan of which wine and particularly red wine are an integrated component of that healthy lifestyle. I found this book useful, if a bit detailed in the science, but it is the explanation of the science that makes it credible. Minimally, this book reduced guilt associated with drinking wine almost every day and has encouraged me to continue to enjoy wine as part of a healthy lifestyle.

Age Gets Better With Wine: New Science for a Healthier, Better & Longer Life (Richard Baxter, MD): This text is similar to *The Red Wine Diet*, but easier to read. It focuses less on the scientific understanding of 'why' to follow the diet and focuses more on 'how' to follow the diet. However, it is still credible.

Either one of these wine diet books is a great read. Since it involves your health and your passion for wine, I recommend reading both as they provide somewhat different perspectives, and the combination of both books provides a number of useful tips, some which may work best for your situation.

Thomas Jefferson on Wine (John Hailman): A personal journal and review of Jefferson's wine experience during his travels to Europe and his personal taste in wine and food. Jefferson had exquisite taste in fine wines and a very nice collection privately and for the White House. He was an American who was truly a global wine expert.

Passions: The Wines and Travels of Thomas Jefferson (James Gabler): Another book on Jefferson and his love of fine wine as experienced through his wine travels across Europe.

Notes on a Cellar Door (George Saintsbury): This is an interesting book of notes and reflection on Saintsbury's cellar and its composition. He wrote this as a consumer and enthusiast for fine wine. While it refers to inaccessible wines from the early- and mid-19th century, the book expresses an understanding and love for drinking wine and is an enjoyable read.

Food and wine matching:

There exists thousands of books on food and wine matching. Most of these books provide a short overview (similar to what is presented in this book) on how and why food and wine matching works and is worth understanding and pursuing. The books will likely present some summary guidelines on 'rules' to follow when matching a suitable wine to food.

There are also numerous articles and blogs available that provide reviews on what wine worked well with what food. The books, blogs and articles can provide some insight into good combinations of food and wine. They also can provide an understanding of why one combination works better than another.

However, there is no substitute for experience, especially in this area of wine appreciation. I use wine and food matching books as references, not as textbooks to deepen my understanding. Many of these books are written by 'foodies' and in my opinion, provide decent, but not optimal pairings. However, some of the best 'foodies' also have a passion for wine, and are capable of doing a better job matching wines. But the combination of finding someone who is a good writer, and knows both their food and their wine is rare.

Having said that, there are a number of good books available and if you are willing to consider the recommendations in the books as a starting point to be supplemented by your experimentation and experience, they can be very useful.

Blogs will vary in quality on this topic. I have written frequently on matching wine to food in my blog *SAZ in the Cellar*. In every case, I present why or why not the wine worked in my opinion. I also try to get the input of others in the field if I can, and accept feedback / criticism on my selections. Further, I link my description of the wine post to my wife's blog *DAZ in the Kitchen* to provide the recipe for the food. This provides the reader with the ability to understand and either agree or question my selections. I have usually tried several different wines with food and vary the combinations to provide comparisons which can be evaluated. I put several hours into these posts plus the time it takes to prepare and consume the food and wine.

Many blog writers are quite prolific, but write what's on their mind without further research or validation of what they are writing. They are sharing experiences which may be useful. However, I have read a number of wine blogs or independent articles published over the Internet which are naïve, if not downright wrong, when it comes to food and wine matching. Therefore, while there is a plethora of sources available, you should be selective and as you gain more experience, you will be able to tell right from wrong, and insight from nonsense (which is probably a better choice of words as there is no absolute right or wrong when it comes to tasting).

Having only purchased and reviewed several books (out of the thousands of books available) on matching wine to food, it would be unfair of me to make any recommendations of the books in general on the topic. You can look online and start by searching for 'food and wine pairing' on the Internet or through Amazon and come up with more responses than you will be able to consume. The listings provide wine and food wheels and books in the 'Dummies' and 'Idiots'' range of books (yes, the book *Pairing Food and Wine for Dummies* does exist!) to specialty books focusing on specific food groups and types of wine. It would be difficult for me to recommend general books on the topic as individual interests differ, but you can easily find several that should be suitable.

However, I do want to provide some references for specialty books as these are more often than not a more difficult category of food or wine to create optimal pairings. These are not the only books

Further Wine Education

on the topic, but are ones that I have reviewed and am comfortable to highly recommend.

Asian Palate (Jeannie Cho Lee MW): Thirty years ago in a Chinese restaurant in Singapore, I was challenged to pick out a couple of bottles of good wine to go with our meal. Having limited knowledge of either Chinese food or wines to match, I guessed on a couple of bottles based on the grapes involved and my memory of Chinese flavors. But wines that match well with oyster sauce, chili, soy sauce, Chinese vegetables, are difficult at best! The great thing about Asian food is that the spices are more dominant than the main ingredients such as pork, chicken, prawns, beef, tofu, etc. This is what makes selecting wines to match Asian food so difficult. *Asian Palate* provides a great overview and list of suggestions to help. Jeannie Cho Lee is the first Asian to be awarded the prestigious Master of Wine (MW) certification. She is also one of the few females to be honored as an MW. Asian Palate won out against 6,000 other food and wine pairing books submitted from 136 different countries to be selected as the *Gourmand Award's Best Food and Wine Pairing book in the World* in 2009. While expensive at about $100 for the book, Asian Palate really helps solve the mystery of what wines to serve with Asian food. It is also a beautiful picture book and makes a unique and beautiful gift for the wine lover who has almost everything else!

Williams-Sonoma Wine & Food: A New Look at Flavor (Joshua Wesson): Most food and wine pairing books start with the premise of what we will be eating and then recommends wines to be selected to match the food. This books starts with the type and varietal of wine you want to drink and recommends food with associated recipes to match the wine! For meals we want to celebrate, I like to select special wines first and then determine what to eat with them. This book helps guide you through that process. For those of us who consider wine to be the centerpiece of the meal, this book is highly recommended.

Cheese & Wine: A Guide to Selecting, Pairing and Enjoying (Janet Fletcher): This book has global applicability and covers all aspects of selecting the right cheese courses for the occasion and the right wines to match. Given the great diversity of cheese types and ingredients, the book does an outstanding job on pairing combinations. Most of us love cheese on its own and wine on its own, so it seems natural that any combination of wine and cheese would do well together. But cheeses vary greatly in terms of acidity, sharpness, hardness and many other characteristics which make one wine work better with a particular cheese than another. It seems that wine and cheese pairing is no easier than the broader topic of wine and food pairing in general. One of life's pleasures is to sit with friends and enjoy wine and cheese together and by using the knowledge in this book, you should have a great time doing it!

The All American Cheese and Wine Book (Laura Werlin): This book is similar to the previously described book, but focuses on American cheeses and wineries. However, I use it effectively in Australia as most of the cheese types and wine varietals are available here. Therefore, it is easy to make substitutions that still provide a complimentary pairing of cheese with wine. This book also has a lot of cheese-related recipes to provide tapas and appetizers to really enliven your cheese tasting.

Savory Pies (Greg Henry): We love our pies, especially in winter time! This is a great little book covering all sorts of pie types from tarts and appetizers to main meal pies including meat, seafood and vegetarian. This is an excellent book containing over 60 recipes with great suggestions for matching wines.

Sweet Wines: A Guide to the World's Best with Recipes (James Peterson): This is a sweet book on sweet wines and can be used to understand different sweet wines around the world. It also provides matching recipes from tapas to desserts to breakfast fare and which sweet wines to select. If you like sweet wines and like eating, you will love this book.

Miscellaneous:

Wine & Conversation (Adrienne Lehrer): Lehrer provides a systematic linguistic approach for describing and discussing wine. A linguist by background, Lehrer helps provide linguistic scales to choose which words to use to describe various degrees of sweetness, acidity, etc. This is a unique book which attempts to make more consistent wine conversation between wine drinkers with varying degrees of experience and semantic capabilities. The book was originally written in 1983, and updated in 2009. It also includes a review of interesting winery and wine names which is humorous. *Wine & Conversation* is required reading if you want to improve your ability to describe what you taste and share your views with others using similar language and descriptions.

1001 Wines You Must Try Before You Die (Neil Beckett): This book defines your wine drinking bucket list! I wonder if anyone has tried to drink every wine listed, or even calculated the total cost, as for most of us, it would be an impossible goal. However, a quick review and reference to this list is always useful. I have drunk or have in my cellar eight of the 1001 bottles mentioned by brand and exact vintage. It is always a pleasure to see listed a bottle you had or can pull out to have at a later date. It also provides a great overview of the best world wines, and even if you cannot find that exact vintage, you may be able to find one of similar quality. I have used this book as a tour guide to trying better wines in regions I am less familiar with. I no longer buy wine guides or annual reviews as they are quickly out of date (I use annual and cumulative wine research subscriptions instead). However, this book never goes out of date, so it is worthwhile to have a copy in your wine library. When I have an upcoming special event which requires great celebration, I look to this book to find a wine to help me celebrate!

How to Drink (Victoria Moore): This is not a book on wine, but more broadly a book on how to drink – wine, spirits, coffee and tea, etc. It provides a good overview of how to achieve pleasure in drinking in general, the aesthetics of drinking and how to be prepared for and get the most from drinking. By reading this book, you can better understand why many consider wine to be a unique beverage with special powers, and also come to appreciate and improve your non-wine beverage drinking.

There are a variety of other books on wine humor and lifestyle which in my opinion enhance the drinking experience by providing anecdotes about wine and other examples of how to improve life by being around and drinking wine. Many of these are presented in history books, biographies, and travel books which have a large and obvious intersection with wine regions or the wine industry. I have read some fascinating journals and biographies of Thomas Jefferson and other gustatory travel journeys from $18^{th} - 20^{th}$ century travel which shows how much wine played in the lifestyles of discerning, yet famous people. A number of people throughout history were passionate about wine and liked to share their experiences with others. I find reading these wine lifestyle books enlightening and also provide a certain level of validation that I appreciate and drink like others that I greatly admire!

Research Subscriptions

The books I reference in the previous section stand the test of time and their content does not change over time. These books are useful for as long as you live. Other information associated with wine changes and is updated annually. Each year new vintages are released, tasted and ranked, prices adjusted, new tasting notes updated, and wineries opened and closed. Books on annual vintage rankings become useless quickly; wine atlases and reviews of wineries soon thereafter. For information which is changing annually, I subscribe on an annual basis.

I subscribe to four different wine research services:

- *Wine Searcher Pro* (mainly for wine prices and wine valuations globally)
- *Robert Parker Online* (for tasting notes of global and American wines and research)
- *Jancis Robinson Purple Pages* (for tasting notes of global and European wines and research)
- *James Halliday's Australian Wine Companion* (for tasting notes of Australian wines and limited research)

Wine Searcher comes in a free and subscription version, with the subscription version called *Wine Searcher Pro*. The free version provides a limited listing of where to source the wine you are looking for and its price. You are limited to the first five listings that are displayed. The main difference is that *Wine Searcher Pro* provides every known listing and its price which gives you a much better chance of sourcing a wine at the best possible price no matter where you are globally. It includes retailers and wine auction sites, with individual prices. It also provides community tasting notes for your review.

Wine Searcher Pro links to other wine review sites such as Parker, Robinson and Halliday if you have subscribed to them. Therefore, when I am considering buying a bottle of wine at a bottle shop or in a restaurant, I pull up my smartphone version of the application to get pricing information and tasting notes. This has saved me a number of times from purchasing the wrong bottle or paying too much per bottle. This is a great service and I have been using it for several years.

Robert Parker has developed a reputation as one of the highest integrity and experienced wine reviewers globally. His subscription service *Robert Parker Online* is a premium service. It provides a global focus, has over 225,000 tasting notes, global vintage charts, online magazines, almost daily publication of new articles and many other features. I found the service to be easy to navigate and use. It surprised me with the amount of additional features provided. It also provides a capability to create your own cellar inventory if you like.

Robert Parker Online may be the most comprehensive set of tasting notes you can find. I use it primarily to review the quality and drinkability (timeframe) of a particular wine. He also has a substantial team behind him which contributes a lot of articles, research information, and other wine related sources. This team has created the most comprehensive set of tasting notes around the world. If I was limited to one subscription service, this would be it.

Jancis Robinson is another icon in the wine industry. She was the first woman to achieve her MW. *Jancis Robinson Purple Pages* is another comprehensive research site. It also has a global focus, an excellent overview of European wines, about 85,000 tasting notes, over 10,000 articles and wine-related research. It also provides almost 200 wine maps online sourced from *The World Atlas of Wine*, plus online access to one of the best wine encyclopedias available, *The Oxford Companion to Wine*. *Purple Pages* also has a member's forum for wine enthusiasts globally to share information and help each other. It is a great social media site for wine enthusiasts.

I found *Jancis Robinson Purple Pages* initially a bit difficult to navigate and search for particular wines, but was able to overcome that by using the menus to drive me through the selections and then become more pedantic in the search criteria I entered. The search engine is not anywhere as sophisticated as Google's and that is a bit problematic as the specific spelling of wine regions, châteaus, etc. are easy to misspell and get a *'your search produced no results'* message or retrieve a record for a completely different wine!

With all the research available, *Jancis Robinson Purple Pages* offers a significant ongoing wine education in addition to providing tasting notes and is a great asset.

James Halliday's Australian Wine Companion is localized to Australian and New Zealand wines and wineries. For those living in Australia or elsewhere who likes Australian wine, it is a tremendous asset. More and more Australian wines are available around the world and Australia is now considered one of the finest winemaking countries in the world.

The *Australian Wine Companion* provides over 70,000 tasting notes with only a few for wines outside of Australia and New Zealand. It also provides vintages maps for each major Australian wine producing region which is extremely handy to make sure you are picking up the right vintage of your favorite wines. Halliday offers access to numerous articles of interest and quick overviews of wine styles, food and wine matching and more, but it is limited and not effectively organized.

I find all three wine review (Parker, Robinson and Halliday) subscriptions services to of great value for me as they all work together and serve over-lapping, but different purposes. I have considered and subscribed to some other services in the past that were sub-standard. The three that I have mentioned here along with *Wine Searcher Pro* have tremendous content which is constantly updated. Additionally, they come with smartphone and tablet applications or can be opened in a mobile browser to provide access to critical information no matter where you are.

Each of the four services to which I subscribe has general availability access which is limited, but can be useful for wine education. I explored this and used some of the services provided, but quickly found out that it was well worth paying for annual subscriptions. Based on when you purchase them and currency exchange rates, each of the three wine review services cost about $100 per year, more or less, with Halliday being the least expensive and Robinson being the most, while *Wine Searcher Pro* is under $50 annually. Currently, I am paying about $300 per year for all four services. This may seem expensive when you could put that money into some more wine, but I have found each service to have saved me a lot of money by avoiding purchasing mistakes, especially by avoiding purchasing an over-priced wine in a restaurant and making a far better selection.

Further Wine Education

Both Parker and Robinson have trade memberships which cost more, but are unnecessary for even the most enthusiastic wine drinker among us! Also, note that both Parker and Robinson are set up as automatic renewals on the anniversary date, so you need to proactively change your account settings to stop the renewal process and terminate your subscription.

Wine Magazines

<u>Gourmet Traveler (GT) Wine</u>: Published as a complimentary guide to Gourmet Traveler with a focus on wine for Australia and New Zealand. Provides reviews of recently-released wine, upcoming events and in-depth articles.

<u>Wine Estates</u>: Review of current releases of wines from Australia and New Zealand by price categories and varietal.

<u>Decanter</u>: International wine magazine published in UK with a focus on European wines.

<u>Wine Advocate</u>: Robert Parker's magazine on wine.

<u>World of Fine Wine</u>: A more expensive wine magazine subscription for the high-end wine collector and consumer.

<u>Wine Companion</u>: James Halliday's wine magazine covering mostly Australia and New Zealand.

As mentioned previously, magazines are enjoyable to read and for relaxing. I enjoy getting my monthly magazines. However, much of the information contained in these magazines is available through the research services you may want to subscribe to or through Internet searches. Wine Advocate and Wine Companion can be purchased as part of a research package, so if you are looking to subscribe to research from Parker or Halliday, you may also be able to subscribe for the magazine at a marginal cost.

Wine Movies

What could be more fun than to learn about wine than watching a wine movie with a glass in your hand! I have learned about wine, the wine industry, wine regions, and the wine lifestyle from watching movies.

Sideways: Interesting movie about two guys exploring and enjoying Napa Valley prior to one of the men getting married. There is a particular focus on the mystery and joy of drinking Pinot Noir.

Bottle Shock: A movie about how Californian wines achieved worldwide prominence by beating out French wines in a head-to-head competition in 1976. Based on the book *Judgment of Paris* by George Taber.

Mondovino (the movie): Portrays the challenges and intrigue of the wine industry as seen through multi-generational family businesses.

Mondvino (the complete series): Provides an expanded version and more stories of the multi-generational family wine business.

Somm: Provides a humorous, yet emotionally consuming look into the pursuit of passing the Master Sommelier Exam. Very few people qualify to become Master Sommeliers and this movie helps you understand why!

Red Obsession: Mystery and intrigue about the wine business, especially as it is impacted by the growth of wine consumption in China.

Wine for the Confused: A humorous introduction into understanding and learning to appreciate wine.

Grapes of Wrath: A remarkable classic on the struggles of American migrant workers during the depression.

There are also a number of excellent YouTube channels on wine education too numerous to mention. Just launch YouTube, enter 'Wine' and start browsing. YouTube wine channels cover wine reviews, wine education, and even videos featuring winery dogs!

Guided Gustatory Tours

Continued reading and research using the resources described above provides an ongoing improvement in our cognitive wine knowledge which is critical to improving wine drinking enjoyment and appreciation. But that on its own is not pleasurable unless you actually do some wine drinking along the way!

Further Wine Education

Earlier in the book, we discussed different methods to gain wine drinking experience as part of our everyday existence. Additionally, there exists other avenues for concentrated and intensive wine education which comprise eating and drinking great wines in great locations. More and more food and wine tours are being organized to provide extreme gustatory experiences embodied as vacations. These can be in duration from several days to several weeks or longer. They usually involve traveling to a place relevant to the food and wine that will be discussed and consumed. Many occur in places such as Tuscany or Provence or take place on cruise ships featuring intensive cooking or wine tasting courses that are great fun and great education.

While you can select your own destinations and visit different wineries and partake in different tasting experiences, having an expert aware of the region, its food and wine styles, and with access to the best venues and instructors can be a real help, both in terms of what you learn and how enjoyable it is. You can easily find out more by looking online or talking with a travel agent. I like to organize my own trips and have not used any wine tour companies, but know of people who have and they highly recommend the experience. Therefore I am providing a few links to these companies that you may want to check out, but many more can be found online or by talking with a travel agent.

On the Road Culinary Adventures (www.ontheroadculinaryadventures.com/) combines a love of food and wine with a love of travel to provide culinary travel adventures. These include several-day events hosted in the US and longer overseas trips, including cruises. *On the Road Culinary Adventures* combine a relaxing vacation experience which focuses on teaching you more about food and wine through providing a tremendous culinary experience complimented by increasing your cognitive knowledge through lectures, instruction by guest chefs, and a hands-on teaching experience where you are preparing the food and the meals under the tutelage of culinary experts.

And if you like your Champagne (or your Cognac), then you should reach out to *The Champagne Dame* (www.thechampagnedame.com/), Kyla Kirkpatrick. *The Champagne Dame* organizes one-week exclusive tours of the Champagne region with lodging and Champagne drinking experiences not available to the general public. This is an indulgent, but educational week that will immediately make you an 'expert' in all things Champagne!

The Wine Experience (http://thewine-experience.com/) provides a comprehensive set of wine tours around the globe, ranging from one-day to one-week trips. They also organize wine cruises and can customize a wine-related vacation to meet your needs in terms of location, varietals and food experiences.

Pure Food Wine and Cooking Tours (http://purefoodcookingtours.com.au/) is another excellent source of various global wine and food vacations.

Gustatory vacations can provide intense and in-depth experiences in a relaxing environment. You should come back from this type of experience with deeper knowledge and increased abilities to recreate similar experiences at home to share with friends. A gustatory vacation also increases your visibility of what is possible and heightens your expectations of how to be involved and even host similar events in the future.

More Advanced Wine Training

There are a number of different options to continue to learn more about wine beyond what has been presented earlier in the book. It is certainly not necessary to partake of further education to increase you wine drinking enjoyment and appreciation. Yet, if you have made it this far in the book, you probably share a similar passion and love of wine with me. This means you may want to explore further education, and there are a number of ways to do that.

Technical and trade schools and specialty schools in Hotel and Hospitality Management offer courses open to the public for continued education, or for a longer-term program of multiple courses and certification. These often focus on learning a trade such as become a bartender or a sommelier. Many trade schools and college or university programs provide training as do specialty Hotel and Hospitality Management colleges.

This is an excellent way to continue to develop your wine drinking and appreciation skills in the evenings if you are working in a full-time job. I have taken these courses with work colleagues and it has provided real bonding experiences and improved our relationships at work as it has evolved another dimension of our relationship in addition to our work pursuits. Having several friends or work colleagues take the courses with you is a great way to learn more about wine while having fun.

There are more intensive and internationally recognized courses available providing sommelier training which run over a three-to-six-month duration and you are expected to participate in these close to full-time. These are available in a number of locations around the world, but may require travel or temporary relocation. While trade schools are available in almost any large city center and provide an easier next step to enhancing your wine education, longer-term, specialized programs may be more challenging to fit into your life's schedule.

Any general training in the direction of becoming a sommelier or courses in becoming a wine judge will certainly provide you with deeper wine knowledge which should continue to improve wine drinking and appreciation. Even if you are not planning on entering the field of wine, this type of coursework is fun in addition to being educational.

Court of Master Sommeliers

Studying to become a Master Sommelier (MS) or a Master of Wine (MW) is a tough and rare accomplishment. The MW is harder and more prestigious, even though there are more MW's globally than there are MS's. If you want to learn more about what it takes to become a MS, watch the movie mentioned previously entitled *Somm*. It is about four guys studying to become MS and the focus it requires.

There are four levels of certification:

- Introductory Sommelier Certificate (3-day course including examination)
- Certified Sommelier Examination (1-day exam)
- Advanced Sommelier Certificate (five days of which half time is spent testing)
- Master Sommelier Diploma (several days of examination)

The study and the exams focus on three main components:

- Theoretical knowledge
- Practical knowledge
- Tasting knowledge and awareness

To reach the Certified or Advanced level, you need to pass 60% for each section, and then obtain a 75% pass rate in each section for your Master Sommelier Diploma. For your Master Sommelier Diploma, you take each part of the examination separately and must pass all three parts within a three year period. You have multiple tries to pass all three parts. If you do not, then you must take all three parts over again.

If you already have significant knowledge and experience, you may be able to achieve all four levels quite quickly. The Court of Master Sommeliers provides details for the structure and knowledge required in each area to provide you guidance in preparing for the coursework and examinations. The most difficult would be to learn and remember the facts and characteristics of various important (and many!) wine regions around the world. This then needs to be complimented by your practical skills and your tasting experience.

Becoming an Advanced or Master Sommelier is focused on a balanced approach to equip you with the skills to be able to serve wine to others at the highest level. The Court of Master Sommeliers schedules courses and examinations regularly and frequently in Europe and the US. It is also now possible to take the Introductory Sommelier Certificate and Certified Sommelier Examination in Australia. However, the Advanced Sommelier Certificate and Masters Sommelier Diploma must be sat in Europe or the US.

If you are so inclined, with a little time and a little money, it is possible for almost everyone to become a Certified Sommelier. Much more practical experience and cognitive knowledge is required to obtain the Advanced Sommelier Certificate or Masters Sommelier Diploma. There are only about 200 MS globally.

Master of Wine (MW)

For the rare breed who wants to reach the top of their wine drinking game, there is always the pursuit of a MW (Master of Wine). This goal is more elusive and expensive than climbing to the top of Mt Everest. It is an intensive minimal three-year study program, and I have heard that the purchase of wine you need to taste will cost you about $200,000 over the course of the program! I know this from someone who made it through the first year of study, but did not find the time or energy to dedicate to getting through the entire program. There are only a few over 300 members who have passed the exam to be certified as an MW. You certainly do not need to be an MW to be considered an icon or expert in the wine industry. Neither Robert Parker nor James Halliday is an MW, even though they would be considered as foremost wine experts globally.

I have met a few MW in my life and am connected to a few more online through a shared passion for wine. There is great advantage in having someone studying for the MW as a friend. The person I mentioned earlier who was not able to finish the course, still enabled and shared some great experiences with me. She had a great palate and I learned a lot tasting with her. Additionally, she would pull out a number of bottles of a particular type and style of wine for us to sample and compare. She is a great deal of fun with whom to drink wine! I always have a great time and learn a lot drinking some very fine wines when with her.

Even if you are not interested in pursuing an MW, it is worth reviewing their website to learn more about the programs and course of study, and to find out if any MWs are located near you who you can meet and get to know.

Winemaking

Another method you may want to consider is to learn more about winemaking. I learned a great deal about food and wine flavors from taking cooking classes and the same is true for winemaking. If you have the time to be able to work through a vintage, you will learn a great deal about wine and how to appreciate it more. Wineries are always looking for help (sometimes paid, sometimes volunteered) and there are plenty of interesting jobs to participate in that help you understand how the grapes are grown and harvested, and how the wine tastes and why. And the physical labor and camaraderie is always a plus!

We have our home as part of a cooperative vineyard in Australia's Hunter Valley. Initially we had staff handle every job which was reflected in more expensive strata fees. However, with recent changes in the Homeowners Executive Committee, they ask for volunteers to help with a variety of winemaking activities, including picking grapes, netting vines, removing slugs from vines, bottling and working the cellar door (if you have your RSA). These activities have provided real insight into when to pick the grapes and why and what to do if the grapes are picked early or late. It also provides great insight into how to identify which plots and vines should be put aside for reserved wines versus mass-produced wines or to be used in blends.

I volunteer to take part in these activities and I am not just helping out our homeowner's association (and lowering our strata fees!), but I am learning a lot which makes me appreciate wine more. I am also now volunteering my time to help some of the other established and prestigious vineyards in the area so I can continue to learn more.

Wine, for many, becomes a lifelong passion and part of an ongoing wine lifestyle. By reading and researching the references provided earlier in this chapter and by taking some continuing wine education and participating in more aspects of winemaking, you can continue to learn more and appreciate wine more. Most importantly, it will continue to improve your wine drinking pleasure.

Working in the Wine Industry

There is no better form of education than just doing it, by learning on the job and be provided training for doing the job. There are many ways to become more involved (and get paid instead of paying!) for being associated with the wine industry. Minimally, you need to spend about $100 - $150 to obtain your RSA (Responsible Service of Alcohol) certificate if you are going to work in a position of serving alcohol to others. If you work as a bartender, or at a cellar door, then you require your RSA. You can take courses online or in a class room setting and the course takes between four and six hours to complete. You also may be required to take a bartending or a sommelier course if you want to serve wine in a restaurant or serve drinks more broadly at other functions.

The key path to learning by working is that you will be associated with people with much more practical knowledge who are sharing with and training you. It is that simple. There are important reasons as to why you may want to consider being educated in wine as recommended previously. It helps provide a foundation and you also achieve certification which is useful in actually finding a job in the wine industry. Or you may just find attending classes or reading books to be the most enjoyable way to learn. But it does beg the question of why pay for education when you can get paid for doing a job that educates you! Practical on-the-job training can be more effective

Further Wine Education

than classroom training, so if you like wine and have the time, you may want to consider some part-time work in the wine industry even if you have another job.

There are many different avenues you can pursue. We have done graphic design for wine labels and learned about what a winemaker is trying to accomplish through the style of wine they make. You can get a part-time job selling wine and be trained on the characteristics of the wine you are selling and how they compare to the competition. (You also may be able to secure employee discounts or wholesale rates when buying the wine!) I have recently started working a cellar door which has put me in contact with a number of people who are experts in the wine industry and also their patrons who have provided tremendous insight into how a large and diverse group of different people react to certain wines. You may also volunteer to work at wine events such as tastings, or to work in the shipping department of a wine distributor. By doing so, you will learn how to package wine for safe handling, possibly learn the price points for various wines when sold at different volume levels, and a few other things along the way.

If you have a passion for wine, then getting any job in the industry can be of interest and it would provide contacts to others in the industry. You may not think you have time to work with wine in addition to your already full life, but there are many opportunities to either work or volunteer for wine-related jobs that only require several hours per week and provide great training or insights that you would not otherwise obtain.

Chapter 21
Other References

When drinking wine, you really only need two things: your mouth and a bottle of wine. However, there are a number of other aspects which improve the wine drinking experience, including the glassware you use, the type of cellar and wine storage facilities you have, the decanters and corkscrews involved, and many other things that can enhance the experience. This chapter provides links to some of those products and services.

The list is certainly not inclusive nor meant to imply any sort of recommendation of the products or services provided. I can personally attest to the value I received or perceive in these products and services, so I believe it may be a good starting point for others with similar interests who want to explore more. The list has been assembled to provide links to further your ability to review and determine if these or similar products and services may help improve your wine drinking experiences. I apologize in advance to a number of the links being of more use to readers in Australia than elsewhere. However, with a little imagination, you should be able to find similar links to products and services local to where you live.

There are many links to wineries and wine-related information on Facebook and LinkedIn, and are too numerous to mention. However some of these may be of interest to you and you are likely to find out about them if you make any mention of wine on your Facebook or LinkedIn walls. The services will start to inundate you with sponsors in the wine industry, which you can choose to 'Like" or not. I also follow quite a few wine-related people and organizations on Twitter. Twitter like Facebook and LinkedIn attempts to identify others you will be interested in and make recommendations.

Many of the links presented below for retail or direct distribution are Australian based. However, there are many similar vendors in all geographies. Use Google or some other search engine to find suitable alternatives wherever you live.

Here are a variety of links you may find useful:

Wine Research:

Robert Parker Online (https://www.erobertparker.com/): One of the most comprehensive online tasting research databases with loads of extras including forums, vintage charts, columns and research articles. Global focus with best overview of American wines

Jancis Robinson Purple Pages (http://www.jancisrobinson.com/): Another comprehensive online tasting research database with load of extras including articles and insights by Jancis and online access to her Encyclopedia and Wine Maps. Global focus with best overview on European wines.

James Halliday Australian Wine Companion (http://www.winecompanion.com.au/): Great tasting database of Australian and New Zealand wines with limited tasting notes on international wines outside Australia. It also includes a good overview of Australian vintage charts.

Wine Searcher (Pro) (http://www.wine-searcher.com/index.lml): Free or professional version is available to provide pricing and availability of a particular wine. Very well designed system with links to community and professional (if you are a subscriber) tasting notes plus Cellar Tracker for integrated wine management and inventory.

Glassware and Other Wine Paraphernalia:

Riedel – The Wine Glass Company: The international Riedel website.

Riedel Australia Online Shop: For Riedel purchasers in Australia.

Riedel USA Online Shop: For Riedel purchasers in USA.

Riedel UK Online Shop: For Riedel purchasers in UK.

Victoria's Basement: An Australian discount kitchen supply store with wide range of glassware and other wine related paraphernalia.

Peters of Kensington: Online kitchen supply distributor in Australia.

Messermeister: Known for knives, but also sells the best Sommelier corkscrews I have used.

IKEA: Wide assortment of inexpensive glassware.

Based on what country you live in, there are a number of other kitchen and home ware stores which have a wide assortment of decanters, glassware and other wine paraphernalia. These include Williams and Sonoma, House, and so forth.

Cellaring Systems:

Vintec: Excellent wine storage systems from two-bottle counter-top systems for open bottles to free-standing units to walk-in cellars (based in Australia).

Wine-ark: Dedicated wine storage cellars around Australia for ranging from small to very large.

Coravin: Device which allows you to extract a glass at a time from a bottle and keep the rest of the bottle for later drinking.

Auction Sites for Buying and SellingWine in Australia:

Wickman's Fine Wines Auction: Monthly wine auction except for months of December and January.

Langton's: Both an auction site and exchange which is a fixed-priced site.

Cracka Wines: Auctions in addition to online wine merchant.

Greys Online: Broader seller of many goods, but direct wine sales and auction.

MW Wines: Auction site plus premier back vintage wines.

Miscellaneous:

<u>Cellartracker</u>: Best wine social media site and inventorying system available in my opinion.

<u>Le Nez Du Vin</u>: Sets of various liquids which represent wine smells and characteristics to practice and improve your ability to smell. (A number of different distributors carry it in many countries.)

<u>Spectrum Direct</u>: Sells Breathalysers for individual use.

      The wine industry has many options in terms of wine, wine related products, storage, and so on. Make sure to do proper research and that you are dealing with reputable vendors. The Internet is extremely useful is identifying and validating which companies to do business with.

Chapter 22
Final Thoughts

What is wine? Is it a drink, part of a symbiotic, shared pairing with a meal, a sensual pleasure, an aesthetic art form, or a lifestyle? The answer to this varies based on who you are and where you have traveled during your wine drinking journey. During my life, wine has grown in importance to become an integrated part and feature of my day-to-day existence. That may not be true for you (yet!), but if you have made it this far in the book, I expect that you certainly enjoy drinking wine and have the desire to drink more and drink better. I hope this book has provided you the tools and ability to be able to appreciate wine more fully and understand why.

Peynaud states, "Wine is a series of complex inter-relationships, between man and nature, between an area and its community, between ecology and society. It is not surprising, therefore, that it is infinitely varied."[117] He goes on to say "The art of drinking, like the art of eating, is thus part of the art of living."[118] Scruton says, "In my view wine is an excellent accompaniment to food; but it is a better accompaniment to thought...Wine, drunk at the right time, in the right place, and the right company, is the path to meditation, and the harbinger of peace."[119] Smith proclaims: "When I taste a wine of extraordinary beauty I want to share this experience with someone else. I may have a specific person in mind...We understand something about the wine and about each other. When someone else recognizes the pleasure we take in things, we know there are others who have that pleasure also."[120]

Final Thoughts

While wine is often on my mind and often in my body and spirit, like any pleasurable pursuit, too much of a good thing may become a bad thing. I drink responsibly, and I drink a little at a time. I also like to have food while drinking to ensure that I am not absorbing too much alcohol and that it is metabolizing and diluting as or almost as quickly as I am drinking it. I think in terms of tasting wine instead of drinking wine. While wine provides antioxidants and has an acceptable amount of calories per volume, too much wine will fuel you with alcohol and put on weight. Drink responsibly in terms of your health and ability to function.

I avoid mediocre wine; I do not drink wine for the sake of ingesting alcohol. I drink wine as I love the taste and appreciate and ponder the craftsmanship that goes into growing and maintaining the vines, and making and cellaring the wine.

While I drink regularly and frequently, I drink only a little. I look for friends to share a good bottle with. Through social discourse or pursuing other activities such as reading or writing, I sip my wine over a long period of time. Neither fine wine nor food is meant to be ingested quickly. They are meant to be enjoyed and savored. They are meant to be an integrated part of life.

I hoped you enjoyed this book and received great value from it. I also hope your love of wine and ability to enjoy it has both increased from what you have read. And I truly hope that we can continue to share our wine drinking experiences with each other and maybe even some day sit and enjoy a glass or two together!

Notes

117. Peynaud, *The Taste of Wine*, 87.
118. Ibid, 252.
119. Scruton, *I Drink Therefore I am*, 134.
120. Smith, "The Objectivity of Tastes and Tasting," 60.

Appendices

Appendix A
Castro's Categories of Wine Odors

W1	W2	W3	W4	W5	W6	W7	W8	W9	W10
FRAGRANT	WOODY, RESINOUS	FRUITY, OTHER THAN CITRUS	SICKENING	CHEMICAL	MINTY, PEPPERMINT	SWEET	POPCORN	SICKENING	LEMON
FLORAL	MUSTY, EARTHY, MOLDY	SWEET	PUTRID, FOUL, DECAYED	ETHERIC, ANAESTHETIC	COOL, COOLING	VANILLA	BURNT, SMOKY	GARLIC, ONION	FRUITY, CITRUS
PERFUMERY	CEDARWOOD	FRAGRANT	RANCID	MEDICINAL	AROMATIC	FRAGRANT	PEANUT BUTTER	HEAVY	FRAGRANT
SWEET	HERBAL, GREEN, CUT GRASS	AROMATIC	SWEATY	DISINFECTANT, CARBOLIC	ANISE (LICORICE)	AROMATIC	NUTTY (WALNUT ETC)	BURNT, SMOKY	ORANGE
ROSE	FRAGRANT	LIGHT	SOUR, VINEGAR	SHARP, PUNGENT, ACID	FRAGRANT	CHOCOLATE	OILY, FATTY	SULFIDIC	LIGHT
AROMATIC	AROMATIC	PINEAPPLE	SHARP, PUNGENT, ACID	GASOLINE, SOLVENT	MEDICINAL	MALTY	ALMOND	SHARP, PUNGENT, ACID	SWEET
LIGHT	LIGHT	CHERRY (BERRY)	FECAL (LIKE MANURE)	PAINT	SPICY	ALMOND	HEAVY	HOUSEHOLD GAS	COOL, COOLING
COLOGNE	HEAVY	STRAWBERRY	SOUR MILK	CLEANING FLUID	SWEET	CARAMEL	WARM	PUTRID, FOUL, DECAYED	AROMATIC
HERBAL, GREEN, CUT GRASS	SPICY	PERFUMERY	MUSTY, EARTHY, MOLDY	ALCOHOLIC	EUCALIPTUS	LIGHT	MUSTY, EARTHY, MOLDY	SEWER	HERBAL, GREEN, CUT GRASS
VIOLETS	BURNT, SMOKY	BANANA	HEAVY	TURPENTINE (PINE OIL)	CAMPHOR	WARM	WOODY, RESINOUS	BURNT RUBBER	SHARP, PUNGENT, ACID

Appendix B
Wine Database Format and Field Listing

This is the format of the database I use to track wine inventory. It is in MS Excel format, but could be in a database language like MS Access if that works better for you. I selected Excel because the primary content can be easily listed in spreadsheet rows and is similar for each bottle in inventory. I can easily use drop down filters to query by varietal, brand, vintage, etc. or some combination of them to locate specific bottles quickly. I have created simple formulas to manage my inventory financially for insurance and investment purposes, as required. The main purpose though has to been able to plot how many bottles I have by drinking period (defined annually) so as to know when is the best time to drink the wine and over what period. This shows me if I have a period in the near future where I may have an excess of wine which will become past due. I can then plan ahead to use the wine for larger functions or to sell it.

You do not need to go to this level to manage your inventory. Hopefully, the format presented here provides a superset of what you require should you elect to build your own database. However, other viable options have become available as discussed in *Chapter 19: Tools and Systems for Managing Wine Inventory* and *Chapter 21: Other References*.

The Database comprises six individual spreadsheets:

Spreadsheet	Description
Inventory	This is the main database used to enter and manage wine assets. It contains over 20 fields describing each wine in inventory.
Varietals	A list of all grape varietals in inventory (may differ significantly from region to region) and is used only for documentation purposes.
Categories	What type the wine is: single variety, blend, sparkling, dessert, etc., and is used only for documentation purposes.
Producer Information	This spreadsheet is only used as a notepad to record notes not found in public databases, such as notes related to changes in personnel, who the winemaker is, treatment of customers, etc.
Drinking and Consumption Notes	Alert and notice system regarding at-risk wines, wines to focus on drinking soon, if a bottle was bad and others may be at risk, etc. Used only as a notepad and 'to-drink' list.
Design Notes	Specific to my database design, to-dos to improve usefulness, explanation of functions and reports used.

You only really need the Inventory spreadsheet to have a useful wine inventory management system. The Varietals and Categories spreadsheets describe acronyms used in the Inventory spreadsheet. The final three spreadsheets are 'notepads' and very specific to my experiences; therefore, they are not described further.

The content of each of the first three spreadsheets are defined on the following pages.

Appendix B: Wine Database Format and Field Listing

Inventory Spreadsheet Definition

Field Name	Format	Description
Producer	Text	Main brand name for the wine producer.
Wine Name	Text	Format varies by region and sometimes is only 'Grand Cru,' or 'Superior.' Important when there are several different quality levels by varietal with same producer.
Vintage	Number	Year grapes were harvested.
Volume (# bottles)	Number	Number of bottles in inventory. Added to if more is purchased and subtracted when removed from inventory.
Current Value	Number	(Formatted as Currency) Derived from research databases, auction prices, or general assessment. I use Wine Searcher Pro as an initial indicator.
Purchase Price	Number	(Formatted as Currency) What you paid for it. Be consistent based on VAT, GST, or other sales tax. Since I live in Australia, all my prices for Current Value and Purchase Price are inclusive of GST.
Varietal	Text	Acronym for grape variety or blend of grapes as defined in the Varietals spreadsheet.
Category	Text	What type or style of wine as it is defined in the Category spreadsheet.
Rating	Number	May be based on 20-point or 100-point system or 5-star ranking system. It may also reflect your own view of the quality of the wine.
Rating System	Text	I usually use Halliday, Parker or Robinson, but also some others such as Oliver or my own assessment or scores from Cellartracker community tastings and assessments. (If you have multiple Ratings from different systems, you may enter multiple lines for Rating and Rating System.)
Bottle Size	Text	Usually 375, 500, 750 ml or 1.5, 3 or 6 liters.

Field Name	Format	Description
Provenance	Text	VP (for Verified Provenance), CP (for Certified Provenance) or CE (Caveat Emptor) as entry. I use the system used by Wickman Fine Wine Auctions (http://www.wickman.net.au/provenance).
Provenance Links	Hyperlink	Your own links to copies of purchase receipts or logs putting the wine into storage. May also be a link to a photo of the wine's label, cork or ullage for older wines.
Description	Text	More detail regarding the wine, such as the percentages of a blend, how it was acquired or anything else you find useful to better describe the wine. This field is blank for most of my entries, but comes in handy every now and then.
Personal Tasting Notes	Text	This is used to provide your own comments.
Links to other Tasting Notes	Hyperlink	Used to point to other tasting notes from research databases such as Parker, Robinson and Halliday or Cellartracker.
Start Drink Year	Number	Based on research of vintage and varietal, bottle size and storage conditions.
End Drink Year	Number	Based on research of vintage and varietal, bottle size and storage conditions.
Optimal Drink Year	Number	Usually the mid-point (or slightly later) of Start Drink Year and End Drink Year.
Country	Text	Country where grapes are sourced and wine is made.
Region	Text	Region within country where grapes are sourced (may be different from the region where the wine is made).
Specific Vineyard	Text	Often blank, but useful for single vineyard wines.

Appendix B: Wine Database Format and Field Listing

Varietals Spreadsheet Definition

Abbreviation	Grape Name
CH	Chardonnay
RS	Riesling
SM	Semillon
SB	Sauvignon Blanc
GT	Gewurtztraminer
PG	Pinot Gris
VD	Verdehlo
VG	Viognier
MC	Muscat
RS	Rose (not a varietal, but useful for definition)
CS	Cabernet Sauvignon
SH	Shiraz
PS	Petite Shiraz
ML	Merlot
MC	Muscato
PN	Pinot Noir
MB	Malbec
CF	Cabernet Franc
GN	Grenache
BB	Barbera
DU	Durif
MV	Mourvedre
PV	Pinot Verdot
TN	Tannat

Abbreviation	Grape Name
TP	Tempranillo
SV	Sangiovese
ZF	Zinfindel
SB/SM	Sauvignon Blanc / Semillon
GT/RS	Gewurtztraminer / Riesling
CS/SH	Cabernet Sauvignon / Shiraz
CS/ML	Cabernet Sauvignon / Merlot
CS/ML/PV	Cabernet Sauvignon / Merlot / Pinot Verdot
GSM	Grenache/Shiraz/Mouvedre
CS/CF/ML	Cabernet Sauvignon / Cabernet Franc / Merlot
CS/SH/CF	Cabernet Sauvignon / Shiraz / Cabernet Franc
PN/CH	Pinot Noir / Chardonnay
SM/CH	Semillon / Chardonnay
SM/BL	Mostly Semillon but other things blended in
CH/BL	Mostly Chardonnay but other things blended in
GT/MC	Gewurtztraminer/Muscat

Appendix B: Wine Database Format and Field Listing

Categories Spreadsheet Definition

Abbreviation	Wine Category
SV	Straight Varietal
SP	Sparkling
CP	True Champagne Style
RS	Rose
PT	Port (Tawny)
PV	Port (Vintage)
FT	Fortified
BL	Blend
DS	Dessert
BT	Botritys
BL/SP	Blend/Sparkling

It is easy to add more varietals and styles as you see are required for categorization purposes. I use Pivot Tables to report on how many bottles I have of certain varietals and styles to review and determine if I have too many of a particular type or need to consider topping off a varietal or style in accordance with the principles defined in *Chapter 17: Buying and Storing Wine*.

Bibliography

Amerine, Maynard A., and Edward Biffer Roessler. *Wines, Their Sensory Evaluation*. Rev. and enl. New York: W.H. Freeman, 1983.

Bach, Ken. "Knowledge, Wine and Taste: What Good is Knowledge (in enjoying wine?)." In *Questions of Taste: The Philosophy of Wine*, edited by Barry C Smith. Oxford; New York: Oxford University Press, 2007.

Brochet, Frederic. "Tasting: Chemical Object Representation in the Field of Consciousness." application presented for the Grand Prix of the Academie Amorin following work carried out towards a doctorate from Faculty of Oenology, General Oenology Laboratory, 351 Cours de la Liberation, 33405 Talence Cedex, 2001

Castro, Jason B., Arvind Ramanathan, and Chakra S. Chennubhotla. "Categorical Dimensions of Human Odor Descriptor Space Revealed by Non-Negative Matrix Factorization." Edited by Andreas Schaefer. *PLoS ONE* 8, no. 9 (September 18, 2013): e73289. doi:10.1371/journal.pone.0073289.

Charters, Steve. "On the Evaluation of Wine Quality." In *Questions of Taste: The Philosophy of Wine*, edited by Barry C Smith. Oxford; New York: Oxford University Press, 2007.

Crane, Tim. "Wine as an Aesthetic Object." In *Questions of Taste: The Philosophy of Wine*, edited by Barry C Smith. Oxford; New York: Oxford University Press, 2007.

Deroy, Odelphia. "The Power of Tastes: Reconciling Science and Subjectivity." In *Questions of Taste: The Philosophy of Wine*, edited by Barry C Smith. Oxford; New York: Oxford University Press, 2007.

Dutton, Denis. "Aesthetic Universals." In *The Routledge Companion to Aesthetics*, edited by Berys Nigel Gaut and Dominic Lopes, 2nd ed. London ; New York: Routledge, 2005.

Gaut, Berys Nigel, and Dominic Lopes, eds. *The Routledge Companion to Aesthetics*. 2nd ed. London ; New York: Routledge, 2005.

Goode, Jamie. "Wine and the Brain." In *Questions of Taste: The Philosophy of Wine*, edited by Barry C Smith. Oxford; New York: Oxford University Press, 2007.

Jackson, Ron S. *Wine Science: Principles, Practice, Perception*. San Diego [etc.]: Academic Press, 2008.

Jefford, Andrew, and Paul Draper. "The Art and Craft of Wine." In *Questions of Taste: The Philosophy of Wine*, edited by Barry C Smith. Oxford; New York: Oxford University Press, 2007.

Korsmeyer, Carolyn. *Making Sense of Taste: Food & Philosophy*. Ithaca, NY: Cornell University Press, 1999.

------. "Taste." In *The Routledge Companion to Aesthetics*, edited by Berys Nigel Gaut and Dominic Lopes, 2nd ed. London ; New York: Routledge, 2005.

------. "The Meaning of Taste and the Taste of Meaning." In *Arguing about Art: Contemporary Philosophical Debates*, edited by Alex Neill and Aaron Ridley, 3rd ed. London ; New York: Routledge, 2008. Kindle edition.

Lee, Jeannie Cho. *Asian Palate: Savouring Asian Cuisine & Wine*. Hong Kong: Asset Publishing and Research Ltd, 2009.

Lehrer, Adrienne. "Can Wines Be Brawny?: Reflections on Wine Vocabulary." In *Questions of Taste: The Philosophy of Wine*, edited by Barry C Smith. Oxford; New York: Oxford University Press, 2007.

Lehrer, Adrienne. *Wine & Conversation*. 2nd ed. Oxford ; New York: Oxford University Press, 2009. Kindle edition.

Neill, Alex, and Aaron Ridley, eds. *Arguing about Art: Contemporary Philosophical Debates*. 3rd ed. London ; New York: Routledge, 2008. Kindle edition.

Peynaud, Emile. *The Taste of Wine: The Art and Science of Wine Appreciation*. San Francisco, CA: The Wine Appreciation Guild Ltd, 1987.

"Poll: Which of the five senses would you give up?," The Escapist Magazine Online Forum, accessed May 7, 2014, http://www.escapistmagazine.com/forums/read/18.300236-Poll-Which-of-the-five-senses-would-you-give-up

Robards, Terry. *The New York Times Book of Wine*. New York: Quadrangle/New York Times Book Co, 1976.

Robinson, Jancis. *How to Taste Wine*. London: Conran Octopus, 2008.

Schuster, Michael. *Essential Winetasting: The Complete Practical Winetasting Course*. London: Mitchell Beazley, 2009.

Scruton, Roger. *I Drink Therefore I Am: a Philosopher's Guide to Wine*. London ; New York: Continuum, 2009.

------. "The Philosophy of Wine." In *Questions of Taste: The Philosophy of Wine*, edited by Barry C Smith. Oxford; New York: Oxford University Press, 2007.

Sibley, Frank. *Approach to Aesthetics: Collected Papers on Philosophical Aesthetics*. Oxford [England] : New York: Clarendon Press ; Oxford University Press, 2001. Kindle edition.

Smith, Barry C. "The Objectivity of Tastes and Tasting." In *Questions of Taste: The Philosophy of Wine*, edited by Barry C Smith. Oxford; New York: Oxford University Press, 2007.

------. *Questions of Taste: The Philosophy of Wine*. Oxford; New York: Oxford University Press, 2007.

Spence, Charles. "The color of wine – Part 1." *The World of Fine Wine* 28 (June 2010): 122–129.

Svans, Peter. "The 10 Most Common Wine Cellar Problems and How to Overcome Them." The Gurdies Winery, 2001. http://www.winebase.com.au/problems.pdf.

"The Seven Senses," SPD Australia, accessed July 7, 2013, http://www.spdaustralia.com.au/the-seven-senses/.

Telfer, Elizabeth. "Food as Art." In *Arguing about Art: Contemporary Philosophical Debates*, edited by Alex Neill and Aaron Ridley, 3rd ed. London ; New York: Routledge, 2008. Kindle edition.

Todd, Cain Samuel. *The Philosophy of Wine: a Case of Truth, Beauty, and Intoxication*. Montreìal [Queìbec] ; Ithaca [N.Y.]: McGill-Queen's University Press, 2010.

Wikipedia, s.v. "Golden ratio," accessed July 28, 2013, http://en.wikipedia.org/wiki/Golden_Ratio.

Wikipedia, s.v. "Polish Hill River, South Australia," accessed August 3, 2013, http://en.wikipedia.org/wiki/Polish_Hill_River,_South_Australia.

"Woman dies after drinking 10 liters of Coke a day," Fox News, accessed June 30, 2014, http://www.foxnews.com/health/2012/04/19/woman-dies-after-drinking-10-liters-coke-day/

Zraly, Kevin. *Kevin Zraly's Complete Wine Course*. 2012 ed. New York: Sterling Epicure, 2011.

www.ingramcontent.com/pod-product-compliance
Lightning Source LLC
Chambersburg PA
CBHW071302110426
42743CB00042B/1138